The European Union: Annual Review 2003/2004

Edited by
Lee Miles

General Editors: William Paterson and Jim Rollo

Blackwell
Publishing

First published 2004 by Blackwell Publishing Ltd

British Library Cataloguing-in-Publication Data applied for
ISBN 1 4051 1919 5

Set in the United Kingdom by Photoscript, Deddington, Oxon
Printed and bound in the United Kingdom by J.W. Arrowsmith Ltd, Bristol

The publisher's policy is to use permanent paper from mills
that operate a sustainable forestry policy, and which has been
manufactured from pulp processed using acid-free and
elementary chlorine-free practices.
Furthermore, the publisher ensures that the text paper and cover board
used have met acceptable environmental accreditation standards.

For further information on Blackwell Publishing, visit our website:
http://www.blackwellpublishing.com

CONTENTS

Editorial: The Paradox of a Popular Europe

LEE MILES
University of Liverpool

Introduction

In many ways, 2003 can be regarded as the 'year of referendums' as regards European Union (EU) questions. First, after the successful completion of the accession negotiations with ten candidate countries at Copenhagen in December 2002, the next stage in the enlargement process required full ratification of accession terms in the existing Member States, the ten candidate countries and also by the European Parliament (EP). Hence, 2003 also saw the holding of nine public referendums primarily in central and eastern European countries (CEECs) on the question of approving full membership status. As Henderson indicates (in this *Annual Review*) all nine produced – albeit to varying degrees – affirmative answers, and thus the enlargement of the Union to 25 members in 2004 became a certainty. To many pro-EU observers, the 2003 series of referendums on questions of EU accession can be regarded as a striking success.

Second, there was a referendum in Sweden (14 September 2003) on the issue of that country adopting the European single currency and thus, eventually joining the euro area. The year 2003 encompassed the prospect of the euro area eventually being enlarged in the latter part of the decade. However, just as most of the referendums largely in central and eastern Europe expressed a deafening collective public voice in favour of being part of the existing Union, the Swedish plebiscite produced an equally resounding rejection of the euro. It could, in many ways, be construed as a commentary on the merits of aspects of further political integration and the concern of at least some of the European public with the future direction of Europe. Indeed, the size of the categorical 'No' from the Swedes has been interpreted widely as a defeat for the Swedish governing elite and, to a lesser extent, the European Union.

Third, the year also saw domestic debates in many Member States relating to the ongoing process of agreeing an EU Constitutional Treaty. More specifically some continued the theme of the 'year of referendums' by discussing openly whether any eventual EU agreement would and/or should be exposed to public scrutiny through the holding of specific referendums on the Treaty. This aspect continued to bubble away irrespective of the EU governments being unable to agree the final draft of the envisaged Treaty in December 2003 (see Dinan in this *Annual Review*).

To some degree, we can place the three differing elements of the 'year of referendums' within the confines of the 'One EMU Europe', 'One Enlarged Europe' and 'One Constitutional Europe' that I alluded to in the editorial to last year's *Annual Review* (see Miles, 2003). In each case, we see a growing demand on the part of the European electorates to comment on the parameters of European integration. This is further evidence that the days of the 'permissive consensus' are now long gone. The gap between the governing and the governed is closing, at least in terms of the political elite in Europe increasingly recognizing a growing political danger to their own fortunes if they continue to ignore public frustration and dissatisfaction with parts of EU evolution.

I. The Dynamics of 'Belonging' and 'Becoming'

At first glance, we could perceive that there has been a conflicting and confused message disseminating from the European electorates in 2003. Nevertheless, the numerous referendums also illustrate that public perspectives on EU matters are differentiated. For the nine candidate countries holding referendums on EU accession, the focus was essentially on whether to 'belong' to the Union. Even though, in practice, the governments of the candidate countries were accepting as part of the *acquis communautaire* and *finalité politique*, steadfast commitment to many aspects of further integration (such as eventual participation in the euro area), the overriding question for their publics was comparatively simple – namely, whether to 'belong' to the European Union or not.

Of course, we also need to recognize that the use of a referendum presents a different kind of choice to the voter from that of an election (Leduc, 2002, p. 711). At least on EU issues, the use of a referendum has been designed to present the voter with a simple 'take it or leave it' choice. In 2003, the respective electorates were, for the most part, presented with a negotiated settlement – be it EU accession terms or the rules of the EMU system – and asked either to approve or reject what the governing political elite had decided to recommend. Hence, a referendum can be a means not just for the political elite to avoid their own divisions, but it can also act as a formal litmus test to help define the parameters of national EU policy.

As regards the referendums on EU accession, the electorates in the respective acceding countries were involved in was what can be roughly described as a 'process of belonging'. In the referendum campaigns, certain dynamics were influential (that are incidentally often perceived as competing factors in terms of political theory). On the one hand, identity-related issues presented themselves in which the electorates in, say, Hungary and Poland were giving (final) assent to their respective country formally completing a process begun in the early 1990s: that is, the incorporation of these countries into Europe's most prominent institution that would once and for all confirm their existing credential as post-1989 mainstream European nation-states committed to western liberal democratic values and capitalist market economies.

On the other hand, the campaigns were influenced by hard-edged geo-strategic concerns. These focused on the perception that EU accession, in conjunction with Nato membership, might – in some way – enhance peaceful co-existence in the region, as well as allow the new Member States to import greater political and economic stability as part of being 'in' the Union and further improve relations between these parties and key third countries, such as Russia. In short then, the accession referendums were an integral part of a 'process of belonging' – to a stable Europe with obvious liberal democratic principles, but also to a supranational European Union based on the core policy of the single European market (SEM).

To take this a little further, the political elites in the candidate countries were largely managing and/or trying to offset what I have labelled elsewhere 'EU-scepticism' (Miles, 2001). This translates into opposition to being part of the European Union in general terms, and assumes a high degree of hostility to the whole EU enterprise. It represents opposition to EU membership status and thus to being part of any kind of supranational Europe at all. As Henderson indicates, the political elites in the acceding states were – at least initially – successful in convincing their domestic populations that the 'process of belonging' is a worthwhile endeavour.

For the countries already in the European Union, the referendum dynamics were largely different, at least as regards 2003. Let us take the Swedish referendum experience of 14 September 2003 first. As Bruter highlights in this *Annual Review,* the population rejected participation in the single currency by 55.9 per cent to 42 per cent – a huge 14 percentage point victory. For the most part, the Swedish population was deliberating – implicitly if not always explicitly – about what Laffan *et al.* (2000, p. 193) have called, in connection with the EU, a 'process of becoming'. Such a process recognizes that the Union does not follow the textbook form of either the political or economic order, and thus its trajectory is difficult to plot. It is 'something incomplete' and still on the way to 'becoming something'.

With EU membership in hand, Sweden in September 2003 was deciding whether to accept one route in the 'process of becoming'. This was to be future membership of an ambitious euro area that is becoming ever more closely integrated in both the economic and political spheres, yet remains ultimately ambiguous as to the overall goals that it will deliver in terms of further political integration. Indeed, I agree with the assertions of Leduc (2002, p. 712) who argues that voting choices in referendums are often entangled with other political factors. When the Swedes said 'Nej' on 14 September, they were sending a clear judgement not just on the merits of the euro. They were also expressing their concerns about the existing democratic legitimacy of the Union, and their worries about the vague linkage between economic and monetary union (EMU) and further political integration leading to a 'federal Europe' (see Miles, 2004).

Given that EU membership – with the notable exception of the United Kingdom – is no longer that controversial within many of the (then) EU-15, the issue of 'belonging' is not so important. However, some caveats must be inserted here, most importantly, that the Swedes may not be 'EU-sceptics', but they are prominent 'federo-sceptics' (Miles, 2001). 'Federo-scepticism' assumes that, although belonging to a supranational Europe is acceptable, certain forms of further integration are not desirable. In particular, 'federo-sceptics' do not believe that the goal of the European Union should be a 'federal Europe'. The 'process of becoming' therefore operates within certain parameters.

The Swedish referendum was not so much about 'belonging' to the euro area – even if that is what the Persson government would have preferred. Rather due to the Swedish public's overwhelming 'federo-scepticism', the referendum debates focused much more on the issue of what the EU will 'become' politically, and how Swedish adoption of the single currency might 'lock' the country into an integrative and constitutional pathway leading to a 'federal Europe'.

Similarly, discussions in certain Member States on the merits of holding a referendum on a future Constitutional Treaty are indicative of the sensitivities of some governing political establishments to the increasing demands of their 'federo-sceptic' populations. They want to know how radical and 'constitutional' any future evolution of the EU will be and, put simply, where it will all lead. Although many of the EU governments portray any forthcoming Treaty as essentially about shaping the Union procedurally, so that the next phase of 'becoming' facilitates effective European Union decision-making with at least 25 states, this is not seen as the whole story in the eyes of the electorates. Rather, public discussion also revolves around any future Treaty creating a European constitution that represents – correctly or incorrectly – major systemic change in the relationship between governments and citizens in the Member States.

A distinct message seems to be arising from these two instances – that of a Swedish euro referendum and the discussions on the use of referendums to approve any forthcoming EU Constitutional Treaty: namely that, although 'belonging' may not be so controversial, the populations are far less sure about what the Union may become, and on this basis may seek to restrict its future growth.

II. The Paradox of a Popular Europe

The European Union is therefore confronted by a paradox if its governing political elite wishes to secure popular consent for its future evolution and ultimately ensure that, in the near future, any national referendums on a future EU Constitutional Treaty will not result in its rejection. Of course, part of the reason for any present or future governmental difficulties lies in the fact that the Union today represents what Brunkhorst (2004) calls a 'polity without a state'. Its evolution – until very recent times – was often presented by national politicians as an ambitious, unique, international organization delivering clear welfare outcomes. The government strategy usually highlighted practical economic and political welfare benefits, avoided the language of constitutions and concentrated on the supplementary dimensions of 'governance' and 'polity'. This was fine provided that the elite were happy not to seek popular consent for further integration through referendums. Once these were used – with increasing regularity from the early 1990s – it also became essential for pro-EU national politicians to use political language that the domestic electorates understand, and this is largely 'statist' driven. Affirmative referendums on the euro or on a future Constitutional Treaty increasingly require a change in the mindset not just of a sometimes sceptical EU populace, but also of their national leaders in determining how they want to win the argument.

The future 'becoming' of the Union is also made more difficult precisely because it has been seen as an elite-driven project. As Dinan indicates in this *Annual Review,* the Convention on the Future of Europe may have prompted greater information and discussion amongst Europe's political elite. However, it has had little impact in most countries in bringing the EU and its constitution-building closer to its citizens. Ultimately, the Convention process has been perceived by many as a further exercise in which the elite are seeking 'the construction of a constitutional self-mandate' (Closa, 2004, p. 184).

So how can the governments of an enlarging European Union deal with these varying pressures. On the one hand, they have the task of successfully handling public support for the economic basics of the Union, such as the SEM, and for 'belonging' to a Union of 25. On the other hand, there is often public opposition to the Union seeking ambitious constitutional solutions to improving the working of an enlarging European Union.

For one thing, there seems to be a paradox in trying to appease a largely 'federo-sceptic' electorate, and simultaneously pursue ambitious European integration that brings the EU 'closer to its citizens'. During the Swedish euro referendum, the 'Yes' camp was ultimately unsuccessful in convincing the electorate that joining the euro was a self-contained economic act – even if, as we know, this was never the case in reality. Rather the Swedish 'federo-sceptic' population feared that, through participation in a single currency, they might become locked into a core EU 'hub' which would promulgate further integration while not simultaneously addressing the lack of political accountability and democratic transparency in decision-making – part of what Miles and Lindh (2004) have called a 'Swedish euro paradox'. Overall, it would seem that most opposition to our 'process of becoming' revolves around the weak democratic legitimacy and poor transparency of general EU arrangements.

At face value, the solution seems easy for the governments of the Member States: namely to embark on EU-level reforms that will improve the democratic credentials of the Union and make the institutions more accountable to its citizens. In the national domain, democratic legitimacy issues of this magnitude are usually dealt with through constitutional reform. This is also precisely what the Convention on the Future of Europe was in part seeking to do at the EU level, and the draft Constitutional Treaty sought to provide. The Union was attempting, albeit to a limited extent, to speak the statist and constitutional language that EU electorates could understand. Why then did it attract so little attention amongst the EU population? And when it did, why did it provoke levels of public hostility given that its mandate was partly to resolve the very matters the EU population want to see addressed?

The answer seems to be equally clear. It once again returns to the issue that the Union has charted its past development as being a 'polity without a state' and, on this basis, a 'process of becoming' that avoided explicit constitutional terminology. Rather ironically, although populations would like to see a more 'democratic Europe', the majority do not necessarily want to see a 'constitutional Europe'. More accurately, they often feel happy with an evolving supranational EU with blurry edges, one that is supposedly distinct from a 'federal Europe' that has overtly constitutional implications. In many EU countries, 'EU constitutionalism' in the public domain is equated with a 'process of becoming', leading precisely to a 'federal Europe'. Because of this, the language of EU constitution-building is sometimes regarded largely in negative terms and treated with nervousness by both EU governments and electorates alike.

There lies a paradox at the heart of creating a popular Europe: how can we democratize the Union to appease public criticisms of the democratic legitimacy of the EU without talking honestly and assertively about 'EU constitutions' and thereby inflaming 'federo-sceptic' public opinion? In addition, how can the EU resolve any divisions over its fundamental goals without resorting to explicit constitutional arguments that the EU governments may find difficult to accept as part of an EU Constitutional Treaty? Finally, how can greater democratic legitimacy be bestowed upon the EU through a Treaty without resulting in that Treaty's rejection by public referendum?

With these considerations in mind, it is not surprising that, in late 2003, the IGC on the new EU Treaty failed to reach agreement. The draft presented to the December European Council summit came across as a project racked by tension between key governments, between the EU core and periphery, and divisive within and between existing Member States and/or acceding candidate countries. In any case, the proposed EU agreement represents a modest compromise that lacks ultimate coherence. It can be argued that that draft did not really provide adequate and effective management structures designed to govern the forthcoming EU-25. It also represents – at least for the moment – only a half-hearted attempt at an EU constitution, and fails largely to address fully any of the issues relating to a 'popular Europe' outlined above. Even though agreement was reached in June 2004, the EU Constitutional Treaty is to be put to public referendum in several EU countries, not least Denmark and the UK, where 'federo-scepticism' is rife.

In one sense, we could therefore regard 2003 as a key year for the Union. During that year, we have seen the electorates of the existing EU-15 and the candidate countries sending clear messages to their respective governments. It has also been a time when awareness by the EU political elite of the essential task of building a popular Europe has grown considerably. Yet, what has also been shown is that Europe's governing political elite remains as confused as ever as to how to achieve it.

Acknowledgements

It is once again my honour to act as editor of this prestigious publication. Like the European Union itself, the *Annual Review* is a mixture of continuity and change. As part of this cycle I would, firstly, like to give my sincere thanks to the departed Massimo Beber, Jo Hunt and Hussein Kassim for their long-standing involvement in the *Annual Review*. As editor, I wish them good fortune with future project and endeavours. However, we are extremely fortunate to have Michael Dougan, David Howarth and David G. Mayes join the ranks of the regular contributors, as well as John Peterson who kindly accepted an invitation to write the keynote article on the subject of EU–US relations. The quality of their contributions, alongside those of the regular writers, is testimony to the leading role this publication plays in informing and updating those interested in the European Union.

References

Brunkhorst, H. (2004) 'A Polity Without a State? European Constitutionalism between Evolution and Revolution'. In Eriksen, E.O., Fossum, J.E. and Menéndez, A.J. (eds).

Closa, C. (2004) 'The Convention Method and the Transformation of EU Constitutional Politics'. In Eriksen, E.O., Fossum, J.E. and Menéndez, A.J. (eds).

Eriksen, E.O., Fossum, J.E. and Menéndez, A.J. (eds) (2004) *Developing a Constitution for Europe* (London/New York: Routledge).

Laffan, B., O'Donnell, R. and Smith, M. (2000) *Europe's Experimental Union: Rethinking Integration* (London/New York: Routledge).

Leduc, L. (2002) 'Opinion Change and Voting Behaviour in Referendums'. *European Journal of Political Research,* Vol. 41, pp. 711–32.

Miles, L. (2001) 'Sweden in the European Union: Changing Expectations?'. *Journal of European Integration,* Vol. 23, No. 4, pp. 303–33.

Miles, L. (2003) 'Editorial: Towards a "Hub and Spokes Europe"?'. *Journal of Common Market Studies. The European Union: Annual Review 2002/2003,* Vol. 41, pp. 1–11.

Miles, L. (2004) 'Sweden, "Hitchhiking" and the Euro Referendum'. *Cooperation and Conflict,* Vol. 39, No. 2, pp. 155–65.

Miles, L. and Lindh, M. (2004) ' After the Referendum: A Swedish Euro Paradox?'. *Cooperation and Conflict,* Vol. 39, No. 2, pp. 201–6.

© Blackwell Publishing Ltd 2004

Keynote Article: Europe, America, Iraq: Worst Ever, Ever Worsening?*

JOHN PETERSON
University of Glasgow

Introduction

As Europeans and Americans prepared for the 2003 Christmas holiday, two dramatic international political events appeared to symbolize the diverging fortunes of the European Union (EU) and the United States (US). First, an EU summit in Brussels seeking to agree a new Constitutional Treaty for the Union collapsed on 13 December amidst acrimony and recrimination. The political gash between Donald Rumsfeld's *soi-disant* 'old Europe' (primarily France and Germany) and 'new Europe' (in this case Spain and Poland), uncovered earlier in the year by the war in Iraq, was painfully re-exposed. Dark mutterings by the French and Germans about punishing the recalcitrants – who refused to accept a new, simpler, double-majority voting system – in forthcoming negotiations on the EU's post-2007 budget suggested that the Union was entering a deep crisis.

The morning after the summit, news broke that US forces in Iraq had captured Saddam Hussein, alive and without resistance. At a stroke, the US-led invasion of Iraq was given a powerful new rationale. Even before video footage of a bedraggled, Rip van Winkle-looking Saddam aired in the media, George W. Bush phoned the leaders of the new European allies: Britain, Italy and Spain. Their French and German counterparts, Jacques Chirac and Gerhard Schröder, apparently heard the news through other channels and then had to do their best to send congratulatory messages to Bush that gave no hint of churlishness.

Coverage of the two events by the television channel, Sky News, was indicative of the media's treatment more generally. Literally one minute before Sky was set to air a live, in-studio interview with EU constitutional expert Richard Corbett MEP (along with veteran eurosceptic Bill Cash) on the Brussels

* I am grateful to Matthew Baldwin, Elizabeth Bomberg, Youri Devuyst, Lee Miles, Mark A. Pollack, Elizabeth Pond, and Michael E. Smith for useful comments on earlier drafts. Special thanks are due to interviewees consulted during fieldwork in Brussels, New York and Washington in 2003–04.

summit, the segment was scrapped to make way for 'an unfolding international event of greater importance'. More generally, the juxtaposition of the EU summit breakdown and the arrest of Saddam suggested that the transatlantic rift of 2003 was a product of deep-rooted, intractable problems: the fundamental weakening of the EU by its enlargement from 15 to 25 alongside the emergence of Bush's America as a military colossus with unfettered power and little use for any besides a few selected, submissive European allies.

In fact, a rich variety of reasons existed to doubt that the US and Europe were stuck in a moment – the build-up to the Iraqi war in early 2003 – and unable to get out of it. The breakdown of negotiations on the Constitutional Treaty was almost entirely unhinged from earlier divisions over Iraq and far less dramatic than it looked, since most of the institutional changes being considered would not have taken effect until 2009 in any event. Seasoned observers of the EU insisted that no deal on a Constitutional Treaty was better than another bad deal struck in the middle of the night (see, e.g., Moravcsik, 2003; Crossick, 2004), *à la* Treaty of Nice. Moreover, consensus, or something close to it, existed on nearly all the institutional changes of closest concern to US-EU relations: the creation of a European Council Presidency, an EU 'Foreign Minister', moves towards an EU diplomatic service, and language on a European security and defence policy (ESDP). The Brussels summit even produced a breakthrough on a previously painful issue: an EU defence planning cell that was compatible with Nato, for which American approval was both sought and secured prior to its unveiling at the summit.

Still, there was no denying that 2003 was a year of enormous strife in the transatlantic alliance. It was easy – far *too* easy – to blame the rift on the behaviour of the most aggressive, undiplomatic and unilateralist US administration in modern history. Simplistic or not, Rumsfeld's old *v.* new Europe distinction encapsulated a basic split that appeared and then reappeared within the EU's common foreign and security policy (CFSP), Nato, and the United Nations Security Council with remarkable consistency (see Peterson and Pollack 2003, pp. 135–6). As such, Iraq exposed as empty claims that the alliance between France and Germany, given their anti-war stance and the refusal of most EU states to support it, had been renewed as a source of accepted, legitimate political leadership of the EU (Pedersen, 2003, p. 24).

The central argument developed here is that the 2003 crisis in transatlantic relations was largely, even mainly, a product of European disunity, and not so much concerning Iraq *per se* as on broader questions of European integration. The refusal of any large EU government, particularly those led by Chirac and Schröder (along with Tony Blair's UK and Silvio Berlusconi's Italy), to invest any political capital in the EU, or take the slightest domestic risk to defend it, was long-standing by this point. It did not require a huge leap of imagination to believe that European integration would eventually resume again simply because it always does. As if to illustrate the point, early 2004 saw Blair try to agree a common EU agenda, especially an economic one, with Chirac and Schröder and to inject the Union with a fresh wave of 'trilateral' leadership, even if the idea was scorned in excluded EU state capitals and downplayed by Berlin and Paris.

Yet, one gauge of how much the European project had stalled in the early twenty-first century was widespread agreement amongst senior officials in Washington, Brussels and other European capitals that Iraq was simply not an 'EU issue'. This assessment said something profound about the European Union's aptitude as a player in international politics, and as an interlocutor to the Americans. It also suggested that Europeans needed to stop blaming everything on the eccentricities of the Bush administration, and confront a central problem in transatlantic relations. That is, it is impossible to modernize a largely one-dimensional and Nato-centred alliance constructed mainly for a static purpose – the cold war – as long as the European Union remains weak, rudderless and immature.

I. The Countdown to War

Any comparison of transatlantic relations before and after Iraq must start by acknowledging important lines of continuity. First, there were plenty of signs of trouble in US–European relations long before Iraq rose to dominate the international agenda, including ones that predated the election of George W. Bush in 2000. Widespread predictions of the demise of the transatlantic alliance (for examples, see Peterson and Pollack, 2003, p. 131) were a sign that the relationship was in transition and permanently emerging from its cold war parameters.

Second, Iraq had been a bitterly divisive issue in both transatlantic and inter-European relations for at least ten years. After revelations of an alleged Iraqi plot to assassinate George Bush Sr in 1993, the US had fought what amounted to an almost continual but 'inconclusive war of attrition' with Iraq, mostly with American air power (Bacevich, 2002, p. 152), which was little noticed or commented on in the media. The personal demonization of Saddam in the US, very much fuelled by the George W. Bush administration, often went unappreciated in Europe. It explained why many Americans cared passionately about Iraq and, in the absence of any real evidence, believed claims that Iraq was involved in the terrorist attacks of 11 September 2001.[1]

---

[1] An opinion poll for the *Washington Post* taken in August 2003 suggested that around two-thirds of Americans believed that Saddam was 'personally involved' in the 9.11 attacks (see «http://www.washingtonpost.com/wp-srv/politics/polls/vault/stories/data082303.htm»).

Third, the EU's forthcoming enlargement was raising new questions about its capacity for collective action and thus its institutional importance. Ironically, eastern enlargement had long been the most important American priority in Europe's integration. Yet, even before the Iraqi war, there was a growing sense within the Bush administration that the EU was 'no longer a geopolitical construct, it is disaggregating, because enlargement has diluted Europe'.[2]

The elaborate system for US–EU exchanges constructed under the Clinton administration, the New Transatlantic Agenda (NTA), survived the change of American administration. US complaints that the Union, represented by its troika – the Commission, the High Representative for the CFSP and the Council's rotating Presidency (the latter a source of considerable irritation and confusion to the Americans) – could actually agree to almost nothing in bilateral exchanges were not perceptively more frequent under Bush than Clinton. As one ex-senior US official put it: 'there was plenty of disillusion on our side before Bush got elected. For the EU, the meeting is the message'.[3]

Nevertheless, the June 2001 US–EU summit in Göteborg succeeded in giving a political profile for the first time to bilateral co-operation in justice and home affairs. Of course, participants had no way of knowing that the terrorist attacks of 11 September were only a few months away. Subsequently, at the first post-9.11 transatlantic summit held in Washington in June 2002, it was difficult to pinpoint tangible accomplishments given the summit's focus on long-term counter-terrorism measures.

A few months later, the Bush administration began to focus on Iraq (see Woodward, 2004). In retrospect, a speech by Vice-President Dick Cheney to a military veterans' group in Nashville in August 2002 was a defining moment. Cheney asserted that Saddam Hussein had ongoing chemical and biological weapons programmes and would possess nuclear weapons 'fairly soon'. He also ruled out any possibility that a UN Security Council resolution resuming weapons inspection would be effective, and essentially argued that a pre-emptive attack on Iraq was both unavoidable and imperative. Considered one of the 'Big Four' within the US administration on foreign policy (along with Secretary of State Colin Powell, Defense Secretary Rumsfeld, and Bush himself), Cheney gave the speech after virtually no consultation with the State Department.

The ensuing drift towards war, which shocked many in Europe, became wrapped up in the November 2002 US mid-term election campaign. Numerous Republicans ruthlessly painted Democratic opponents of the war as soft on terrorism. The campaign of one successful Republican Senate candidate in Georgia ran television spots that featured images of his opponent, Max Cleland (who had lost three limbs after wounds suffered in Vietnam), alongside

---

[2] A senior US official quoted anonymously in Grant (2003, p. 13).
[3] Interview, Washington DC, 2 December 2003.

Saddam and Osama bin Laden. Prior to the November US election, resolutions authorizing the use of force in Iraq were approved by resounding majorities in both houses of Congress (296–133 in the House and 73–23 in the Senate), with one Congressional scholar left to lament the 'dark shadow' that had been cast 'over the health of US political institutions and the celebrated system of democratic debate and checks and balances' (Fisher, 2003, pp. 390–1). As 2003 began, '[t]here was no robust policy debate in the United States for Europeans to join' (Pond, 2003, p. 48). More generally, America's Iraq policy illustrated the nostrums that 'foreign policy begins at home' and 'keeping foreigners happy is always low on the agenda' (Cooper, 2003, pp. 103–7).

Still, it would be simplistic to claim that there was no European traction on American policy. In the early autumn, Tony Blair joined Powell and the US State Department in pushing Bush to seek a UN Security Council resolution on Iraq. Bush duly appeared at the UN on 12 September 2002 and laid out a series of tough conditions, including renewed weapons inspections, that Iraq had to meet to avoid war. The actual wording of a UN resolution was subject to several months of negotiations, with the key exchanges between the US and French described by Pond (2003, p. 65) as 'haggling', but characterized as essentially obliging and professional by UN insiders.[4] On 8 November, UN Security Council resolution (SCR) 1441 was passed unanimously, with even Syria supporting it (largely in response to French lobbying). Saddam thus faced 'serious consequences' if Iraq was found to be in 'material breach' of existing UN resolutions prohibiting it from obtaining or developing weapons of mass destruction (WMD).

A few weeks later, the Prague Nato summit welcomed seven new central and eastern European states into the alliance and agreed an ambitious modernization agenda, including the 'Berlin Plus' arrangements for mutual support between the EU and Nato (see Cornish, 2004). After the Bush administration had refused most European offers of military support in Afghanistan in 2002, and fostered doubts about America's commitment to Europe, UN SCR 1441 and Prague appeared to signal that the US still cared about Europe. By extension, it was hoped, Washington might also be willing to deal with Iraq through diplomacy and multilateralism.

II. Old *v.* New Europe?

If, after reviewing 2002, it was 'difficult to imagine a more challenging year for the EU in its relations … with the United States' (Allen and Smith, 2003, p. 111), it was only because it was impossible to foresee how European gov-

---

[4] Interviews at the US, French and British delegations to the UN and the UN Secretariat, 17–18 February 2004.

ernments would almost sleepwalk into the worst transatlantic crisis in memory in 2003. To begin to understand why the EU split over Iraq so irrevocably, and more broadly how the Iraqi crisis seemed to usher in a new era in international politics, it helps to recall one comment on America's decision to bomb Iraq in 1998 as a punishment for its lack of co-operation with UN weapons inspectors:

> The Iraq crisis brought to an end the post-Cold War era. The Bush [Sr]–Gorbachev coalition of 1991 had finally expired. In the UN, the line-up was the Anglo-Americans versus Russia, France, and China. So, too, had the idea of collective security finally collapsed. (Hyland, 1999, p. 192; see also Juster, 1998)

What made the 2003 Iraq crisis (which truly deserved the moniker this time) so dramatically different was the position of Germany. To be fair to the Schröder government, the Bush administration effectively suspended all consultation with Germany on US policy towards Iraq in the latter half of 2002 (see Pond, 2003, pp. 48–9; Grant, 2003, p. 48). The timing was inopportune as Schröder and his Social Democratic Party (SPD) were trailing badly in the German federal election campaign at the time of Cheney's Nashville speech. Afterwards, Schröder stepped up his anti-war rhetoric, to the delight of both his own SPD and fervently anti-war and (often) anti-American east German voters, many of whom Schröder needed to pry away from the Party of Democratic Socialism (the reformed communist party) in order to win re-election. Schröder's main opponent, Edmund Stoiber, the conservative leader of the Bavarian Christian Social Union, went as far as to hint that his government would refuse even to deliver on its Nato responsibilities to the US – primarily, allowing the US the use of German air space – before quickly back-tracking. In a stunning reversal of post-war German policy, Schröder (via his campaign manager) ruled out German support for an attack on Iraq even if sanctioned by the UN. Schröder was hammered in much of the German press for ostracizing Germany from its most important ally (Pond, 2003, p. 58). The anti-war coalition in Germany was always fragile, but may have been shored up by the publication a few days before the German election of the Bush administration's National Security Strategy, which explicitly endorsed pre-emptive military attack as a means of confronting international terrorism and the proliferation of WMD. It was headline news as Germans went to the polls.

The perception that Schröder was playing electoral politics with Iraq caused outrage in Washington, which took most available steps to ostracize Berlin. Meanwhile, France and its President, Jacques Chirac, seemed to revel in Schröder's desperate need for allies. An ostentatious celebration of the 40th anniversary of the Franco–German Elysée Treaty in January 2003 was indicative, the emptiness of which was reflected in a list of mostly symbolic new acts of Franco–German policy co-operation. Chirac seemed actively to close off escape routes from the anti-war corner into which Schröder had painted himself, not least by playing on German fears, apparently real ones,[5] that France might cave at the last minute and join the US coalition. In an illustration of how individual leaders can sometimes override all countervailing pressures and determine foreign policy almost by themselves (see Waltz, 1954; Hill, 2003), Chirac and Schröder, together with very small groups of close advisers, crafted uncompromising anti-war positions on Iraq and thus made the bitterest of clashes with the Bush administration, and much of the rest of the EU, inevitable.

After early 2003, Iraq effectively ceased to be an EU issue. The Greek Council Presidency tried to make the best of an impossible job by brokering an EU common position on the crisis. After a weekend in February that saw millions of protestors on the streets of European capitals, the European Council (2003, p. 1) agreed a stance that was more hawkish than had been expected, stating that 'the Iraqi regime alone will be responsible for the consequences if it continues to flout the will of the international community and does not take this last chance'. But the extremely brief, one-and-a-half page statement also recognized that 'the primary responsibility for dealing with Iraqi disarmament lies with the [UN] Security Council'.

By this point, the Security Council's solidarity on Iraq had already suffered a body blow from what became known as the 'ambush' of Colin Powell on 20 January. France and Germany's invitation to a UN debate on terrorism persuaded Powell, an African-American, to cancel multiple political engagements on Martin Luther King Day. Despite accounts to the contrary, the UN meeting discussed anti-terrorist measures almost exclusively. Afterwards, Powell spoke to the press and acknowledged that 'several of my colleagues have made reference to the situation in Iraq' but also applauded the efforts of France and Germany (amongst others) to counter terrorism.[6] After Powell left the UN for lunch at the French UN Ambassador's residence, Dominique de Villepin, France's flamboyant Foreign Minister, faced the media and zealously stated that France would oppose any further UN Security Council resolution authorizing military action against Iraq. An incensed Powell apparently only learned of Villepin's statement after he arrived back in Washington. By all accounts, the war sceptics lost their only potential ally in the Bush administration, with Chirac's aides claiming that the incident 'destabilised' Powell (Grant, 2003, p. 20).

---

[5] To illustrate the point, a senior French military liaison officer visited General Tommy Franks, the leading US military commander in the Iraq war, in December 2002 to discuss how at least 15,000 French soldiers might be integrated with an allied strike force.
[6] Secretary Colin L. Powell, 'Remarks at the United Nations Security Council Ministerial on Terrorism', 20 January 2003, available from «http://www.state.gov/secretary/rm/2003/16756.htm».

Two days later, in response to a reporter's question about anti-war sentiment in Europe, Rumsfeld replied, 'You're thinking of Europe as Germany and France. I don't. I think that's old Europe ... vast numbers of other countries in Europe ... are with the United States'. Spain's Prime Minister, José Maria Aznar reacted by running with an idea that originated with the Deputy Editor of the *Wall Street Journal Europe*, the most relentlessly anti-EU of all quality US newspapers. Specifically, Aznar took the lead in engineering the 'Letter of Eight', which claimed that Iraq represented 'a clear threat to world security' and was published under his own name, Blair's, and those of the Heads of State or Government of Italy, Denmark, Portugal, Poland, Hungary and the Czech Republic. Soon afterwards, an even clearer statement of support for the US stance on Iraq was issued by the leaders of the 'Vilnius 10' states lined up to join the EU and/or Nato. Later, it was learned that the Vilnius 10 letter was actually written by a shadowy former US military intelligence officer, Bruce Jackson, who 'worked' the governments – of Albania, Bulgaria, Croatia, Estonia, Latvia, Lithuania, Macedonia, Romania, Slovakia and Slovenia – to sign up to it. [7]

Thus, Iraq was an EU issue only insofar as the European Council agreed a slightly more than lowest-common-denominator statement, after which a visibly outraged Chirac bellowed that the Vilnius 10 had missed a good opportunity to 'shut up'. In contrast, Iraq became a major issue within Nato, with Germany and France (joined by Belgium and Luxembourg), blocking a proposal to shift Nato assets to defend Turkey in the event of war. Despite intense mutual recriminations, with Europeans claiming that the move never required a vote and was effectively a US initiative that Turkey supported only half-heartedly, the action eventually was agreed.

For its part, the Bush administration persisted in seeking a second UN Security Council resolution authorizing the use of force against Iraq, in large part because Tony Blair pleaded that one was needed to sustain British public support for a war. France and Germany – joined by Russia – issued a joint statement on 5 March 2003 insisting they would not support any UN reso-lution that sanctioned an attack on Iraq. Five days later, Chirac made it clear that France would use its veto in the UN Security Council 'regardless of the circumstances' because there were 'no grounds for waging war'. Even leav-ing France, Germany and Russia aside, it became clear that a solid majority of UN Security Council members, including traditionally reliable US allies such as Chile and Mexico, opposed a second UN resolution on Iraq, which was subsequently withdrawn.

On 11 March, Rumsfeld caused a *frisson* by stating that if Blair could not secure a majority vote for war in the UK House of Commons, it hardly mat-

---

[7] See *Financial Times* (UK domestic edition), 28 May 2003, p. 19.

tered since the US could just as easily fight the war on its own. Ultimately, Blair received parliamentary backing for sending British forces into combat, despite losing two ministers from his cabinet, prompting Pond (2003, p. 74) to claim that '[a]mong western democracies, Westminster alone conducted a serious, substantive debate about going to war'. As for Schröder, some of his critics were appeased by his commitment to deliver on Germany's Nato obligations, and the actual German contribution to the war effort was considerably more than that of (say) Spain. The involvement of all other EU states in the military campaign, which ended in Iraq's defeat after three weeks, ranged from minimal to none.

The Iraq war was widely viewed as leaving the transatlantic alliance in tatters. The question of whether the Bush administration had reversed long-standing US policy towards Europe and adopted a strategy of 'disaggregation' of the EU, which exercised many in Brussels even before the war, took on fresh urgency. Yet, relations with Europe seemed a relatively low foreign policy priority for the Bush administration, and important only in connection with Iraqi reconstruction and the war on terrorism more generally. In regional terms, the administration was considerably more focused on Asia – particularly North Korea, but also (relatedly) China – and even Latin America, on which US trade policy concentrated following the collapse of the Cancún ministerial meeting of the World Trade Organization (WTO) in September 2003. One senior official in the Bush Sr administration was adamant: 'there's no disaggregation policy – that's giving them [the George W. Bush administration] more credit than they deserve for thinking about Europe'.[8] The leader of the US House subcommittee on Europe and president of the Nato Parliamentary Assembly, Congressman Doug Beureuter, was firm that the old/new Europe distinction was entirely and almost immediately forgotten in Washington, but repeated 'again and again in Europe', in a sign of the EU's sensitivity about its own dignity. Asked whether the Bush administration was seeking to split the EU, Bereuter insisted no, adding 'the EU has done a good job of doing that itself'.[9]

III. EU–US Relations after Iraq

After Iraq, three fundamental questions loomed for the transatlantic alliance. First, was bitter conflict between elites mirrored in declining mutual affinity between ordinary Europeans and Americans? Here, it was important to distinguish between short-term indicators, such as European public opposition to the war (which was overwhelming; see Kritzinger, 2003) or the American consumer boycotts of French and German products (which had little impact),

[8] Interview, Washington DC, 2 December 2003.
[9] Quoted in *European Voice,* 26 June–2 July 2003, p. 1.

and the longer-term evolution of opinion. Schröder and Chirac could both point to solid anti-war majorities in Germany and France, and (had they chosen to) rising anti-Americanism as the war began. Despite some nuances, primarily in the UK and the Netherlands, the war did not meet with noticeably less opposition in new Europe, including Italy, Poland, Spain (where the participation of Spanish forces was opposed by a margin of six to one; see Heywood, 2003) and Turkey (where anti-war opinion ran to 90 per cent or more and parliament voted against allowing US-led attacks to be launched from Turkish soil).

Yet, a careful sifting of evidence about more deeply-held attitudes revealed that Americans and Europeans mostly agreed on the nature of new security threats, even if they diverged on how to respond. Most continued to see each other as partners (see Kennedy and Bouton, 2002; Asmus et al., 2003; Pew Research Center, 2004). Mutual expressions of warmth fell, but only from historic highs in the 1990s. Even in France, polls showed a stronger affinity amongst the French for Americans than for the peoples of nearly all of France's neighbours, with Germans rated only very slightly higher on the 'warmth scale'.[10] Anti-Americanism amongst the French intelligentsia was reinforced by Iraq (see, e.g., Todd, 2002). But a leading French historian argued that it had become 'a routine of resentment, a passionless Pavlovianism' (Roger, 2002, p. 571). Others noted the rise of a counter-revolutionary, 'anti-anti-Americanism' in France (see Revel, 2002; Levy, 2003). Perhaps most importantly, the European backlash incited by Iraq appeared overwhelmingly focused on the Bush administration itself. When asked 'what's the problem with the US', nearly three-quarters of French and German respondents replied 'mostly Bush', as opposed to 'America in general'.[11]

A second question was: would the rift over Iraq damage existing and future transatlantic policy co-operation? Here, there was little evidence to suggest that – leaving aside European defence (see below) – much had changed. The war on terrorism was a mother of necessity in prompting unprecedented levels of exchange and collaboration on justice and home affairs policy, an area which dominated the EU's own internal policy agenda. After 9.11 galvanized the EU into agreeing a common definition of terrorism and European arrest warrant, the Bush administration found the EU able to negotiate acceptable bilateral compromises to cope with the consequences of American attempts to push the policing of US borders outwards from its own shores. Thorny issues such as passenger name recognition (PNR, or data on passengers flying to the US from Europe) and the inspection of cargo containers bound for the US were resolved with creative bilateral solutions. EU officials acknowledged that the

---

[10] See Chicago Council on Foreign Relations and the German Marshall Fund 'Worldviews 2002 Survey' (p.12 of pdf version), available from «http://www.worldviews.org/detailreports/europeanreport.pdf».

[11] See findings from a poll taken by the Pew Research Center taken just before the war in Iraq started, available at «http://people-press.org/reports/display.php3?PageID=681».

transatlantic relationship was extremely one-sided on JHA matters, with the US administration mobilized aggressively and at all levels in pursuit of clear goals, and the Union often on the defensive. Still, given America's long-standing predisposition to work via national capitals in this area, one Commission official at the cutting edge of transatlantic exchanges marvelled at how 'the Americans, even [US Attorney General John] Ashcroft have invested themselves in our nascent JHA structures'.[12]

The June 2003 US–EU summit in Washington brought a serious return on the investment, in the form of a bilateral agreement on mutual legal assistance and extradition. The summit was an unusually productive one more generally, advancing progress on a range of issues from aviation liberalization to WMD counter-proliferation. The Transatlantic Business Dialogue (TABD), which had turned dormant after being an important impetus behind US–EU regulatory co-operation in the 1990s, was relaunched. Perhaps most importantly, a pre-summit meeting between members of Congress and the European Parliament yielded fresh pledges to try to prevent future crises before they occurred by stepping up exchanges between specialized committees prior to votes on new regulations. One EU official involved in organizing the Washington summit observed, 'after Iraq, the whole purpose of the summit was to avoid the spectacular ... but the progress we made on a whole host of dossiers wasn't far short of spectacular'.[13]

The split over Iraq also had the unexpected side effect of inducing the Bush administration to be more co-operative on a range of economic issues. One was US foreign sales corporations (FSC), which allowed American exporters to set up shell companies to avoid tax. Several years earlier, the EU had won a WTO case claiming that FSC amounted to an illegal export subsidy. Fresh US legislation passed in 2001, ostensibly designed to be WTO compliant, was greeted by howls of protest in Brussels as no less pernicious than that which it replaced. After sending mixed signals about US intentions, the Bush administration – and in fact Bush himself – declared at the 2003 Washington summit that the US was wrong about FSC and would 'fix it'.

Six months later, the administration's lifting of punitive tariffs on steel imports, again in response to a WTO case brought by the EU (and others), was politically difficult heading into an election year. But the move was at least partly spurred by alliance considerations. Even the breakdown of the WTO Cancún meeting in August 2003 could be viewed as a product of *too much* transatlantic co-operation. Specifically, a joint US–EU paper on agriculture produced before the summit contained virtually no figures quantifying proposed

[12] Interview, European Commission Directorate-General for Justice and Home Affairs, Brussels, 11 November 2003.
[13] Interview, European Commission DG RELEX, Brussels, 14 November 2003.

European or American trade concessions, and thus became a lightning rod for the so-called Group of 20 developing states who were primarily responsible for the summit's collapse. More generally, if policy co-operation was used as a gauge, it was tempting to view transatlantic relations as being repaired with surprising speed after Iraq. But it was probably more apposite to conclude that Iraq had never infected US–EU relations as it did Nato or the UN.

That said, Iraq clearly had a significant hang-over on military policy. The 2003 US National Defense Authorization Act, described by one EU official as 'a hastily drafted piece of revenge legislation',[14] proposed blatantly to discriminate against European (and all other non-US) defence manufacturers. However, the Bush administration – even Rumsfeld himself – lobbied hard and successfully against it in Congress, threatening a Presidential veto if it passed in its initial form.

Two issues that touched more directly on European security – the proposed transfer of the US-led peace-keeping force in Bosnia to the Union and plans for an EU military planning cell – brought raw-nerved clashes within Nato. To the surprise of many in European diplomatic circles, the US began expressing fresh hesitations about transferring to the EU command of the Bosnia SFOR force in 2004 as planned. Yet, the announcement in early 2004 by the UK and France (with, eventually, Germany) that they would create new, joint, flexible intervention forces which would combine their hard, national combat capabilities for specific military tasks seemed to assuage American concerns, if not completely to dispel them.

On the other side of the ledger, the so-called 'chocolate summit' held just after the Iraqi war, at which France, Germany, Belgium and Luxembourg discussed creating a new EU military headquarters in a Brussels suburb, seemed designed to provoke the Americans. If so, it was a resounding success: the Bush administration reacted with fury despite widespread consensus in Europe that the summit was little more than political theatre, which was taken seriously by few within European (particularly German) military circles. Ultimately, the issue was defused by the agreement at the December 2003 Brussels summit on a military planning cell that did not undermine existing Nato structures.

If policy co-operation was mostly untouched by political tensions over Iraq, it was also clear that Europe was prepared to contribute relatively little where the Bush administration most wanted co-operation: in the reconstruction of Iraq. Here, the EU remained utterly divided, with (especially) the UK as well as Poland, Italy, Denmark and other states contributing significantly to post-war military policing. Meanwhile, the comments of the former French Foreign Minister, Hubert Vedrine, were indicative of the persistence of the anti-war coalition elsewhere: '[i]t's hard to take responsibility for a war we thought was

---

[14] Interview, European Commission DG Relex, Brussels, 14 November 2003.

wrong, now that the United States finds itself in a traditional colonial trap'.[15] It did not help that the US Defense Department, which increasingly seemed at war with the American State Department, barred French and German firms from Iraqi reconstruction contracts. If Iraqi reconstruction was considered a litmus test for transatlantic reconciliation (see Grant, 2003; Stokes, 2003), it was one the EU and US had still failed well into 2004.

A third question concerned the war's effect on the EU: was it enough to goad member governments into transforming the Union into a truly effective global actor? As one EU Council official put it: 'every cloud has a silver lining: our history is all about reacting to failure. Without the Balkan wars, we never would have had the CFSP. Without Kosovo, we never would have had ESDP'.[16] There were three reasons to think that Iraq would have its own ratchet effect and lead to an upgrade in the EU's external capabilities. The first was the European Security Strategy endorsed at the Brussels summit at the end of 2003, which echoed the US National Security Strategy's emphasis on the need for preventive action (if not 'pre-emption') to deal with terrorism and the spread of WMD. For once, the EU showed itself capable of agreeing on something like actual doctrine, as opposed to merely creating yet another institutional framework.

A second reason to believe that the EU might emerge from the Iraq crisis as a more effective international actor was the planned overhaul of its foreign policy institutions. In particular, the creation of an EU Minister of Foreign Affairs was widely viewed as upgrading the post of High Representative for the CFSP that it was replacing. Whenever the EU's new Constitutional Treaty was finally agreed, its main foreign policy provisions were effectively sealed by the end of 2003.

Third, and perhaps ironically, an act of European foreign policy that appeared to sideline the EU and its institutions entirely – the visit to Iran by the Foreign Ministers of France, Germany and the UK in November 2003 – gave cause for hope that large EU member governments were re-engaging with each other post-Iraq. The delegation, which convinced the Iranian government to accept tighter controls on its nuclear development programme, did *not* include the CFSP's High Representative (Javier Solana) or any representative of the Italian Council Presidency. Still, it did nothing that was inconsistent with a previously agreed EU common position on Iran and, ultimately, succeeded in both its diplomatic mission[17] and in reuniting the Big Three on a foreign

---

[15] Quoted in *National Journal*, 20 December 2003, p. 3833.

[16] Interview, Council General Secretariat, Brussels, 12 November 2003.

[17] The long-term success of the initiative was never assured. In early 2004, evidence of Iranian misinformation about its nuclear programmes, as well as revelations of a black market nuclear procurement network headed by Abdul Qadeer Kahn (the 'father' of Pakistan's nuclear bomb) which had channelled nuclear technology to Iran, put the durability of the European–Iranian agreement in doubt.

policy issue that, arguably, was a more important test case for European foreign policy than Iraq. One effect was to make Blair's attempts at trilateralism in early 2004 seem more credible. Whether they were or not, the experience of 2003 made it difficult to deny that the EU was in serious need of both fresh leadership and renewed unity, especially if Europeans wanted Washington to take Brussels seriously.

American political commitment to an integrated Europe, regardless of the short-term costs to US interests, was a more or less consistent principle underpinning post-war US foreign policy. A potentially major shift occurred in the transition from Clinton to George W. Bush, with the US reverting mostly to ambivalence on most questions of European integration, leaving aside the significant exceptions of European defence and justice and home affairs. Yet, claims that the US had adopted a new European policy of 'disaggregation' assumed that the Bush administration had a strategic vision of Europe's future, when the hallmark of its foreign policy appeared to be unalloyed pragmatism about working with whatever alliance – large or small – best served its own ends.

In this context, it was difficult to overestimate how much attitudes towards the EU in Washington were shaped by the words and actions of the UK. By the end of 2003, the Blair government suddenly seemed to disown the Convention on the Future of Europe and the Constitutional Treaty to which it gave birth, and to be running scared from both after ferocious attacks on them by the eurosceptic UK Conservative Party. The German-born British MP, Gisela Stuart (2003), a staunch Blairite who had served on the præsidium of the Convention, lashed out at the Convention as a 'self-selected group of the European political elite' and openly criticized the Constitutional Treaty just before the Brussels summit.

Far more debatable was the extent of London's influence on US foreign policy decision-making. Whether or not the special relationship had become a liability that damaged British interests in Europe and the Muslim world, one European diplomat spoke for many in complaining that 'British diplomacy now devotes so much time and energy to the US that they are disconnected from the rest of the world, and can no longer explain to the Americans why, for example, Germany, Chile and Mexico all opposed them on Iraq'.[18]

Putting the special relationship to one side: how, and how permanently, was the transatlantic relationship changed by Iraq? It was clear that the reservoir of mutual trust drained to depths not seen since Suez. However, it was also hard to argue that Iraq transformed the US–European relationship in structural terms anywhere near as much as the end of the cold war did. By the end of 2003,

[18] Interview, UN, New York, 17 February 2004.

there were signs on both sides of a genuine desire to move on and become reconciled. If the rift between the transatlantic allies over Iraq was the worst ever in the 50-odd year history of European integration, it did not appear to be ever worsening a year later.

Conclusion

If many Europeans were mystified by the Bush administration's behaviour in 2003, it was perhaps a sign, more than anything else, of how few Europeans appreciated that the US was always likely to go to war with Iraq at some point after 9.11, even under an Al Gore Jr administration.[19] Western intelligence, faulty or not, strongly suggested that Iraq maintained extensive WMD programmes and was close to a nuclear capability (see Pollack, 2004). Saddam Hussein had used chemical weapons around 200 times in the 1980s against Iran and Iraqi Kurds. Crucially, in domestic American political terms, Saddam continued to reward financially the families of Palestinian suicide bombers who struck Israel, a country viewed by many Americans as facing the same threat from terrorism as the US post-9.11, right up until the invasion of Iraq.

Obviously, we lack counterfactuals. But if there was always going to be a war with Iraq, two further, hypothetical, 'what if' exercises are enlightening. First, what if an EU of 25 had actually put the question of support for US policy towards Iraq to a vote? American officials claimed to have done the maths, and to have found a qualified majority in support of US policy. Second, what if the EU had privileged its unity and/or more directly responded to public opinion and united in opposition to a US attack on Iraq? Moisi's (2003) answer is unequivocal: the war would have happened regardless. Others were less sure. One senior European official insisted that 'a common EU position on Iraq would have made a massive difference. At the end of January and early February, Bush was completely isolated internationally and at home. Blair played a crucial role in giving him international cover'.[20]

Ultimately, it is unlikely that the European Union, united or otherwise, could have prevented a war in Iraq. What does seem clear is that regardless of its position, as long as it was unanimous, the EU would have emerged out of the war with more respect in Washington. If Europe had united against the war, the transatlantic rift certainly would have been worse in the short term. But the Bush administration's desire for reconciliation, given its need for European support to 'win the peace' in Iraq (as well as Afghanistan) might well have been stronger in the medium term. If we take a long view – and Hill (2004,

---

[19] This view was suggested or seconded by three former Clinton administration officials during interviews conducted in Washington in December 2003.
[20] Interview, 17 February 2004.

p. 161) is insistent and consistent in the view that 'European foreign policy is a long game' – it plausible to think that *any* EU position, in terms of shaping views about Europe in America, would have been preferable to its embarrassing disunity over Iraq.

Future historians might still conclude that Iraq will end up having an effect similar to that of Vietnam in the 1970s: that is, plunging transatlantic relations into crisis but, paradoxically, consolidating the alliance in the long run because of Europe's desire for leverage on US policy and will to achieve it through greater internal unity.[21] Even so, the EU emerged from 2003 in danger of prompting ever more disillusion and loathing in Washington – a sad result given how much it was admired (if often poorly understood) within the American political class in the decade after 1989. The central problem of transatlantic relations was not a growing cultural gap with which some commentators seemed obsessed (see Kagan, 2003). In fact, the best evidence suggested that Europeans and Americans still liked and even admired one another. Arguably, the real problem was that many American elites, including those who had once found the rhetoric of European unity seductive, had turned sullen and cynical about the European project, especially given talk of using it to achieve 'multipolarity' and the tendency of European elites to 'fuss endlessly with their wet noodle of a European Union' (Pond, 2003, p. 42).

There was much about the EU that was authentically innovative and always would be. Nevertheless, the radical EU enlargement of 2004 meant that the costs of non-investment in measures to make the Union work better were rising. One senior official's *cri de coeur* was indicative:

> We've reformed the Council but it is not enough. The European Council keeps violating all the rules they agreed at Helsinki[22] (in 1999), such as having only two delegates per state and avoiding long European Council conclusions … Blair and Chirac don't care and no one is looking after the system. Meanwhile, enlargement is already here: it is very cumbersome and we simply cannot negotiate with 25.[23]

By March 2004, a new Spanish government and the horror of the Madrid terrorist bombings seemed to have galvanized European governments, and even spurred them to action on strengthened counter-terrorism measures and early agreement on the Constitutional Treaty. By this point, a critical mass of EU member governments, particularly those of its largest states, showed signs of realizing that the Union risked being locked into a path of institutional decline.

---

[21] I am grateful to Helmut Sonnenfeldt, a long-time adviser to Henry Kissinger, for suggesting this point to me.

[22] 'An effective Council for an enlarged Union: guidelines for reform and operational recommendations', approved by the Helsinki European Council, 10–11 December 1999.

[23] Interview, Brussels, 12 November 2003.

One of the EU's greatest assets – its 'power of example' for other regions and regional organizations (Cooper, 2003, p. 42) – is a primary source of the Union's reputation for originality in Washington. It is also easily squandered, especially when, in the words of Luxembourg's respected Prime Minister, Jean-Claude Juncker, '[w]e have a certain illness in Europe. We do not love each other any more'.[24]

References

Allen, D. and Smith, M. (2003) 'External Policy Developments'. *Journal of Common Market Studies. The European Union: Annual Review 2002/2003*, Vol. 41, pp. 97–114.

Asmus, R., Everts, P.P. and Isernia, P. (2003) *Transatlantic Trends 2003: Power, War and Public Opinion* (Washington DC/Turin: German Marshall Fund and Compagnia di San Paolo), available at «http://www.transatlantictrends.org/».

Bacevich, A.J. (2002) *American Empire: The Realities and Consequences of US Diplomacy* (Cambridge MA/London: Harvard University Press).

Cooper, R. (2003) *The Breaking of Nations: Order and Chaos in the 21st Century* (London: Atlantic Books).

Cornish, P. (2004) 'Nato: The Practice and Politics of Transformation'. *International Affairs* Vol. 80, No. 1, pp. 63–74.

Crossick, S. (2004) 'Failed Summit Unfortunate, but not Disastrous'. *European Voice*, 18 December 2003–14 January 2004, p. 7.

European Council (2003) *Cover Note from Presidency to Delegations: Extraordinary European Council, 17 February,* EN 6466/03, 21 February, available at «http://www.ue.eu.int/ueDocs/cms_Data/docs/pressData/en/ec/74554.pdf».

Fisher, L. (2003) 'Deciding on War Against Iraq: Institutional Failures'. *Political Science Quarterly,* Vol. 118, No. 3, pp. 389–410.

Grant, C. (2003) *Transatlantic Rift? How to Bring the Two Sides Together* (London: Centre for European Reform).

Heywood, P. (2003) 'Desperately Seeking Influence: Spain and the War in Iraq'. *European Political Science* Vol. 3, No. 1, pp. 35–40.

Hill, C. (2003) *The Changing Politics of Foreign Policy* (Basingstoke/New York: Palgrave).

Hill, C. (2004) 'Rationalizing or Regrouping? EU Foreign Policy since 11 September 2001'. *Journal of Common Market Studies,* Vol. 42, No. 1, pp. 143–63.

Hyland, W.G. (1999) *Clinton's World: Remaking American Foreign Policy* (Westport CT/London: Praeger).

Juster, K.I. (1998) 'Iraq: An American Perspective'. In Haas, R.N. (ed.) *Transatlantic Tensions: The United States, Europe, and Problem Countries* (Washington DC: Brookings).

---

[24] Quoted in *European Voice,* 18 December–13 January 2004, p. 15.

Kagan, R. (2003) *Of Paradise and Power: America and Europe in the New World Order* (New York: Knopf).

Kennedy, C. and Bouton, M.M. (2002) 'The Real Transatlantic Gap'. *Foreign Policy* November–December, pp. 66–74.

Kritzinger, S. (2003) 'Public Opinion in the Iraq Crisis: Explaining Developments in the UK, France, Italy and Germany'. *European Political Science*,Vol. 3, No. 1, pp. 30–4.

Levy, B.-H. (2003) *Qui a tué Daniel Pearl?* (Paris: Grasset et fasquelle).

Moïsi, D. (2003) 'The Statesman and the Unstoppable War'. *Financial Times*, 23 December, p. 15.

Moravcsik, A. (2003) 'Viewpoint: Kick the Can Please!', *Newsweek International* (Atlantic edition), 22 December, available from «http://www.people.fas.harvard.edu/~moravcs/library/kick.doc».

Pedersen, T. (2003) 'Keynote Article: Recent Trends in the Franco–German Relationship'. *Journal of Common Market Studies. The European Union: Annual Review 2002/2003*, Vol. 41, pp. 13–25.

Peterson, J. and Pollack, M.A. (2003) 'Conclusion: The End of Transatlantic Partnership?'. In Peterson, J. and Pollack, M.A. (eds) *Europe, America, Bush: Transatlantic Relations in the 21st Century* (London/New York: Routledge).

Pew Research Center (2004) *A Year after Iraq War: A Nine-Country Survey* (Washington DC: Pew Research Center for the People and the Press) 16 March (available at «http://people-press.org».

Pollack, K.M. (2004) 'Spies, Lies and Weapons: What Went Wrong'. *Atlantic Monthly Online*, January/February (available from «http://www.theatlantic.com/issues/2004/01/pollack.htm».

Pond, E. (2003) *Friendly Fire: The Near-Death of the Transatlantic Alliance* (Pittsburgh/Washington DC: European Union Studies Association/Brookings).

Revel, J.-F. (2002) *L'obsession anti-americaine: Son fonctionnement, ses causes, ses inconsequences* (Paris: Editions Gallimard).

Roger, P. (2002) *L'Ennemi Americain* (Paris: Editions du Seuil).

Stokes, B. (2003) 'Trans-Atlantic Repairs Needed in 2004'. *National Journal*, 20 December, pp. 3832–3.

Stuart, G. (2003) *The Making of Europe's Constitution* (London: Fabian Society).

Todd, E. (2002) *Après l'Empire: Essai sur la decomposition du système americain* (Paris: Editions Gallimard).

Waltz, K. N. (1954) *Man, the State and War* (New York: Columbia University Press).

Woodward, B. (2004) *Plan of Attack* (New York: Simon and Schuster).

JCMS 2004 Volume 42. Annual Review pp. 27–42

Governance and Institutions: The Convention and the Intergovernmental Conference

DESMOND DINAN
George Mason University

Introduction

The Convention on the Future of Europe and ensuing Intergovernmental Confer-ence were major developments in 2003. Following a lengthy preparatory stage in 2002 the Convention – consisting of 105 representatives of the Commission, national governments, national parliaments, and the European Parliament – be-gan in early 2003 to put together a Constitutional Treaty for the EU, based on the reports of several working groups and an outline that its chairman, Valéry Giscard d'Estaing, had submitted in October. There was some concern that the Convention would not finish by the stipulated deadline of June 2003. In the spring, when the Convention's workload seemed insurmountable, Giscard asked for an extra couple of months, but the European Council refused. Hop-ing to show that the EU could still make progress despite divisions over Iraq, and believing in the importance of their undertaking, the delegates knuckled down in April and May to produce an acceptable text.

The result, even under the best of circumstances, was bound to be sub-optimal. After all, the Convention was constrained by 50 years of history and could not simply redesign the EU from scratch. The Nice Treaty, the EU's most recent reform, was part of the historical baggage. Indeed, Nice haunted the Convention and undercut the Intergovernmental Conference. Although widely reviled as a highly unsatisfactory agreement, a number of Member States wanted to stick to the Nice package of institutional reforms for which they had fought so tenaciously in 2000. As the Convention progressed and institutional issues became increasingly contentious and, later, as the Intergovernmental Conference headed toward derailment, most participants must have regret-ted that the Irish government (with the support of the EU and other national governments) had successfully pressured the electorate for a 'Yes' vote in the second referendum on the Nice Treaty, in October 2002.

© Blackwell Publishing Ltd 2004, 9600 Garsington Road, Oxford OX4 2DQ, UK and 350 Main Street, Malden, MA 02148, USA

Notwithstanding the Nice fiasco, what do the Convention and the Inter-governmental Conference tell us about politics and governance in the EU? Treaty reform is commonplace in EU history, or at least in recent EU history, but not using the convention method, pioneered in the drafting of the Charter of Fundamental Rights in 2000. By including representatives of various EU and national institutions, the Convention on the Future of Europe sought to open up the process of treaty reform and break the national governments' stranglehold. As well as diversifying the participants in the reform process, the Convention attempted to interest the EU's notoriously uneasy citizens in what was happening in Brussels. The Convention could not replace the Intergovernmental Conference, which alone has the authority to change the treaties. But the Convention could prepare the work of the Intergovernmental Conference and, precisely because of widespread dissatisfaction with the Nice Treaty, present national governments with a *fait accompli*. How well did the Convention succeed? What were the political and institutional dynamics at play? How effective was the Convention's leadership and what was the basis of its authority? Could the Convention have exorcised the ghost of Nice? Was the Intergovernmental Conference bound to break down? This article attempts to answer those questions.

I. The Convention

The Convention's members were experienced politicians used to fighting their corner but used also to making deals. Nevertheless, such a large and disparate body needed strong direction and leadership. The formal leadership structure consisted of a præsidium of 13 representatives of the Convention's constituent parts, including the chairman and two vice-chairmen. Giscard did not simply chair the Convention; he presided over it in regal splendour drawing on all his attributes and experience – a noble bearing, an imperious nature, a keen intelligence, and the aura of being a former head of state – to overawe the conventioneers and impress upon them the magnitude of the undertaking. He derived his authority not only from the mandate of the European Council, but also from having once been the directly elected President of France, histori-cally the EU's most important Member State. No matter that he was an old man epitomizing a youthful endeavour, or that he was a self-styled aristocrat trying to popularize and democratize the EU. No matter either that he unapolo-getically championed the cause of the big Member States and the EU's more intergovernmental institutions (the Council of Ministers and the European Council). He did so on the grounds that the big Member States represented the vast majority of the EU's citizens and that the balance between equality of citizens and equality of states in the EU had tipped too far in favour of the small countries. Regardless of his personal predilections and institutional out-look, few members of the Convention questioned Giscard's competence and conviction, or his determination to reach a satisfactory conclusion that would assure their place in EU history.

Giscard employed an array of emotions and affectations to get the job done. He swept into meetings of the præsidium and into plenary sessions after the others had taken their seats. With a nod here and a handshake there, Giscard would make his way to the chair. He kept an ornamental turtle with a dragon's head – a Chinese symbol of longevity and wisdom and a reminder that the Convention would eventually reach its goal despite a slow start – on his desk during plenary sessions (at the final plenary in July 2003, he ostentatiously fed it some lettuce leaves).

Giscard had strong views about what the Constitutional Treaty should and should not contain. His priorities were reform of the Council Presidency, a smaller Commission, and a new assembly linking the European Parliament and national parliaments. He also wanted to include a religious reference in the pre-amble. He was realistic about what he could achieve, although he misjudged the fierce attachment of most of the small Member States to maintaining national representation in the Commission and widespread resistance to establishing a new EU-level body. Hoping to keep his preferences in the draft document, Giscard included proposals that he willingly sacrificed later in the Convention. Giscard used every trick of the trade, including a judicious leak of controversial proposals for institutional reform to *Le Monde* in mid-April, to bolster his case. He was ably assisted by Sir John Kerr, Secretary-General of the Convention and a former British permanent representative in Brussels.

Giscard and Kerr were a formidable and intellectually intimidating team. They easily dominated the præsidium which, despite internal disagreements, was united in its determination to wrest an agreement from the heterogeneous Convention. Based on the reports of the working groups, amendments from convention delegates, and their own ideas, Giscard and Kerr drafted articles for submission to the præsidium, whose members sometimes complained that the articles in question bore no relation to the work of the Convention so far. But few members of the præsidium had the will or the means to redraft the articles entirely, choosing instead to see how the Secretary-General's – and now the præsidium's – draft would fare on the Convention floor.

The plenary sessions, which took place more often as the deadline for com-pletion of the draft Constitutional Treaty approached, were large and unwieldy affairs. Their most striking characteristic was a perceptible spirit of enterprise and enthusiasm, most of the delegates being conscientious and optimistic about the eventual outcome. There was much lobbying on and off the floor. Delegates from the candidate countries did not have an equal voice, but most participated actively in the proceedings. Indeed, the Convention provided a good opportunity for them to get to know Brussels and become acquainted with their counterparts from the existing Member States. As the deadline approached, delegates redoubled their efforts to whittle down the options and reach a consensus on the Convention's outstanding issues.

Whereas the European Council had appointed Giscard and the two vice-chairmen to act in an individual capacity, the other members of the præsidium and the Convention played an institutional role as representatives of the Convention's constituent parts (the Commission, the national governments, the European Parliament and the national parliaments). Of these, the national governments were easily the most influential and the Commission the least, with the national parliaments being closer to the Commission and the European Parliament being closer to the national governments in terms of shaping the Convention's outcome.

Actors and Interests

The Commission's position in the Convention epitomized the Commission's position in the EU: apprehensive and insecure. The Commission's institutional authority had been on the wane for over a decade. Almost everyone in the Convention claimed to want a stronger Commission. For those who advocated a smaller college and/or a better institutional foundation for the Commission Presidency, the current Commission provided a compelling object lesson. Inevitably, the Commission's two representatives in the Convention were relatively uninfluential. The college was divided over several key issues and the President, Romano Prodi, provided poor leadership. The Commission never recovered from Prodi's gaffe in December 2002 when he submitted a draft treaty without the knowledge, let alone support, of the entire college.

By contrast, the European Parliament was bullish. Here was an institution in the ascendancy, used to faring well in successive rounds of treaty reform. The Parliament relished the possibility of electing the Commission President if only to undermine the President's independence (without ever admitting as much) and strike a blow against the European Council. As usual, the Parliament sought to extend the applicability of co-decision and extend its budgetary authority not least by ending the anachronistic distinction between compulsory and non-compulsory expenditure. Like the Commission, however, the Parliament was not a unitary actor. Its delegation included representatives of the main political groups whose institutional preferences were similar (a stronger Parliament, if necessary at the expense of the other institutions, including national parliaments) but whose policy preferences sometimes differed.

The European Parliament delegation had ample opportunity to meet, for instance at plenary sessions of the Parliament and on the fringes of the

Convention – especially as the Euro-parliamentarians lived in Brussels. The Parliament's political groups monitored proceedings in the Convention, and the relevant parliamentary committees issued regular reports. As a result, the Parliament's delegates in the Convention were bombarded with instructions and exhortations, often of a contradictory nature. Pat Cox, President of the Parliament, generally urged a conciliatory line, which did not endear him to some of the Parliament's more aggressive delegates.

National parliaments were relative newcomers to the Brussels scene. National parliamentarians strongly resented their institutions' exclusion from EU decision-making, despite efforts since the Amsterdam Treaty to give them a more meaningful role. National parliaments and the European Parliament may seem like natural allies, but the European Parliament has flourished at the expense of national parliaments and is instinctively unwilling to share power with or otherwise strengthen its national counterparts. National parliamentary delegates made perfunctory efforts to co-ordinate their positions, which differed considerably from country to country depending on the degree of each national parliament's involvement in EU affairs, domestic institutional arrangements, and national preferences on a range of EU issues. Membership of European political parties or groupings occasionally brought national parliament, European Parliament, and national government delegates together, but those ties were generally weak. Nationality proved a stronger bond, often uniting national parliament and national government delegates (if not delegates of the European Parliament) in pursuit of a perceived national interest or preference.

The conduct of the Convention was instructive in that regard. Altogether, delegates drafted hundreds of amendments, both editorial and substantive. The governments of the existing Member States proposed amendments on almost every agenda item. National parliamentarians were less active than Euro-parliamentarians, although many amendments came from European political parties (the European People's Party and the Party of European Socialists), which attracted support from national and Euro-parliamentarians alike. Germany's national and Euro-parliamentary representatives were particularly active. National parliamentarians in many cases endorsed their governments' positions. Indeed, although the purpose of the Convention was partly to curb the Member States' monopoly of treaty reform, discussions in the plenary sessions and in the præsidium increasingly reflected national priorities as the deadline for completion approached.

If not masters of the Convention, national governments definitely made most of the running. Institutionally, they were best equipped to do so, having the resources of government ministries behind them. Also, as Giscard occasionally reminded some of the more disputatious delegates, national governments would ultimately decide the fate of the draft Constitutional Treaty in the

Intergovernmental Conference. Many delegates, in turn, accused Giscard of giving preferential treatment to national government representatives. Giscard made no secret of his affection for the European Council (his own creation) and respect for national leaders. He also appreciated the participation in the Convention of some Member States' foreign ministers, to whom he showed due deference.

The participation of foreign ministers – more joined as the Convention gathered speed – showed that national governments generally appreciated the relevance of the Convention and the importance of trying to shape its outcome. Needless to say, national governments did not come together as a group, as national parliamentarians or Euro-parliamentarians did. Discussions of the Convention in the Council of Ministers or the European Council were not efforts to forge a common position among national governments, but to assess the state of the Convention and its likely result. Nevertheless some national governments grouped together and agreed common positions. There was an obvious distinction between the big and the small Member States. Yet neither group was united on more than one or two key issues or made a collective démarche. There were joint proposals from some of the big Member States and joint responses from most of the small Member States, but there were also joint proposals from a big and a small Member State (for example France and the Netherlands, traditionally suspicious of each other, submitted a joint proposal on justice and home affairs). As the Convention proceeded, the essential distinction among Member States seemed to be not between the big and the small countries, but between the original Six (the founding Member States) and the rest, particularly those about to join in 2004.

The big–small Member State divide, which opened so alarmingly during the Intergovernmental Conference that preceded the Nice Treaty, was bound to resurface in the Convention, especially when it addressed contentious institutional questions which Giscard, precisely because they were so controversial, had not consigned to a working group and left for discussion until the end. Other EU developments in 2003 exacerbated tension between the big and small countries. At the beginning of the year, the Iraqi crisis caused a rift among the big Member States, but also between two of the biggest Member States (France and Germany) and most of the small Member States. At the end of the year, French and German disregard for the Stability and Growth Pact (SGP), which supposedly underpinned economic and monetary union, alienated many of the other Member States in the euro area.

A joint proposal by France and Germany in January 2003 – an important element in the celebrations of the 40th anniversary of the Elysée Treaty – brought the big–small country divide starkly to the fore. Its main features were an endorsement of the call, already made by the UK, France and Spain, for a standing President of the European Council (for a period of up to five years), elected by the European Council, and for the election of the European Commission President by the European Parliament (a long-standing German demand). Many of the small Member States (plus the Commission) immediately cried foul, resenting what looked like a Franco–German diktat, presuming that the standing President of the European Council would come from a big Member State, and fearing that the proposed European Council Presidency would undermine the Commission Presidency and therefore undermine the Commission, traditionally a champion of the small Member States.

Britain and Spain weighed in with a joint proposal in March reiterating the call for a standing President of the European Council, but rejecting the idea of the European Parliament electing the Commission President. They favoured the *status quo:* Euro-parliamentary approval of the Commission President who would be selected (if necessary elected) by the European Council. The avowed support of four of the biggest Member States (Italy and Poland, the other two big Member States, were also on board), together with Giscard's enthusiasm for it, ensured that the draft Constitutional Treaty would call for an elected European Council President. The opposition of three of the biggest Member States, together with Giscard's lack of enthusiasm for it, ensured that the draft Constitutional Treaty would *not* call for the election of the Commission President by the European Parliament.

There was general agreement among all Member States that a new position – that of EU Foreign Minister – should replace those of High Representative for the Common Foreign and Security Policy and Commissioner for External Relations. The same person would therefore chair meetings of the Foreign Affairs Council and co-ordinate the Commission's external relations responsibilities. The advent of the elected European Council President and the EU Foreign Minister would mean the end of the rotating Council Presidency, as currently constituted. Other Council formations would still need presiding over, but the six months' rotation would be replaced with a new system that would provide greater continuity and predictability, or what Giscard called 'stability'.

The rotating Presidency is a symbol, cherished by the small countries, of equality among Member States. Small countries also relish being in the international limelight during the Presidency. If they had to give it up, they were more determined than ever to maintain another symbol of equality among Member States: representation in the Commission. Of course the Commission was never intended to be a representative institution, although from the beginning (despite the efforts of Jean Monnet) its members were drawn from each of the Member States. Based on the rationale that an ever-expanding Commission in an ever-expanding EU was inherently inefficient and ultimately unworkable, the Nice Treaty finally broke the link between the number of Member States and the number of Commissioners. In return for giving up the right to nominate a second Commissioner, the big Member States prevailed on the small Member States to reduce the Commission's size to fewer than the overall number of countries as soon as the EU expanded to 27. Most of the small Member States mounted a fierce rearguard action to reverse that decision and maintain the right always to nominate a full Commissioner.

With the support of the big Member States, Giscard nevertheless pushed through a provision for a college of 13 Commissioners, selected on the basis of equal rotation among Member States, plus the Commission President and the EU Foreign Minister (the Commission Vice-President). The Commission would also include non-voting members from the other Member States, selected on the basis of equal rotation. Having lost the battle over the Commission's size and composition in the Convention, the defenders of one Commissioner per Member State resolved to win the war in the Intergovernmental Conference.

Whereas the big Member States were informally united on the questions of the European Council Presidency and the Commission, the small Member States were not, despite a number of efforts by them to form a common front. All opposed the idea of a standing European Council President and all agreed as well on the principle of equal representation in the Commission, but not that each Member State should continue to appoint a full Commissioner. Sixteen current and candidate countries – not including the Benelux countries – signed a letter in mid-March defending the rotating Presidency, the only point on which they could unequivocally agree. The so-called 'Athens 16', a different group of current and candidate small Member States – this time including the Benelux countries – met before the opening of the informal European Council in Athens in mid-April, where the accession treaties were signed, to oppose the election of a standing President of the European Council. Regardless of their composition, these groups of small countries, and another that met in early May, demanded that their preferences prevail because they represented a majority of Member States in the EU. As Giscard reminded them, they nonetheless represented a minority of the EU's population.

Just as the image of a confrontation in the Convention on institutional issues between united groups of big and small Member States was misleading, so too was the supposition that, on most other issues, the British stood alone. Peter Hain, the UK government's representative, was pilloried in Britain for surrendering sovereignty and pitied in Brussels for sticking rigidly to archaic positions. British euroscepticism certainly cast a shadow over the Convention, where most of the delegates sympathized with Hain's predicament. Ironically, fear throughout the EU of the force of euroscepticism strengthened Britain's hand in the proceedings.

Hain's utter rejection of the 'F' word (federalism), reminiscent of Prime Minister John Major's equally allergic reaction to it during the Maastricht Treaty negotiations, drew a predictable response in the Convention. While acknowledging that the EU had obvious federal features, most delegates were willing to sacrifice the 'F' word in the draft text in order to help Hain out and mollify the eurosceptics baying for his blood. Hain's other protestations elicited a mixed response. Oversensitive to eurosceptical complaints, at one point Hain objected to a reference in the draft document to the supremacy of Community law, a principle first established some 40 years earlier. The other delegates refused to humour him on that score. Many British positions were more defensible and won varying levels of support, however. Thus Hain argued that the disappearance of the pillar system did not mean the end of differentiated decision-making on foreign and security policy. On justice and home affairs the British were quite accommodating, appreciating the perils of unanimity for collective EU action.

Although often on the defensive in the Convention, Hain was rarely in a minority of one. The French and German representatives were in a stronger position, not least because they held the rank of Foreign Minister. Joschka Fischer and Dominique de Villepin may not have attended every plenary session, but their participation in the Convention lent additional weight to their countries' inherently influential positions. French and German officials co-ordinated their work closely, giving the appearance at the Convention of a concerted Franco–German drive, despite differences between them on a range of issues.

Italy was relatively unassertive throughout the Convention. Silvio Berlusconi, the country's mercurial Prime Minister, restrained himself and his country's representative in the hope of hosting the signing ceremony for the Constitutional Treaty in Rome. Spain, by contrast, felt no such compunction. In keeping with Prime Minister Aznar's generally forceful approach to EU issues, the Spanish government pushed certain points, notably preservation of the voting weights agreed in the Nice Treaty. Thus Spain resisted the Franco–German proposal, supported by Giscard, for a new definition of a qualified majority in Council decision-making (a majority of Member States and at least three-fifths of the EU's population). Having secured 27 Council votes compared to 29 for Germany in the Nice Treaty, Spain's position was understandable yet ominous for the outcome of the Intergovernmental Conference.

II. The Draft Constitutional Treaty

The draft Constitutional Treaty included a preamble and four parts. Formulating Part I, the quasi-constitutional section covering such key provisions as the EU's competences, institutions, membership, objectives and values, took up most of the Convention's time and effort in 2003. Part II came ready made in the form of the Charter of Fundamental Rights, and Part III consisted mostly of the existing treaties, with some important changes. Part IV (general and final provisions) included protocols and other ancillary material.

The results of the main institutional battles – the standing European Council President, the smaller Commission college, and the EU Foreign Minister – were incorporated into Part I. These were not the only contentious institutional issues. The size of the European Parliament was once again up for grabs, with the Convention agreeing on a limit of 736 members. The Constitutional Treaty emphasized that the EU is a representative democracy in which the principle of equality of citizens would have to be respected. Accordingly, seats in the European Parliament would need to be redistributed in order to correct the over-representation of citizens from the small Member States. Rather than settle the issue now, the Convention decided that the European Council would have to reapportion the seats sometime before the 2009 direct elections, in a 'digressively proportional' way with a minimum threshold of four Euro-parliamentarians per Member State (a protocol attached to the Constitutional Treaty allocated seats among Member States for the 2004–09 parliamentary term).

Increasing the participation of national parliaments in EU affairs was another means of strengthening citizens' links to the European level of governance. Indeed, given the continuous decline in the turnout for direct elections, engaging national parliaments more closely in EU decision-making seemed essential if the EU was ever to close the gap between the governed and the governing. The Convention therefore sought to engage national parliaments in a meaningful and constructive discussion of EU affairs. Giscard's idea of a joint national–European Parliament congress was not a bad one, but inevitably encountered opposition on the grounds that the very citizens to whom it should appeal would baulk at the establishment of yet another EU body. National parliaments nonetheless won the right to vet Commission proposals for conformity with the principle of subsidiarity. Henceforth, according to a new protocol, the Commission would send proposals to all national parliaments as well as to the Council and the European Parliament; if at least one-third of national parliaments challenged the proposal, the Commission would have to review and possibly withdraw it. That risked raising another hurdle in the already cumbersome process of legislative decision-making, but it raised the possibility of turning national parliaments into a locus of debate and lobbying on the EU, thereby stimulating greater citizen interest.

In another institutional innovation, the Convention proposed revising the Council's formations. In future there would be only two 'standing' Councils: the General Affairs and Legislative Council and the Foreign Affairs Council.

In its general affairs mode, the General Affairs and Legislative Council would prepare meetings of the European Council; in its legislative mode it would, together with the European Parliament, enact EU laws. The Foreign Affairs Council, chaired by the EU Foreign Minister, would deal with the EU's external relations. The European Council would establish other formations in which the Council could meet. The presidency of the General Affairs and Legislative Council and any additional council formations would rotate between Member States for periods of at least a year.

The Convention agreed that, except where the Constitutional Treaty provides otherwise, the Council would reach decisions by qualified majority vote. Thus the Luxembourg compromise (a Member State's right to prevent a decision being taken in the Council) would be scrapped entirely. As for the mechanism for qualified majority voting (QMV), the old weighting system would be replaced by a majority of Member States representing at least three-fifths of the EU's population, with provision for a super-qualified majority in some cases. Not only did the Constitutional Treaty extend the range of QMV, it also permitted the European Council to decide, albeit by unanimity, to change to QMV those issues still subject to decision-making by other means. That was a potentially powerful tool to facilitate deeper integration without recourse to tricky national ratification procedures, including referendums.

The Laeken declaration of December 2001 mandated the Convention, among other things, to simplify the EU's legal instruments. The Convention obliged by limiting the EU to five legal acts: European laws; European framework laws; European regulations; European decisions; recommendations and opinions. A European law, binding in its entirety and directly applicable (therefore not requiring transposition at the national level) would be the most common legislative act. A European framework law, the other legislative act, would be binding as to the intended result, leaving Member States free to choose the form and means of achieving it. European regulations and European decisions would be used to implement legislative acts (the former having general application, the latter specific application), whereas recommendations and opinions would be non-binding.

Institutional issues – whether or not mandated by the Laeken declaration – predominated towards the end of the Convention, but were by no means the only sticking points. A number of other items that eventually formed Part I of the Constitutional Treaty proved equally contentious. In particular, the question of EU competences and responsibilities – one of the Convention's main undertakings, according to the Laeken declaration – preoccupied the Convention in the first ten weeks of the year and demonstrated the difficulty of demarcating EU-level and national powers in a process as politically and historically muddled as that of European integration. The Convention eventually agreed on a short list of exclusive responsibilities (monetary policy, trade policy, the customs union and part of the common fisheries policy) and a long but not exclusive list of shared responsibilities (ranging from agricultural policy to economic and social cohesion). In addition, the EU would have the competence to promote and co-ordinate national economic and social policies and define and implement a common foreign and security policy, including the progressive framing of a common defence policy. Finally, the EU could take supporting, co-ordinating, or complementary action in areas such as industry, culture and civil protection. The limits of EU competences were governed by the principle of conferral – at British insistence, conferral by the Member States – and the use of those competences by the principles of subsidiarity and proportionality.

The values and objectives of the EU were relatively uncontroversial, apart from a heated discussion about whether and how to recognize the EU's religious heritage. The Catholic Church took a keen interest in the work of the Convention, especially in this issue. It did not go unnoticed that mention of an explicit Christian heritage would hinder (if not prevent) Turkish accession to the EU. In the end, the preamble merely included a reference to Europe's religious 'inheritance'. Membership of the EU would be open to all European states that respected the EU's values and were committed to promoting them together – hardly clear-cut criteria, either geographically or normatively.

Most delegates wanted to include the Charter of Fundamental Rights directly in the Constitutional Treaty in order to emphasize the EU's values and possibly increase the EU's appeal to citizens. The British and Irish governments were unenthusiastic about the Charter, doubting that it would have any effect on public opinion (except perhaps to provide more ammunition to eurosceptics), and fearing that strict adherence to it would raise business costs in the EU. But the Charter's location in the Constitutional Treaty, whether as a free-standing part or in a protocol, did not become a make-or-break issue. Notwithstanding the Charter's incorporation into the Constitutional Treaty, a majority of delegates agreed that the EU should accede to the European Convention for the Protection of Human Rights and Fundamental Freedoms.

Outcome

Bringing the various bits and pieces together and concluding the Constitutional Treaty was a Herculean task for a Convention of over 100 members from 28 countries. Undoubtedly democratic, the convention method was unavoidably awkward. It needed autocratic leadership to succeed. Giscard was determined to submit to the Intergovernmental Conference a single draft text instead of alternative versions of controversial provisions. He could not hope for unanimity, only for majority support from each of the Convention's constituent parts. By emphasizing the Convention's historic importance as the deadline fast approached, Giscard won the approval, grudging or otherwise, of most of the delegates for the general secretariat's final text (only a rump faction of eurosceptics formally dissented).

Even when tidied up in July before being submitted officially to the Italian Presidency, the Constitutional Treaty was inelegant and ungainly, rather like the EU itself. Nevertheless merging the treaties into a single text, abolishing the pillar structure, and granting the EU legal personality were important steps forward. In general, the Constitutional Treaty's provisions were a significant improvement on what currently exists. It promised a more intelligible, efficient and transparent EU. In short, it was a harbinger of better governance.

But would it succeed in appeasing the eurosceptics? Would it make the EU more likeable and less threatening? The 'F' word, with its connotations of excessive centralization at the expense of national sovereignty, was sacrificed on the altar of euroscepticism, although the 'C' word (constitution) survived. Given that the EU has state-like characteristics, 'constitution' is an appropriate word to use. It appears as an adjective rather than a noun, however, because the EU ultimately rests on the basis of a treaty negotiated between sovereign states. Yet even in adjectival form, 'constitutional' was bound to alarm eurosceptics and possibly cause some unease among the EU's otherwise indifferent citizens.

Also in deference to eurosceptics, the Convention dropped the well-known phrase 'ever closer union' from the Constitutional Treaty (while keeping it in the Charter of Fundamental Rights), substituting for it a vague reference to the 'peoples of Europe … united ever more closely'. The most striking change intended to mollify eurosceptics, however, was the inclusion of an exit clause: an elaborate procedure for a country to withdraw from the EU. As one national parliamentarian put it, this was intended to undermine the argument that the EU was a prison from which there was no escape.

By their nature, however, eurosceptics are impossible to appease. It is difficult to imagine an implacable foe of the EU changing his or her mind on the basis of the Constitutional Treaty. It is equally implausible that the vast majority of citizens will become enamoured of the EU because of the Convention and its outcome. Judged on their merits, however, the Convention was a useful exercise and the Constitutional Treaty a potentially important step forward. Although its institutional and other reforms may have been inadequate and were bound to be picked apart in the intergovernmental conference, the Constitutional Treaty was a marked improvement on what preceded it and a fitting testimonial to the EU's political maturation.

III. The Intergovernmental Conference

The Intergovernmental Conference was unlike any before it. Dissatisfaction with the narrowness and high-level haggling of recent Intergovernmental Conferences accounted in large part for the decision to set up the Convention. But the Convention could not substitute for the Intergovernmental Conference, only lay the groundwork and possibly reach a global agreement for the national governments to endorse. As the Convention came to an end, it was clear that many governments were dissatisfied with the institutional provisions of the draft Constitutional Treaty and wanted to reopen them in the Intergovernmental Conference. That risked repeating the Amsterdam and Nice debacles. At Amsterdam, EU leaders argued late into the night without reaching an agreement on institutional reform; at Nice, they argued at similar length before concluding an unsatisfactory agreement. Could the 2003 Intergovernmental Conference have ended successfully, with an agreement that improved the EU's institutional efficiency and legitimacy without alienating one or more of the Member States?

The legacy of Amsterdam and Nice should have benefited the Intergovernmental Conference. None of the EU's leaders wanted to relive those painful episodes. Yet most wanted to reopen the Nice package in some way or other. For many of the small Member States, especially those about to join the EU who had not participated in the pre-Nice conference but were affected by its outcome, the new Intergovernmental Conference presented an opportunity to reclaim the right to representation in the Commission even after the EU expanded to 27 countries. For Spain and Poland, the Nice agreement on voting weights was a major and, in Spain's case, hard-fought victory. Why should Spain surrender such an advantage, to which the other Member States had agreed, especially as the Laeken declaration had not specifically put the Nice package on the Convention's agenda? The Poles were equally justified in claiming that, having recently won a referendum on the terms of EU membership, it would be wrong (and politically risky) to give away the prize of near-equality of voting weights with France and Germany.

What about the much-vaunted 'common European interest'? Unlike the Commission, the Member States are not obliged to take that nebulous consideration into account. There is a presumption, nonetheless, that Member States will not deliberately harm or undermine the common interest. By any stretch of the imagination, it is difficult to see how Spanish and Polish intransigence on the question of QMV was harmful to the EU. After all, the two countries were defending an arrangement which, when arrived at less than four years previously as part of a deal intended to facilitate enlargement, was hailed in the EU as a major breakthrough. Perhaps France, rather than Spain or Poland, deserves criticism for acting against the common interest by adamantly refusing to explore the possibility of a compromise on the formula for qualified majority voting.

Ideally, the legacy of Amsterdam and Nice should have extended beyond the personal experiences of the EU's leaders and included strong public pressure to get the EU's institutional arrangements right this time round. Yet for all the talk of closing the democratic deficit and connecting with Europe's citizens, national governments know that most people are uninterested in the vagaries of QMV. Not only that, but governments can make political capital at home by pushing their countries' institutional positions in the EU – by securing more votes in the Council or retaining the right to nominate a Commissioner – but are unlikely to help their domestic situations by improving the EU's institutional arrangements without gaining, let alone sacrificing, perceived national advantage.

Whereas the Council Presidency played little part in the Convention, the Presidency usually plays a pivotal role in an Intergovernmental Conference. The Intergovernmental Conference of 2003 was ill served by having Italy in the chair. Desperate to conclude the Intergovernmental Conference in December, Italy tried to ram through the draft Constitutional Treaty instead of mediating between Member States and attempting to broker a compromise. To some extent Italy's approach was understandable. Revisiting the Convention's institutional proposals meant 'opening a Pandora's Box'. Yet the strength of national positions on various institutional issues meant that a negotiation of them could not be avoided. Italy wasted precious time at the beginning of the Intergovernmental Conference denying the existence of deep divisions between the Member States. By the time that Italy took its responsibilities seriously, it was probably too late to rescue the December summit from failure, although the depth of French and Spanish feelings in any case made a breakdown appear inevitable.

The European Council is rightly celebrated for its indispensable directorial role in the EU. Yet its strength – regular, close encounters of the EU's leading politicians – is also its weakness. Personalities are important in politics. Highly successful, headstrong national politicians, used to getting their own way at home, often grate on each other in the European Council. The personalities of the national leaders most centrally involved in the Intergovernmental Conference exacerbated the problem. By December 2003, Chirac had thoroughly alienated the small Member States, plus the big Member States that did not side with France over Iraq. Never missing an opportunity to put down the Commission President (Prodi is a bitter domestic rival), Berlusconi lacked the credibility to be an effective Council chair. Aznar's obduracy was legendary in the European Council. Rarely have personal factors contributed so negatively to a decisive political development.

Threats by France and Germany to link the result of the Brussels summit to the new financial perspective (by implication cutting funds to Spain and Poland) and to forge ahead with a 'core' or 'pioneer' group of like-minded Member States (by implication excluding Spain and Poland) clearly backfired. Spain drew a more pertinent parallel between the pious incantations of France and Germany in the Intergovernmental Conference and their disregard for the Stability and Growth Pact outside it. As Aznar observed, perhaps there is already a two-tier EU, the key distinction being between the economic reformers and the recalcitrants; between Member States that are improving employment, growth and productivity, and those that are not.

The breakdown of the Brussels summit cast a pall over politics and government in the EU. The state of the Intergovernmental Conference mirrored the state of the EU as a whole, with Member States at loggerheads over a range of internal and external policies. The conduct of the Intergovernmental Conference, in which 25 countries participated, although ten of them had not yet formally acceded to the EU, illustrated the difficulties awaiting the EU after enlargement. All the more reason for the Member States to surmount the challenges ahead by reconvening the Intergovernmental Conference, resolving the institutional issues, and reaching agreement on the Constitutional Treaty as soon as possible.

Not that the EU is in danger of falling apart without it. Even if agreed upon once the Intergovernmental Conference resumed in 2004, the Constitutional Treaty would face formidable hurdles on the road to ratification. Failure to implement the Constitutional Treaty, however, would not be disastrous for the EU. For the Constitutional Treaty is desirable but not essential; the EU would be poorer, but not unworkable, without it. Even with the Constitutional Treaty in place, strong national interests, a wilful European Parliament, and a weak Commission would continue to impair the EU's effectiveness. The EU needs better leadership and a more congenial political and economic environment, not simply the palliative of a Constitutional Treaty, to restore its lustre and sense of purpose.

The Greek Presidency: In the Shadow of War

DIONYSSIS G. DIMITRAKOPOULOS
Birkbeck College, University of London
ARGYRIS G. PASSAS
Panteion University of Social and Political Sciences, Athens

Introduction

Greece took over the Council Presidency on 1 January 2003, just when the US-led war on Iraq was looming, almost a year after the establishment of the Convention on the Future of Europe, and just days after the decision of the European Council in Copenhagen to let ten central, eastern and southern European countries into the EU. Faced with this set of challenges was the most maturely pro-European Prime Minister Greece has had since its accession in January 1981. Veteran Social Democrat Premier Costas Simitis was widely considered in European political circles as a 'safe pair of hands'. He was regarded as an experienced statesman, and one of the most senior members of the European Council 'with a quiet authority that his colleagues respect' (Ludlow, 2002, p. 21) who had led his country into the final stage of EMU. This was matched by the profile of the Greek Foreign Minister, George Papandreou, widely credited for radically transforming Greek foreign policy *vis-à-vis* Turkey with Simitis' active support.

This was the first Presidency to work under the new arrangements agreed by the Fifteen in Seville in June 2002. The new arrangements emphasize a combination of annual operating programmes of Council activities with a multi-annual strategic programme agreed every December (see Dinan, pp. 27–42 in this *Review*). This, in turn, reduces the ability of Presidency holders to pursue their own preferences (Ludlow, 2002, p. 2) and places greater emphasis on those of the Council. Acting in this context, the Greek government identified five priority areas that reflected a mixture of national and European issues, namely, enlargement, the implementation of the Lisbon strategy, immigration and asylum, the debate on the future of Europe and the role of the EU as an international actor.

I. Foreign Affairs and Defence: Herculean Tasks

The open disagreement between the Member States on the cardinal issue of war in Iraq cast a shadow on both the EU's long-term capacity to act in this area and the Greek Presidency. These divisions and the deep-rooted, historically defined anti-US feeling in the domestic political context reduced the capacity of the Greek Presidency to act as honest broker. The active support of the US-led policy line on Iraq by eight European states (the UK, Italy, Spain, Portugal, Denmark, Poland, Hungary, and the Czech Republic) broke with consultation practice established within European Political Co-operation and the common foreign and security policy. It also clearly undermined the capacity of the Greek government to mend any fences and earned them public criticism from Prime Minister Simitis (*Guardian*, 31 January 2003, p. 4). Therefore, the Presidency's highly contested (*Financial Times*, 13 February 2003, p. 8) decision to convene the extraordinary meeting of the European Council of 17 February 2003 (the so-called 'war summit') could only reaffirm the long-held view that the UN should remain 'at the centre of the international order' and highlight the fact that war was not inevitable. However, it did not manage to identify a common way forward.

Nevertheless, the lengthy process of institution-building in the area of defence continued. There was agreement amongst the Fifteen to establish in 2004 an intergovernmental armaments agency, subject to the authority of the Council, with a view to promoting competition in the European defence market.

II. Enlargement

Although the negotiations for the accession of ten new states were concluded in December 2002, two issues remained: first, the formalization of the agreement reached in Copenhagen in December 2002 as regards the adjustment of the 2000–06 financial perspective for the purposes of enlargement; second, the interrelated concerns regarding Cyprus and Turkey. The decision of 19 May 2003 (*OJEC* L147, 14 June 2003) resolved the first issue, and the accession treaties were signed in Athens on 16 April 2003. The quest for a political solution to the thorny issue of the reunification of Cyprus (a full Member State as of 1 May 2004) remained part of the Greek government's successful strategy to 'Europeanize' its relations with Turkey. In that context a revised EU accession partnership with Turkey was adopted, and the Union emphasized the actual implementation of the legislative reforms duly adopted by the Turkish government.

III. Economic Reform

The European Council endorsed the revised Broad Economic Policy Guidelines and Employment Guidelines that, for the first time, cover a three-year period. In addition to further steps taken in the liberalization of the energy market, the agreement on taxation of income from cross-border savings which ended a ten-year stalemate was a significant success. Twelve of the Fifteen will have to share data on money that EU citizens have abroad so as to enable taxation of that income in the savers' country of origin (exceptional arrangements were agreed for Austria, Luxembourg and Belgium). Furthermore, a significant decision was reached in June 2003 whereby the Commission will be responsible for negotiating international agreements in the area of air transport. The agreement on the reform of the CAP (June 2003) is also noteworthy as it generalizes the notion of decoupling and the principle of single farm payments.

IV. Immigration, Judicial Co-operation and Institutional Reform

Two significant agreements were reached in the area of immigration: the agreement in principle to finance the EU's action in this area at least in part from the common budget (after 2006), and the EU–US extradition and mutual assistance agreements (June 2003). The end of the fourth Greek Presidency saw the submission by Convention President Giscard d'Estaing of the draft Constitutional Treaty prepared by the Convention on the Future of Europe. The European Council approved the candidacy of Jean-Claude Trichet for the Presidency of the European Central Bank. In addition, the Fifteen reached agreement on the statute and the financing of European political parties. Last, but not least, there was political agreement on the reform of the staff regulation reached in the General Affairs and External Relations Council of 19 May 2003.

Conclusion: Managing Political Divisions

These issues were not politically contentious in the Greek context. The fourth Greek Presidency became a core governmental argument in the run-up to the electoral contest of March 2004 and the last major political event under Simitis' premiership. Any attempt to evaluate the rotating Presidency must be very cautious, especially when it comes to using the notions of success and failure. Failure is improbable due to the organizational and political features of the Union's system (in particular those of the Council). Rather, it is a question of the political and administrative capacity of the Presidency to increase the pace of integration in first pillar issues and its ability to manage political divergence in the intergovernmental arena. The fourth Greek Presidency has a very positive record in both.

References

Ludlow, P. (2002) *The Greek Presidency*, Briefing Note No. 9 (Brussels: Euro Comment).

JCMS 2004 Volume 42. Annual Review pp. 47–50

The Italian Presidency

LUCIA QUAGLIA
University of Limerick

Introduction

Italy held the rotating Council Presidency from July to December 2003, at a
very critical juncture in the process of European integration, and for Italy's
trajectory therein. The 2004 enlargement was imminent, diplomatic relations
between EU Member States and between the EU and US had been soured
by the war in Iraq, economic growth remained a major challenge for Europe,
and an Intergovernmental Conference (IGC) was held to negotiate the new
Constitutional Treaty. The Council Presidency was particularly significant
for Italy in that it was the first held by the Italian centre-right government of
Silvio Berlusconi, whose governing coalition is usually portrayed as more
eurosceptic than its predecessors. A review of the activity and performance of
the Italian Presidency can be organized under three main headings: the IGC,
the external relations of the EU, and relations with other EU institutions and
the Member States.

I. The Intergovernmental Conference

The programme presented by the Italian government when it took over the
Presidency in July 2003 highlighted five 'priority objectives', the first and most
important of which was the completion of negotiations at the IGC on the new
Constitutional Treaty. The ten accession states participated fully in the work
of the IGC, whereas the three candidate countries – Bulgaria, Romania and
Turkey – participated only as observers.

The negotiations were complex and were affected by many structural
factors, such as time constraints – the IGC lasted less than three months (4
October–13 December 2003); the negotiating positions of 25 countries with
different preferences on core issues; and several controversial points unresolved
or inherited from previous negotiations, such as the voting system agreed in

the Nice Treaty in December 2000. These factors limited the President's room for manœuvre and ultimately determined the failure of the IGC to agree on the new Treaty. On the other hand, the performance of the Presidency in the IGC was negatively affected, especially in the final stage of the negotiations during the European Council in December 2003, by the over-confident style of the Italian Prime Minister and his limited familiarity with EU dynamics. Internationally, Berlusconi did not have the necessary authority to gather consensus for difficult compromises on the Constitution for Europe. This, however, does not detract from the considerable expertise and competence demonstrated by senior Italian officials throughout the Presidency.

The working method adopted by the Italian Presidency in the IGC was not to reopen negotiations on the whole draft Treaty as agreed by the Convention in June 2003, but to focus instead on the points that had not been settled. A tight timetable was set by the Presidency in order to reach overall agreement by December 2003, aiming to sign the Constitutional Treaty before the EP elections in May 2004 (*Agence Europe*, 4 September 2003).

The main stumbling block in the IGC were the negotiations on the EU institutional framework. Principally, these were: the voting weights in the Council; Council voting rules, i.e. the increased usage of qualified majority voting (QMV) in several policy areas; the size of the Commission and the European Parliament; the creation of a President of the European Council and the status of the EU Foreign Minister; and constitutional revisions. The preamble, too, was the object of intense discussion concerning a reference to God and Europe's Christian heritage. However, it was disagreement on the voting weights in the Council that ultimately led to the collapse of the negotiations.

Besides the institutional issues, 'focal points' of negotiations in the IGC concerned the EU common security and defence policy and judicial co-operation. In the end, agreement was reached on both issues. However, on judicial co-operation, an 'emergency break' was inserted by the Presidency with the support of some of the Member States.

II. Other Activities of the Presidency

As part of the activities of the Presidency, Italy chaired the meetings of Ecofin and the Euro Group, where the Stability and Growth Pact (SGP) was the defining issue on the table. In November 2003, the Italian Presidency, after calling for a vote on France and Germany's breach of the Pact, went on to work out a political declaration that gave France and Germany more time to comply with the SGP, while suspending the threat of fines should they subsequently fail. The conduct of the Presidency in this matter was criticized by some of the smaller Member States, and by the Commission, which decided to bring the case before the European Court of Justice.

Major divergences between the Italian Presidency and the rest of the EU emerged over questions pertaining to the external relations of the EU, as well as EU inter-institutional relations. Two important meetings between the EU and Russia (October) and the EU and the Ukraine (November) took place in 2003. During these summits, the positions expressed by the Italian Prime Minister in his role as Council President were at odds with the stance adopted by the Commission (and some other Member States), causing tensions amongst the institutions.

More generally, relations between the Presidency and the Commission and, in particular, between the Italian Council President, Berlusconi, and the Italian President of the Commission, Romano Prodi, were difficult. This was not so much because of conflicts of power between EU institutions. Rather it stemmed from the likelihood that both leaders would compete for the office of Prime Minister at the next Italian general election. Domestic political rivalry thus led to a novel form of 'politicization' of the Presidency, whereby the EU arena became an extension of the Italian political space.

The relationship between the Italian Presidency and the European Parliament began disastrously when, during the stormy session in which the Italian government presented its programme to the EP in July 2003, the Italian Prime Minister likened a German MEP to a 'concentration camp guard'.

On the whole, relations between Italy and the main Member States were uneasy. After Berlusconi's gaffe at the EP, relations with the German government were strained further as a result of several anti-German statements made by a Northern League junior minister. Relations between Berlusconi and French President Jacques Chirac had never been good, and those with the British Prime Minister Tony Blair deteriorated over time. The lukewarm relationship between Italy and the other main EU players was also illustrated by the fact that, on the important matter of defence and security policy, the Italian government, was systematically excluded from discussions taking place between France, Germany and the UK.

Conclusion

Overall, the 2003 Italian Presidency was characterized by three key inter-related features: first, its uneven performance in the various EU activities in which it was engaged; second, the idiosyncratic and controversial style of its President; third, a novel form of politicization, in which the Presidency was affected through an externalization of domestic Italian politics. Domestically, the 'dog that did not bark' was the breaking out of major disagreements within the Italian government. A potential for conflict on core issues, such as the Constitutional Treaty, was present within the heterogeneous centre-right coalition, not least because the coalition represented the cohabitation of the old Christian Democratic tradition (strongly pro-EU), the National Alliance (recently converted to Europe), and the unstable and populist Northern League (with its newly-embraced eurosceptic rhetoric). Notwithstanding the IGC setbacks, considerable progress was made across a broad range of issues, on which the Irish Presidency proceeded to build.

Internal Policy Developments

DAVID HOWARTH
University of Edinburgh

Introduction

2003 marked the tenth anniversary of the internal market and new priorities were established for the next three years. The Lisbon process, set out in March 2000, continued to structure action in several policy areas, and the looming enlargement of the EU required various policy adjustments. The open method of co-ordination was simplified and streamlined with regard to the European Employment Strategy (EES), the Broad Economic Policy Guidelines (BEPG) and social policy within a three-year time-frame. The sixth framework research programme was launched providing several billion euros of funding for several hundred projects. On economic and monetary union (EMU), 2003 witnessed decisions seriously undermining the credibility of the fiscal policy rules governing macroeconomic policy co-ordination. In competition policy, the Commission developed a modernized anti-trust and merger control. Several significant developments in EU budgeting also feature in 2003. The mid-term review of the common agricultural policy (CAP) was finally adopted after French blockage during 2002.

I. Economic and Related Policies

The Lisbon Process: Competitiveness, Growth and Employment

A great deal of emphasis – rhetorical and otherwise – was placed on progress with the Lisbon strategy objectives. In January, the Commission adopted its review identifying priorities for further progress in the context of an enlarged EU and Ecofin highlighted priorities with regard to competitiveness and the EU employment strategy. The March European Council insisted on the implementation of sound macroeconomic policies in order to restore confidence and economic growth, and the closer co-ordination of budgetary policies. A group of independent experts prepared and presented the Sapir report. It sets out a six-point agenda to achieve the objectives of the strategy and enable enlargement to be a success. This covers: making the single market more dynamic; boosting investment in knowledge; improving the macroeconomic policy framework; redesigning policies for convergence and restructuring; achieving effectiveness in decision-taking and regulation, and refocusing the EU budget. In July, following a request from the Thessaloniki European Council, Ecofin launched the European action for growth initiative based on stimulating investment in trans-European networks (TENs), infrastructure and research and development (R&D) projects. The need to take into consideration environmental issues was an ongoing theme of the strategy.

Employment and the European Employment Strategy (EES)

In January, the Commission launched a broad consultation exercise on the future of the employment strategy. In July, on the basis of the March Council and Commission report on achievements in employment in 2002 and a March European Council agreement, Ecofin presented a simplified and more effective European Employment Strategy (EES) within a three-year perspective. Ecofin adopted ten new guidelines to achieve the EES objectives of full employment, labour quality and productivity, and social cohesion:

- devise active and preventive measures for the unemployed and inactive;
- create jobs and foster entrepreneurship;
- address change and promote adaptability in work;
- invest in human capital and strategies for lifelong learning;
- increase labour supply and promote active ageing;
- ensure gender equality;
- promote the integration of and combat discrimination against people at a disadvantage in the labour market;
- make work more financially attractive through incentives;
- transform undeclared work into regular employment; and
- tackle regional employment disparities.

The Council adopted specific recommendations for each Member State.

The Commission established a European employment task force charged with recommending reform measures likely to have a direct and immediate effect on the ability of the Member States to implement the revised EES. Delivered to the Commission in November and welcomed by the December European Council, the task force's report underlined the need to accelerate employment-related reforms, establishing four priorities:

- increase the adaptability of workers and enterprises;
- attract more people to the labour market;
- invest more efficiently in human capital; and
- ensure effective implementation of reforms through better governance.

The Commission engaged in an ongoing analysis of the accession countries' employment policies. Finally, the Commission continued its efforts to improve job mobility: in April it adopted the EURES (European Employment Services) Charter to improve the provision of employment information; in July it adopted guidelines on skills and mobility for the 2004–07 period; and in September it opened the European job mobility portal.

Enterprise

The Lisbon goal of making the EU economy the world's most competitive in 2010 continued to determine enterprise policy. The March European Council reiterated oft-made calls to improve competitiveness, reduce the administrative burden on firms, and create and encourage small businesses. In January, the Commission issued a Green Paper on entrepreneurship intended to launch debate in this area in the Parliament and consultative assemblies, while in March the Council recommended a co-ordinated approach to entrepreneurship policy. The Commission also continued the work started in 2002 on defining an industrial policy for an enlarged Europe. The 2003 European Competitiveness Report and the 2003 version of the enterprise policy scoreboard were published in October. The October European Council called on the Commission to develop an integrated strategy for European competitiveness, presented in a November communication. On 9 December, a high-level conference organized by the Commission discussed the main findings of the report and the study on 'European productivity and competitiveness: a European perspective'. At sectoral level, the Commission fleshed out its strategy in the field of chemical products outlined in 2001, and presented communications calling for strengthened defence equipment and pharmaceutical industries. Progress was made on the preparation of legislation relating to vehicles and their safety equipment.

A Knowledge-based Economy

There was progress on 'information society' initiatives at the Community level, especially through the establishment of a Network and Information Security Agency. The EU continued to implement the '*e*Europe 2005' action plan, with the aim of promoting access to the internet for all, the dissemination of best practice, and the improvement of network and information security. In a February report, the Commission welcomed what it called the success of the *e*Europe 2002 action plan and the recent connection to the internet of a large number of households, businesses and schools. The report also set out various scenarios for the transition from analogue to digital broadcasting. The October European Council endorsed the importance of developing telecommunications to stimulate growth in the enlarged Europe and the availability of widespread broadband. In March, the Council agreed with a February Commission reminder to Member States of the need to complete rapidly the process of defining and implementing the measures adopted in March 2002 in the sector of electronic communications ('Go Digital' initiative). With regard to network and information security, in February the Council called for a comprehensive European strategy and the Commission proposed the establishment of a European agency to gather and analyse data on information security, advise Member States and encourage co-ordination. In November, the Council consented to establish the agency which the Heads of State and Government agreed at the December European Council to locate in Greece. In the realm of e-government, in September the Commission proposed 18 measures to speed up the development of online administration and, in November, the Council adopted conclusions advocating the reinforcement of measures to promote the supply of pan-European services, innovation and the exchange of best practices.

Research

The most important development in Community research policy was the implementation of the sixth framework programme with the launch of several hundred projects with a total budget of €17.5 billion for the period 2002–06. In the first few months of the year, the Commission adopted the model contracts and guides to the proposal evaluation and selection procedures needed for the execution of the specific programmes. This achievement was accompanied by several important developments in Community research policy. In January, the Commission presented a Green Paper to launch a debate on the future of Europe in space. Following favourable responses from the Council and Parliament, in November the Commission adopted a White Paper on space policy, calling for increased spending and the stimulation of research activities. The EU and the European Space Agency (ESA) signed a co-operation agreement in November with the aim of facilitating joint activities.

The Commission, responding to a call by the Barcelona European Council in 2002, issued a communication in March assessing the progress made in implementing Europe's strategy on life sciences and biotechnology defined in 2002. Although stressing that progress had been made, the Commission pointed out that it was necessary to improve research and to make more financial resources available, and that the EU was lagging behind in the area of genetically modified organisms (GMOs). With regard to poverty-related diseases, in

June the Parliament and Council adopted Decision No. 1209/2003/EC. This focused on Community participation in a research and development programme aimed at developing new clinical interventions to combat HIV/AIDS, malaria and tuberculosis with a maximum Community financial contribution of €200 million, to be met by the Member States.

With the aim of meeting the Barcelona European Council commitment to raise EU-wide investment in R&D to close to 3 per cent of GDP by 2010, the Commission presented an action plan in April to improve intergovernmental co-ordination in the area. In another project, in August the Commission launched a pilot project with a budget of €2.5 million in 2003 to develop experimental activities involving networks of European regions, with a view to creating 're-gions of knowledge' (KnowREG), which will provide a blueprint for regional implementation of the Lisbon strategy.

Economic and Monetary Union (EMU)

2003 will stand as the year the Stability Pact was effectively undermined through the incomplete application of the excessive deficit procedure (EDP) with regard to Germany and France. On 21 January, Ecofin adopted a decision noting the existence of an excessive deficit in the case of Germany and launched the early warning procedure against France. Finance ministers recommended that within four months, by 21 May, the German authorities take necessary measures to eliminate the excessive deficit in the course of 2004 at the latest. On 3 June, Ecofin launched the EDP against France. With sluggish economic growth in the two largest euro area economies, and the inability of the French and German governments to meet the required 2004 target, the Commission called on the Council (21 October, 18 November) to extend the target by one year. In its 25 November conclusions, Ecofin decided to suspend the EDP altogether while taking into account the French and German commitment to bring their deficits below the 3 per cent threshold by 2005 at the latest. This decision met with the Commission's objection, but the Parliament expressed its concern.

In the meantime, throughout the year, the Commission, Parliament, Eu-ropean Council and Ecofin all continued to advocate tightened macroeconomic policy co-ordination and the need for more rapid structural reforms in several of the Member States. Ecofin adopted a code of best practice in February on data compilation and reporting to the Commission in the context of the EDP. In March, on the basis of a Commission communication from 2002, Ecofin presented a report on co-ordination, and the Parliament adopted a resolution supporting the Pact, but in favour of an 'intelligent and flexible application in the manner proposed by the Commission in 2002'. In December, the Commission proposed a regulation which would require Member States to provide data on their quarterly government debt to allow closer monitoring. From January to July, the Council adopted a series of opinions on the updated stability and convergence programmes of the euro area countries. On 21 May, the Commission adopted its 2003 report – its fourth – on public finances, reviewing the Member States' budgetary results in 2002 and assessing their prospects in the short and medium term.

For the first time the Broad Economic Policy Guidelines (BEPG) were drawn up for a three-year period (for 2003–05) as an effort to streamline key policy co-ordination instruments, and were formally adopted by Ecofin on 26 June. BEPG objectives remained the same as in previous years emphasizing the need to:

- maintain sound macroeconomic policies geared to supporting growth and employment and safeguarding price stability, while promoting competitiveness and dynamism through investment in human capital, knowledge and innovation;
- press ahead with reforms aimed at increasing the growth potential in the EU and employment by facilitating job creation and improving the operation of the labour market via measures to make work more attractive, to organize work in a more flexible and innovative way and to increase labour mobility; and
- to strengthen the sustainability of public finances in particular by further reducing government debt ratios and reforming pension and healthcare systems.

In July, Ecofin identified the key structural reform challenges in the future Member States that would be included in the BEPG update from 2004 and the implementation report from 2005.

Despite sluggish economic growth in the three largest economies of the euro area, half-hearted structural reforms and deteriorating budgetary positions, 2003 also witnessed the steep assent of the euro in relation to the dollar. The euro's value rose from approximately \$1.05 (US) at the start of the year to slightly above \$1.25 by its end, exceeding in May the important \$1.17 figure at which the currency was launched on 1 January 1999 (see Mayes, pp. 73–6 in this *Annual Review*).

In July, the Commission presented its report on financial assistance to third countries in 2002 and, on the basis of a Court of Auditors' special report, the Council stressed the need for a more harmonized approach between the different instruments of macroeconomic financial assistance, and for improved transparency and economic monitoring. During the year the Commission raised the maximum amount of further macrofinancial assistance for Serbia and Montenegro, and increased the small and medium-sized enterprises (SME) finance facility for accession countries with an additional Phare commitment. The European Investment Bank granted loans in 2003 totalling €42.4 billion in support of EU objectives (compared to €39.6 billion in 2002), of which €34.2 billion (81 per cent of the total) were in the Member States, €4.6 billion in the candidate or accession countries, and €3.6 billion in partner countries, including the western Balkans and African, Caribbean and Pacific (ACP) countries.

Internal Market Developments

2003 marked the tenth anniversary of the internal market (see Kassim, 2003). At the request of the March European Council, in May the Commission set out ten priorities as part of the internal market strategy for the next three years, with a particular view to:

- achieving full transposition by the Member States of legislation already adopted at EU level – in November 2002 the Commission had reported on the serious implementation deficit in several Member States;
- gaining as much as possible from the internal market in terms of competitiveness, growth and employment; and
- meeting the challenges posed by enlargement and an ageing population, and the EU's goal of becoming the world's most competitive economy by 2010.

The October European Council requested the Commission to come up with new proposals needed to complete the internal market and exploit its potential to the full.

In 2003, drafting work continued on the Commission's strategy in the area of services that had been defined in 2000. However, considerable progress was made in implementing the action plan for financial services, with 36 of the 42 original measures being completed by the end of 2003 and focus shifting to implementation and execution. In February, the Council set up an internal Financial Services Committee (FSC) to make recommendations on the legislative process and sensitive issues in this area. In November, the Commission proposed a directive to modify the committee's structure so as to ensure a more rapid Community legislative process to react more quickly and effectively to financial developments and ensure consistent implementation and execution of rules. In November, the Commission also presented its final report on the implementation of the risk capital action plan (RCAP) covering 2002 and, for certain areas, the first three quarters of 2003. Despite great progress in this area, the Commission lamented the fragmentation of the Community's risk capital markets.

In the area of transferable securities, in November the Parliament and the Council adopted Directive 2003/71/EC concerning the prospectus to be published when securities are offered to the public or admitted to trading. The new legislation aims to establish a 'single passport' for issuers of securities and to harmonize the requirements for drawing up, approving and distributing the securities prospectus in order to protect investors. In March, the Commission proposed the amendment of Directive 2001/34/EC on the admission of securities to official stock exchange listings and on the information to be published on those securities, seeking to improve the harmonization of transparency requirements. At the request of the March European Council, in May the Commission presented a Green Paper advocating a substantial review of Community policies relating to services of general interest and in particular an examination of the possibility of establishing a Community legal framework for such services, as envisaged at the Barcelona European Council. In a November report on the transposition and application of Directive 2000/31/EC on electronic commerce and its impact on the internal market, the Commission proclaimed its overall satisfaction.

There was significant progress in the construction of a Community tax regime. The Council adopted the legislative package which had been under discussion for several years, paving the way for more effective combating of perceived 'harmful' tax practices and for the reduction of distortions in the internal market, essentially with regard to the taxation of savings and company taxation. In October, the Council adopted Directive 2003/93/EC to extend the scope of Council Directive 77/799/EEC concerning mutual assistance by the competent authorities of the Member States in the field of direct and indirect taxation. The amendment will allow Member States to exchange information regarding the taxation of insurance premiums. The Council also adopted Regulation (EC) No 1798/2003 to strengthen mutual co-operation between the tax authorities of the Member States to combat VAT fraud. In December, the Commission proposed a further amendment to Directive 77/799/EEC to adapt it better to the needs of the internal market with regard to excise duties. In the field of direct taxation, in June the Commission adopted Directive 2003/48/EC which seeks to ensure that savings income in the form of interest payments made in one Member State to persons residing in another Member State are taxed in accordance with the latter's legislation. Also in June, the Council adopted Directive 2003/49/EC on a common system of taxation applicable to interest and royalty payments made between associated companies of different Member States, with the elimination of all such taxation in the Member States in which the payments originate.

The Commission looked into modifying existing legislation on taxation in the event of mergers, divisions and transfers of assets and exchanges of shares.

It assessed the achievements of the current Community strategy regarding company taxation. In particular, the Commission presented a report in November assessing the results of the Fiscalis programme implemented between 1998 and 2002 to improve the operation of indirect taxation systems within the internal market through more efficient co-operation between the administrations in question. The Commission recommended more complementary activities in the new Fiscalis programme for 2003–07 (see the 2002/03 *JCMS Annual Review*). Other tax measures included a Decision (No. 1152/2003/EC) to combat fraud and simplify the system of Excise duties; and in June, the Commission proposed amendments to the sixth VAT Directive (77/388/EEC) to simplify the directive and prevent Council-granted derogation. The Council failed to act on this.

In the field of enterprises, the Commission drew up an action plan for modernizing company law and enhancing corporate governance in the context of the integrating internal market. In September, the Council welcomed the action plan. In July, the Council adopted a regulation (EC No 1435/2003) on European co-operative societies which, following 12 years of preparation, is intended to enable the establishment of new legal bodies to organize certain economic transactions in at least two Member States. In July, the Parliament and the Council adopted Directive 2003/58/EC, amending Directive 68/151/EEC, to speed up public access to information on those companies. Progress was also made regarding accounting regulations, particularly with regard to better integration of international accounting standards. In May, the Council adopted Directive 2003/38/EC amending Directive 78/660/EEC on the annual accounts of certain types of companies to exempt small and medium-sized enterprises from various obligations in this area. The 1978 directive was again amended with the adoption, in June, of Directive 2003/51/EC, in which the Parliament and the Council provided Member States with the possibility of gradually bringing national accounting requirements closer in line with international accounting standards (IAS) ratified in Regulation (EC) No. 1606/2002.

Progress was made with the development of the jurisdictional system for the Community patent on which the Commission proposed two directives in December. In October, after lengthy negotiations lasting seven years, the Council adopted a decision allowing the Community to accede to the 1989 Madrid protocol on international trademarks and a regulation linking this international system with the Community trademark. The regulation will provide non-EU companies with a single procedure to protect their trademarks in the EU. Significant progress was also made in simplifying the legislation on public procurement. The Parliament and Council came to an agreement on a joint draft in the Conciliation Committee on 2 December.

Competition and Industrial Policies

In 2003, the Commission developed the detailed provisions of a modernized regulatory framework for anti-trust and merger control. In September, the Commission adopted several draft texts aimed at completing its overhaul of the application of the Community competition rules, as provided for by Council Regulation (EC) No. 1/2003 of December 2002. It represented the most far-reaching reform of anti-trust norms to date (Articles 81 and 82 of the EC Treaty), allowing national authorities to apply Community competition rules. The Commission made several important decisions in favour of potentially anti-competitive practices including: third generation mobile phone network-sharing in the UK and Germany (site sharing itself not raising competition concerns); the joint selling arrangements of UEFA for the media rights to the football Champions League; and premium pay-TV channels and pay-per-view channels and co-operation between Canal+Nordic, the leading supplier of premium pay-TV channels and Telenor/Canal Digital, the leading satellite TV distribution platform in the Nordic countries.

The Commission also made several important decisions prohibiting restrictive agreements including: an agreement between six federations in the beef and veal sector in France, setting a minimum purchase price for certain categories of cattle and suspending, or at least restricting, imports of all types of beef and veal; and the agreements and practices governing the distribution of musical instruments manufactured and sold by Yamaha which were seen as intended to obstruct parallel trade and fix resale prices. Fines were imposed on French beef and veal federations (of €16.68 million, but reduced given the difficulties in the prices of beef and veal linked to the 'mad cow' disease crisis); Yamaha; four companies producing sorbate; five carbon and graphite producers; five companies producing organic peroxides; the three main copper tube producers in Europe; Deutsch Telekom AG; and Wanadoo Interactive, the French internet provider.

The Commission proceeded with reforms of its merger control system with, in December, the adoption for the first time of guidelines clarifying its analytical approach when assessing the likely impact of mergers on competition. The Commission reached decisions on 13 mergers, allowing all of them but only after the Commission's concerns were addressed by the companies concerned, including: Pfizer Inc. and Pharmacia (creating the largest pharmaceutical company in the world); Stream and Telepiu; and Procter & Gamble's acquisition of Wella AG. The Commission embarked on an in-depth review of the way in which its state aids rules are applied in practice, in order to refocus its efforts on those aid measures that are most liable to distort competition. In April and October, the Commission published updated versions of the state aid scoreboard, and praised what appeared to be a continuing downward trend in aid provided by Member State governments. In 2001, Germany, France and Italy (in that order) provided the most state aids but, as a percentage of GDP, Finland, Denmark and Belgium (in that order) provided the most. In July, the Community and Japan signed an agreement concerning co-operation on combating anti-competitive practices. Terms of reference for future co-operation in the field of competition policy were also agreed between the Community and China in November. In addition to acting in other anti-trust cases, the Commission adopted a number of landmark decisions dealing with the problems raised by the behaviour of certain enterprises enjoying a dominant position. It likewise defended, in several decisions, the importance of consistent and impartial vetting of state aid at the European level. In April, the Commission adopted the XXXII Report on Competition Policy, which takes stock of its activity in the field in 2002.

Structural Funds and Regional Policy

The Commission's 13th Annual Report on the Structural Funds (19 June) noted the delays which had occurred in the programmes and the non-optimal use of resources (yet also called for increased funding for the European Regional Development Fund). In its communication of 25 August, the Commission revised the general indicative guidelines on the structural funds laid down in 1999 for the national and regional authorities responsible for programme preparation. In October, the Commission adopted its 14th report on the implementation of the structural funds. In commitments made during 2003 – as in the previous year – Spain, Greece, Italy, Portugal and Germany (in that order) were the major recipients of objective 1 funding (regions where per capita income is below 75 per cent of the EU average) receiving over 90 per cent of the income. The major beneficiaries of objective 2 funding (regions undergoing structural change) were France, UK, Germany, Italy and Spain; and the major beneficiaries of objective 3 funding (modernization of education, training and employment systems) were Germany, UK, France, Italy and Spain. The Urbact initiative, intended to create networks among the cities of Europe focusing on their experiences of sustainable urban development, was launched as the latest Community initiative. Allocations in 2002 from the cohesion fund were, unlike the roughly even apportionment of 2001, concentrated more on transport (57.6 per cent of the appropriations) rather than the environment. The Council and Parliament reached a decision (9 October) to mobilize €87.905 million from the newly established European Union solidarity fund (EUSF) to three countries suffering from natural and man-made disasters: Spain, Italy and Portugal.

II. Social Policies

The social policy agenda, the programming instrument created at the Nice summit to cover the period 2000–05, reached its midpoint in 2003. The Commission published its third scoreboard on implementation in February and its mid-term review in June recommending changes to take account of developments in society and the labour market, and in view of the forthcoming enlargement. In May, a Commission communication put forward the need to simplify and streamline the open method of co-ordination. This was designed to reinforce the social dimension of the Lisbon strategy, define common objectives structured around the three pillars of social inclusion, pensions and long-term healthcare, produce a joint annual report on social protection and develop agreed indicators and a progressive implementation with a timetable leading to 2009. On 1 December, the Council endorsed the Commission's position.

Following the request of the Barcelona European Council, in February the Commission presented a timetable for the creation of a European health insurance card designed to replace the E111 forms currently needed for health treatment during a temporary stay in a Member State, and to facilitate the movement of citizens throughout the EU. Following the March European Council's endorsement and the Parliament's opinion, in October the Council put forward some recommendations for developing a properly co-ordinated strategy.

In the area of social inclusion, in February the Council called on the social partners to identify possible partnership mechanisms and approaches for specific activities while, in December, the Commission presented a draft joint report presenting its conclusions drawn from the second national action plans for social inclusion (2003–05). 2003 was the European Year of People with Disabilities, in connection with which the Commission presented a European action plan in October for equal opportunities in a range of social and occupational situations. In May, the Council adopted two resolutions underlining the need to improve the integration into society of disabled people. In February, the Commission adopted its third annual programme on the implementation of the framework strategy on gender equality, setting out three priorities: the continuation of impact analysis work; collecting gender-specific data and statistics; and seeking a gender balance in the Commission's various committees and groups of experts. In March, the Parliament came out in favour of an action plan for gender mainstreaming within the Parliament itself.

Further progress was made in the realm of social chapter legislation. In November, the Parliament and the Council adopted Directive 2003/88/EC codifying Directive 93/104/EC concerning certain aspects of the organization of working time. At the end of the year, the Commission adopted a communication concerning the re-examination of specific provisions to lay down minimum requirements in this policy area. In February, the Parliament and the

Council adopted Directive 2003/10/EC laying down minimum health and safety requirements concerning the risks to workers exposed to noise. In March, they adopted Directive 2003/18/EC on risks associated with exposure to asbestos at work which lays down a single exposure limit, and brings the sea and air transport sectors within the scope of the protective provisions. In July, the Council adopted a decision merging the existing two advisory committees for health and safety at work. In its March Decision (2003/174/EC), the Council institutionalized the informal practice of the tripartite social summit of growth and employment involving the social partners examining the implementation of the Lisbon strategy. The first formal summit took place on 20 March in Brussels during the European Council.

III. Finances

2003 was a landmark year for EU finances in several respects: with the application of the new financial regulation involving fundamental changes in the management of Community finances; the preparation of the budget for 25 Member States; and the presentation of the budget for the first time using entirely the activity-based budgeting method. Also, for the first time – despite the Commission's warning and Parliament's reservations – a financial framework for the ten future Member States was included in the Treaty of Accession. After long and difficult negotiations, the Parliament and Council reached agreement on the adjustment of the financial perspective for enlargement, and agreed to raise the ceiling for 'internal policies'. The Council stressed the importance of keeping a tight grip on payment appropriations for 2004, lowering the figures proposed by the Commission which were already a significant drop from 2003. The 2004 budget for the 15 current Member States was adopted by Parliament on 18 December. It totalled €99.528 billion for commitments and €94.618 billion for payments, with an amending budget to be adopted in early 2004 to add the appropriations required for the new Member States, bringing the total budget to €111.3 billion for commitments and €99.72 billion for payments. The final figures demonstrate that the Parliament was willing to be conciliatory in agreeing to the Council's figures for commitments and accepting a compromise closer to the Council's position on payments. Compared with 2003, commitment appropriations were down by 0.3 per cent and payment appropriations up by 2.3 per cent. There was a substantial margin of €7.655 billion for payments and €4.492 billion for commitments. The 2004 payments budget represents 0.98 per cent of Member States' gross national income (GNI), the authorized ceiling being 1.06 per cent, which makes the 2004 budget the smallest initial budget since 1990. The implementation of appropriations for commitment from 31 December for the EU-12 is shown in Table 1 while, on the revenue side, the own resources are shown in Table 2. In April, following a Council recommendation, the Parliament granted the Commission a discharge in respect of implementation of the 2001 budget. During the year there were wide-ranging discussions and preparations concerning the forthcoming post-2006 financial perspective. It was decided not to present the Commission proposal on this perspective until after the December European Council.

On other budgetary matters, in a March resolution the Parliament maintained that the distinction between compulsory and non-compulsory expenditure was inappropriate. It argued that all budgetary items should be adopted on a co-decision basis, although certain details would have to be adapted, for example

Table 1: 2004 Budget

Heading	2004 Budget	2003 Budget	Financial Perspective 2004	% Diff. 2004 over 2003
1. AGRICULTURE				
Agricultural exp. (excl. rural dev't)	39 958 410 000	40 082 450 000		−0.3
Rural dev't and accompanying measures	4 803 000 000			2.2
Total	44 761 410 000	44 780 450 000	47 211 000 000	−0.0
Margin	2 449 590 000	4 698 000 000		
2. STRUCTURAL OPERATIONS (1)				
Objective 1	21 952 101 719	21 577 061 305		1.7
Objective 2	3 573 793 131	3 651 793 231		−2.1
Objective 3	3 793 306 700	3 718 927 200		2.0
Other structural measures (outside obj. 1)	174 900 000	171 900 000		1.7
Community initiatives	1 949 198 650	1 866 017 000		4.0
Innovative measures and tech. assistance	106 699 800	143 301 264		−25.5
Other specific structural measures	p.m.	12 008 240		−00.0
Cohesion fund	2 785 000 000	2 839 000 000		1.9
Total	34 326 000 000	33 980 008 240	34 326 000 000	1.0
Margin	0	−12 008 240		
3. INTERNAL POLICIES (2)				
Research and tech. development	4 312 541 968	4 055 000 000		6.4
Other agricultural operations	43 010 000	44 597 000		−3.6
Other regional operations	15 000 000	15 000 000		0.0
Transport	59 110 000	54 000 000		9.5
Other measures – fisheries and sea	74 290 897	70 420 000		5.5
Education, vocational training and youth	565 300 000	562 682 000		0.5
Culture and audiovisual sector	117 600 000	117 500 000		0.1
Information and communication	98 779 500	110 347 000		−10.5
Social dimension and employment	191 345 189	180 775 000		5.8
Contributions to European parties	p.m.	7 000 000		−100.0
Energy	50 882 000	48 000 000		6.0
Euratom nuclear safeguards	19 279 000	18 800 000		2.5
Environment	241 917 000	237 300 000		1.9
Consumer policy and health protection	18 000 000	22 572 500		−20.3
Aid for reconstruction	340 000	611 000		−44.4

Table 1: 2004 Budget (Contd)

Heading	2004 Budget	2003 Budget	Financial Perspective 2004	% Diff. 2004 over 2003
Internal market	180 909 500	200 256 500		−9.7
Industry	p.m.	p.m.		
Labour market and tech. innovation	114 300 000	122 500 000		−6.7
Statistical information	37 288 000	35 400 000		5.3
Trans-European networks	716 690 000	725 057 000		−1.2
Area of freedom, security and justice	180 464 875	153 635 600		17.5
Measures to combat fraud	9 900 000	7 200 000		37.5
EU solidarity fund	p.m.	104 789 000		−100.0
Reserve for administrative exp. (performance facility reserve)	3 910 822	647 4000		504.1
Total	7 050 858 751	6 894 090 000	7 053 000 000	2.3
Margin	2 141 249	−98 090 000		
4. EXTERNAL ACTIONS (3)				
European development fund	p.m.	p.m.		
Food aid and support measures	419 000 000	425 637 000		−1.6
Humanitarian aid	490 000 000	441 690 000		10.9
Co-operation – Asia	616 125 000	562 500 000		9.5
Co-operation – Latin America	312 125 000	337 000 000		− 7.4
Co-operation – southern Africa & S. Africa	134 000 000	127 000 000		5.5
Co-operation – Mediterranean third countries and the Middle East	842 000 000	753 870 000		11.7
Aid for rehabilitation & reconstruction of Iraq	169 000 000	p.m.		
EBRD Community sub. to the capital	p.m.	p.m.		
Assistance – E. Europe and C. Asia	535 395 000	507 370 000		5.5
Other Community measures in favour of the partner countries of eastern Europe and central Asia and the countries of the western Balkans	−	−		−
Co-operation with the countries of the western Balkans	674 961 000	684 560 000		−1.4
Other co-operation measures	519 400 000	505 470 000		2.8
European initiatives for democracy and human rights	125 625 000	106 000 000		18.5
International fisheries agreements	193 820 520	192 599 000		0.7
Ext. aspects of certain Community policies	91 175 000	86 362 000		5.6
Common foreign and security policy	62 600 000	47 500 000		31.8
Pre-accession strategy – Med. countries	p.m.	25 000 000		−100.0
Reserve for administrative expenditure	324 480	4 403 000		−92.6
Total	5 176 551 000	4 806 862 000	5 082 000 000	7.7
Margin	−94 551 000	165 138 000		
5. ADMINISTRATION (4)				
Commission (excluding pensions)	2 994 522 324	2 780 000 371		7.7
Other institutions (excluding pensions)	2 248 676 790	1 870 598 727		20.2
Pensions (all institutions)	796 539 000	731 372 000		8.9
Total	6 039 768 114	5 381 971 098	6 157 000 000	12.2
Margin	117 231 886	28 902		

Table 1: 2004 Budget (Contd)

Heading	2004 Budget	2003 Budget	Financial Perspective 2004	% Diff. 2004 over 2003
6. RESERVES				
Guarantee reserve	221 000 000	217 000 000		1.8
Emergency aid reserve	221 000000	217 000 000		1.8
Total	442 000 000	434 000 000	442 000 000	1.8
Margin	0	0		
7. PRE– ACCESSION STRATEGY				
SAPARD Pre-accession instrument	226 700 000	564 000 000		–59.8
Instrument for structural policies for pre-accession (ISPA)	453 300 000	1 129 000 000		–59.8
PHARE pre-accession instrument	809 700 000	1 693 000 000		52.2
Turkey (5)	242 600 000	149 000 000		62.8
EU solidarity fund	p.m.	p.m.		
Total	1 732 300 000	3 535 000 000	3 455 000 000	–51.0
Margin	1 722 700 000	–149 000 000		
Appropriations for commitments –				
Total	99 528 887 865	99 812 381 338	103 726 000 000	–0.3
Margin	4 197 112 135	2 503 618 662		
Compulsory expenditure	41 474 399 675	41 504 890 321		–0.1
Non-compulsory expenditure	58 054 488 190	58 307 491 017		–0.4
Appropriations for payments –				
Total	94 618 747 943	95 524 837 098	102 274 000 000	2.3
Margin	7 655 252 057	10 413 162 902		
Compulsory expenditure	41 528 734 313	41 582 214 321		–0.1
Non-compulsory expenditure	53 090 013 630	50 942 622 777		4.2
Payment appropriations as % of GNI	0.98	0.98		1.06

Source: Bulletin EU 12-2003.
Notes:

1. The amount entered in the 2003 budget under this heading exceeds the financial perspective ceiling because of the use of the flexibility instrument, as allowed by the inter-institutional agreement, for an amount of €12 million for conversion of the Spanish and Portuguese fisheries fleet.

2. The amount entered in the 2003 budget exceeds the financial perspective ceiling because of the mobilization of the EU solidarity fund for €104.8 million for Portugal, Spain and Italy.

3. The amount entered in the 2004 budget under this heading exceeds the financial perspective ceiling because of the use of the flexibility instrument, as allowed by the inter-institutional agreement, for an amount of €95 million for the reconstruction of Iraq.

4. The ceiling for heading 5 covers the enlarged Union (EU-25). It also includes €174 million for staff contributions to the pension scheme, in accordance with footnote 1 to Table 1 of the financial perspective (EU-15) as adjusted for 2004.

5. In 2004, Turkey is also entitled to €7.4 million under the TAIEX line included in the PHARE pre-accession instrument, thereby bringing the 2004 total up to €250 million.

Table 2: Budget Revenue

	2003 € million	2004 €million
Agriculture duties	1 012.0	839.1
Sugar and isoglucose levies	383.2	359.9
Customs duties	9 457.5	9 850.0
VAT own resources	21 536.3	13 319.5
Gross national income (GNI)-based own resources	50 906.0	69 444.6
Balance of VAT and GNI own resources from previous years	336.0	p.m.
Surplus available from previous year	7 676.8	p.m.
Other revenue	1 948.4	805.6
Total	93 256.2	94 618.7
	% of GNI	
Maximum own resources which may be assigned to the budget	1.24	1.24
Own resources actually assigned to the budget	0.97	0.97

Source: Commission (2004) *General Report on the Activities of the European Union*, (Luxembourg: OOPEC).

in order to clear the way for a decision in the event of disagreement between Parliament and Council. In a November resolution, the Parliament gave its support to the budget provisions in the draft Constitutional Treaty. In November, Parliament and Council agreed to use the flexibility instrument (provided for in the inter-institutional agreement of May 1999) to mobilize €95 million to the rehabilitation and reconstruction of Iraq. Work on the modernization of the accounting system continued, with the Commission proposing a tightening of internal controls in its synthesis of the 2002 annual activity reports of directorates-general and services.

IV. Agriculture and Fisheries

Agriculture

After the failure to reach agreement on the mid-term review of the common agricultural policy (CAP) in 2002 because of French obstruction, on 29 September the Council succeeded finally in adopting a series of regulations to implement the mid-term review. The reforms furthered the policy shift of the past decade in favour of less price support for farmers and more direct subsidies, with the introduction of a single payment to farmers unrelated to production (except insofar as to maintain some production) and with increased insistence on observing environmental, food safety and animal standards. Despite the failure of the World Trade Organization (WTO) Cancún summit, the Commission argued that the reform of the CAP was a sign of the Community's will to follow through on its commitment in the WTO Doha agenda to open its market to international trade, including agricultural products. The mid-term review also included increased funding for the EU's rural development policy through the reduction of direct payments to large holdings and funding to help farmers apply Community production standards from 2005. To put flesh on the agreements reached in October 2002 on spending, the Council adopted a financial discipline mechanism to ensure compliance with the agricultural budget fixed until 2013 – with the aim of preventing a massive rise in expenditure – with spending rises at only 1 per cent, less than the probable inflation level. The Council agreed on a revision of the CAP's market management policy, mainly through asymmetrical price reductions in the milk sector, the halving of monthly increases in the cereals sector and reforms in the rice and several other sectors. Towards the end of the year, the Commission presented to the Council three agriculture-related regulations to prepare for enlargement: one ensuring that overall CAP reform would take enlargement into consideration; a second that would amend the Act of Accession in the light of CAP reform; and a third to allow the new Member States temporary derogation in complying with standards.

Fisheries

In 2003 Community institutions were preoccupied with giving effect to certain aspects of the reform to the common fisheries policy (CFP). Policy papers were adopted on a range of issues, including the need for uniform and effective implementation of the common policy, and the Commission adopted an action programme on reform in May. In June, the Commission proposed a compliance plan covering the period 2003–05. In July, the Council called for the consolidation of rules on inspection and enforcement of the CFP in a single regulation. In November, fishing ministers met in Venice at a Conference for the Sustainable Development of Fisheries in the Mediterranean, reaffirming the commitment of bordering countries to provide better protection for resources in the area. The Parliament and the Council welcomed the Commission's communication of 19 September 2002 on 'A strategy for the sustainable development of European aquaculture'. In October, the Commission presented a proposal for a Council decision establishing regional advisory councils under the CFP (provided for in Council Regulation (EC) No. 2371/2002) with the aim of involving stake-holders in policy implementation. In August, the Commission adopted the annual report on the results of the MAGPs (multi-annual guidance programmes for fishing fleets), closing the fourth MAGP, and reported on the state of progress of the programmes. In December, the Commission reported a decline in the number of cases of serious breach of CFP rules detected by national authorities in 2002. In April, the Council called on the Commission to prepare strategies and specific measures to ensure the conservation of stocks, and specific measures were adopted by the Council – including regulations on tuna tracking and verification, accidental catches of cetaceans and the management of the European eel – and proposed by the Commission – including regulations on the recovery of several fish species, including cod, northern hake, southern hake, sole and Norway lobster. A total of 77 fisheries were closed for irregular fishing, far exceeding the number in 2002 (24). In January, the Council welcomed the Commission's May 2002 action plan to integrate environmental requirements into the CFP. In November, the Commission proposed amending the regulation (EC No. 2792/1999) laying down the detailed rules and arrangements regarding Community structural assistance in the fisheries sector to make it possible for the financial instrument for fisheries guidance (FIFG) to contribute better to implementing the strategy for the sustainable development of European aquaculture adopted as part of the reform of the CFP. In commitments made during the year through the FIFG (outside areas under objective 1), France, Spain, Denmark, UK, Germany (in that order) received the most funding.

V. Environmental Policy

In 2003, there were developments in the four priority areas of the sixth environmental action programme including steps towards the adoption of an environment and health strategy as a means of identifying and preventing risks and a proposal for a new policy on chemicals (REACH, the registration, evaluation, authorization and restrictions of chemicals). As part of the implementation of the action programme, guidelines were laid down for thematic strategies on resources, waste and recycling. In May, the Commission launched a consultation process with the aim of identifying the most cost-effective measures for sustainable waste management so as to draw up a thematic strategy on the prevention and recycling of waste. In June, the Commission adopted measures to ensure continuity in the implementation of the integrated product policy defined in its 2001 Green Paper, such as greening corporate purchasing and promoting environmental labelling. In October, the Commission proposed guidelines for the development of a Community strategy on the sustainable use of natural resources. In May, the Commission produced a report detailing the gaps in application by Member States of the Community waste treatment policy and, in June, a report noting the gaps in the Member States' application of European regulations on the effects of certain public and private projects on the environment.

Progress was made on the implementation of the Aarhus convention. To bring Community legislation into line with the convention, in October the Commission proposed a package of three pieces of legislation concerning the right to initiate administrative or legal proceedings with a view to application of environmental law and the application of the convention's three pillars to EC institutions and bodies. In May, the Council signed a protocol on pollutant release and transfer registers (PRTRs) aimed at establishing a system for gathering and disseminating environmental data concerning releases and transfers of dangerous chemical products. To promote transparency and public participation in environmental decision-making processes, the Parliament and the Council adopted two directives: in January Directive 2003/4/EC and in May Directive 2003/35/EC.

With regard to the Lisbon strategy, in January the Commission reported on the environmental dimension of sustainable development and continued its work, begun in 2002, on developing an action plan on environmental technology. On GMOs, in July the Parliament and Council adopted Regulation (EC) No. 1946/2003 to incorporate the provisions of the Cartagena protocol into Community legislation. This regulation established a Community system more constraining than the protocol requiring the notification and information of GMO exports to third countries. In September, the Parliament and Council adopted another regulation ((EC) No. 1830/2003) concerning the traceability and labelling of GMOs and products produced from GMOs. On the quality of fuel, in March the Parliament and the Council adopted Directive 2003/17/EC to supplement the specifications for air quality standards provided for in Directive 98/70/EC. The new directive requires Member States to lower the sulphur content of petrol and diesel fuels by 2005 and move to zero-sulphur fuels by 2009.

In October, the Parliament and Council adopted Directive 2003/87/EC establishing a Community scheme for greenhouse gas emission allowance trading to be phased in by 2012. The aim was to enable the EU to meet its obligations under the UN Framework Convention on Climate Change and the Kyoto protocol by achieving a global reduction of emissions without hindering the smooth operation of the internal market and distorting competition. The directive provides for penalties for non-compliance and requirements for the provision of more consistent and accurate information. In a November report, the Commission noted the rise in greenhouse gas emissions for a second consecutive year (up by 1 per cent) – taking them above the Kyoto target path – and proposed various measures to achieve reductions. In September, the Parliament and Council adopted Regulation (EC) No. 1804/2003 bringing EU legislation into line with the Montreal protocol and contributing to the accelerated regeneration of the ozone layer. On forests, in November, the Parliament and the Council adopted Regulation (EC) No. 2152/2003 which defines a four-year (2003–08) comprehensive, harmonized approach for activities relating to monitoring and protecting forests from atmospheric pollution and fires; biodiversity; climate change; carbon sequestration and soils.

At the international level, the EU continued to play a leading role in pushing for ratification of the Kyoto protocol by the key parties and improving pan-European co-operation on environmental matters. The June Thessaloniki European Council made a commitment to integrate the environment into external relations and the December European Council in Rome welcomed the definition of the 'Green diplomacy network'.

References

Commission of the European Communities (2004) *General Report on the Activities of the European Union* (Luxembourg: OOPEC).

Commission of the European Communities (2003) *Bulletin of the European Union*, for several months (Luxembourg: OOPEC).

EU Observer (2003) (various).

Kassim, H. (2003) 'Internal Policy Developments'. In Miles, L. (ed.) *Journal of Common Market Studies. The European Union: Annual Review 2002/2003*, Vol. 41, pp. 53–74.

The European Central Bank in 2003

DAVID G. MAYES
University of Stirling

Introduction

The ECB probably feels quite pleased with its performance during 2003: nothing significant seems to have gone wrong; fears of deflation appear to have been misplaced; and the Iraq war has been weathered with no burst of inflation. However, policy has not been particularly active. Interest rates have changed only twice, with cuts of 0.25 per cent on 7 March and 0.50 per cent on 6 June (see Figure 1). With a final rate of 2 per cent, a noticeable differential has been maintained with respect to the US. Even so, the ECB has not been as successful in holding down inflation in 2003 as it would have liked, especially given the steady rise in the euro during the year. With the benefit of hindsight,

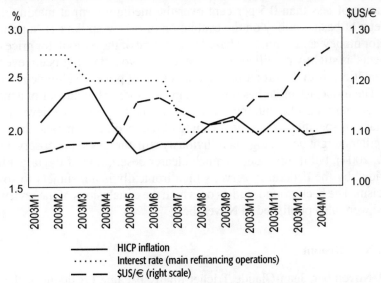

Figure 1: Monetary Policy Settings and Inflation Outcomes, Euro Area 2003

the origin of the problems probably dates back to 1999, when the ECB cut rates initially, before raising them during 2000. Once inflation gathers pace it is difficult to slow. A tighter policy earlier and an easier policy later might have kept both inflation and the exchange rate on a more stable path. That said, the extent of the overshoot has been minor, with monthly inflation lying within the +/–1 per cent range that inflation-targeting countries normally set themselves. In any case, the ECB is not inflation-targeting, except in the sense that everyone who has a measurable price stability target and no secondary objectives is inflation-targeting. It has a medium-term target. If we measure that by a five-year rolling average, it has only just reached the 2 per cent limit right at the end of 2003. However, as the low values in 1999 drop out of the calculation, this average will inevitably rise somewhat even if the results later in 2004 are quite low.

I. The Review of Monetary Policy

In the first part of the year the ECB undertook a review of its monetary policy framework and published the result in May. Those who were hoping for substantial change were disappointed. The medium-term target for price stability of year-on-year inflation in the HICP (Harmonized Index of Consumer Prices) 'below 2 per cent' has now been qualified by the addition of the words 'close to' (2 per cent). Given that the arithmetic for the computation of the reference value for M3 was on the basis of 1–2 per cent inflation, this could only represent a change of less than 0.5 per cent over the medium term at maximum. The strategy of basing policy on the evaluation of the two pillars of 'a prominent role for money' and 'a broadly based assessment of the outlook for price developments' is slightly modified. The order of the two pillars has been reversed in presentation, with the broad-based assessment of price developments coming first. The monetary pillar has now been given more of the flavour of a medium to longer-term check, with the shorter-term emphasis on price developments. The lack of specificity over the meaning of the medium term, and the way the two pillars might be put together obviously still enrages some observers (Galí *et al.*, 2004), but it represents a much clearer description of the target than is provided by the Federal Reserve, which ironically is not subject to so much criticism. The background studies on which the conclusions of the review were based were also published in November.

II. A New Broom

On 1 November, Jean-Claude Trichet finally became President of the ECB, taking over from Wim Duisenberg, who had been President from the ECB's inception. The Duisenberg years have not been free from controversy, but the bank has become firmly established over the period, instituting the monetary policy framework, expanding rapidly and successfully introducing the notes and coins for the euro. The organization has had five years to get entrenched, so a new President has some inertia to overcome. Nevertheless the character of the press conferences has already changed. It is not particularly valuable to speculate about the future course the new President might seek, but his earlier comments (Trichet, 2002) stressing the balance between centralized decision-making and decentralized implementation, and the importance of financial stability might give a guide. The ECB had already strengthened its financial stability team during the year and published a review of EU banking sector stability in November.

In the middle of the year Sirkka Hämäläinen reached the end of her term on the Executive Board and was replaced by Gertrude Tumpel-Gugerell, the Vice-Governor of the Österreichische Nationalbank, thereby leaving the balance of sexes and country sizes on the Board unchanged. Only limited debate surrounded the appointment and the ECB avoided getting swept into broader political concerns.

III. Policy Co-ordination

Perhaps the biggest debate of the year surrounded fiscal policy, with the Governing Council stressing the importance of adherence to the terms of the Stability and Growth Pact. A more credible commitment to fiscal prudence enables a lighter hand on monetary policy. However, in the face of short-run pressures, governments have asked for looser monetary policy in the face of slow growth and fiscal pressure. It is ironic that Galí *et al.* (2004) should be criticizing the ECB for apparently having too much regard for the performance of the real economy compared to their price stability goal, whereas political comment has tended to voice exactly the opposite complaint. The debate has also extended to the exchange rate with fears over the euro area's competitiveness, as the euro rose during the year by 20 per cent from parity with the dollar at the outset. The lack of meeting of minds has continued, with the political debate not being about the relationship between monetary policy, the exchange rate and the prospects for inflation. However, although some changes were proposed in both the report by the Convention and its deliberations, there has been no attempt to alter the terms of reference of the ECB or its role in the system of European institutions.

IV. Voting in the Governing Council

In February, the Governing Council took advantage of the 'enabling clause' (Article 10.6) in the Nice Treaty and formally recommended the way that the Governing Council votes should be amended once the number of participating Member States exceeds 15. Although all governors would have the right to be present and participate, they would be divided into two, and on further enlargement, three, groups according to the economic and monetary size of their countries. The number of votes for governors would remain at 15, and the voting rights would rotate round the members of each group. In the three-group model, the five largest countries share four votes, the next largest countries forming half of the remainder share eight votes and the last group three votes. The six members of the Executive Board retain their voting rights. This complex arrangement breaks the principle of each expert being equal irrelevant of country of origin and does not address the question of the sheer number of participants in monetary policy debates (Svensson, 2001). The Governing Council faced the difficult task of finding an 'equitable efficient and acceptable way' guided by the principles they label as: 'one member one vote'; 'ad personam participation'; 'representativeness'; 'automaticity/robustness'; and 'transparency'. The new Member States, who were not party to the discussion, have at least two years to make their views about this anticipatory arrangement known before it comes into effect.

References

Galí, J., Gerlach, S., Rotemberg, J., Uhlig, H. and Woodford, M. (2004) *The Monetary Policy Strategy of the ECB Reconsidered*, Monitoring the European Central Bank 5 (London: CEPR).

Svensson, L.E.O. (2001) *Independent Review of the Operation of Monetary Policy: Report to the Minister of Finance* (Wellington: Treasury).

Trichet, J.-C. (2002) 'The Eurosystem: The European Monetary Team'. In *Competition of Regions and Integration in EMU* (Vienna: Österreichische Nationalbank).

Legal Developments

MICHAEL DOUGAN
Liverpool Law School, University of Liverpool

Introduction

It is difficult to decide which of the very many important legal developments dating from 2003 deserve attention in this survey. After all, two major texts of profound legal interest were adopted: the Accession Treaty which paved the way for the historic enlargement on 1 May 2004;[1] and the draft Treaty Establishing a Constitution for Europe prepared by the Convention on the Future of Europe.[2] There were also important legislative developments across every field of Community activity, for example: on fundamental reform of the common agricultural policy;[3] modernization of the system for enforcing competition law under Articles 81 and 82 EC;[4] the legal status of long-term resident third-country nationals, and the right to family reunification;[5] a revised prohibition on tobacco advertising and sponsorship;[6] promoting the use of renewable fuels to replace diesel and petrol for transport purposes;[7] and establishing minimum common principles for legal aid in cross-border disputes.[8] And that leaves aside many important proposals for new measures worthy of critical assessment in their own right, for example: concerning free movement for Union citizens and their families;[9] and regulating fairness in business-to-consumer commercial transactions.[10] Nevertheless, attention will focus on the case-law of the Court of

[1] OJ 2003 L 236 and C 227 E. See also, Hillion, C. (2004) 'Commentary on the Accession Treaty 2003'. 29 *ELRev* (forthcoming).
[2] OJ 2003 C 169, p. 1. See also, Dougan, M. (2003) 'The Convention's Draft Constitutional Treaty: Bringing Europe Closer To Its Lawyers?'. 28 *ELRev* 763.
[3] Regulation 1782/2003, OJ 2003 L 270, p. 1.
[4] Regulation 1/2003, OJ 2003 L 1, p. 1.
[5] Directive 2003/109, OJ 2004 L 16, p. 44, and Directive 2003/86, OJ 2003 L 251, p. 12 (respectively).
[6] Directive 2003/33, OJ 2003 L 152, p. 16. Cf. Directive 98/43, OJ 1998 L 213, p. 9; annulled in Case C-376/98 *Germany* v. *Parliament and Council* [2000] ECR I-8419.
[7] Directive 2003/30, OJ 2003 L 123, p. 42.
[8] Directive 2003/8, OJ 2003 L 26, p. 41.
[9] COM(2003) 199 final.
[10] COM(2003) 356 final.

Justice – an endless source of fascination and occasional frustration for lawyers, and an important reference point for all those interested in the workings of the European Union. Even there, with hundreds of judgments to choose from, we must be highly selective. This review will therefore examine just a handful of the most significant rulings delivered by the Court of Justice in 2003.

I. Effective Judicial Protection Against Member States

The Court in *Francovich* established the principle that Member States are obliged to make reparation for damage caused by a breach of Community law for which they can be held responsible.[11] The dispute in *Köbler* raised the question of whether this could cover decisions of a national supreme court. Here, the Austrian Supreme Administrative Court decided that certain loyalty bonuses paid to university professors were compatible with the rules on free movement for workers – an erroneous assessment of Community law, made after withdrawing a reference under Article 234 EC on the basis that the issue was *acte clair* in the light of recent case-law.[12] On an action for damages against Austria, the Court of Justice found that the full effectiveness of the Treaty would be called into question, and the protection of rights derived from Community law would be weakened, if individuals were unable to obtain reparation in respect of infringements resulting from judicial decisions delivered at last instance in respect of which there could be no further possibility of correction. However, liability should be incurred only in exceptional cases, where the court of last instance has manifestly breached Community law, taking into account whether the judges abrogated their obligation to make an Article 234 EC reference. In this dispute, the Court of Justice concluded that no such manifest breach had been established: the compatibility of loyalty bonuses with the treaty rules on free movement of workers had not been clearly addressed at the date of the Supreme Administrative Court's judgment, and the Article 234 EC reference had been withdrawn on the basis of an incorrect interpretation of the Court's recent case-law.[13]

Köbler is undoubtedly an important judgment – not least because of the impact the possibility of *Francovich* liability might have on relations between national and Community judiciaries. For example, *Köbler* clearly increases the incentive for national judges not to abuse their discretion under the *CILFIT* case-law, by refraining from making Article 234 EC references in respect of issues which are not genuinely covered by the *acte clair* doctrine.[14] Similarly, *Köbler* has the potential to shift the goalposts of the supremacy debate: national

[11] Cases C-6 and 9/90 *Francovich* [1991] ECR I-5357.
[12] In particular, Case C-15/96 *Schöning* [1998] ECR I-47.
[13] Case C-224/01 *Köbler* (judgment of 30 September 2003).
[14] Case 283/81 *CILFIT* [1982] ECR 3415.

judges might be more reluctant to shirk their obligation to disapply any provision of domestic law which conflicts with the Treaty, in flagrant defiance of the Court's well-established case-law, if that would almost certainly constitute a manifest breach of Community law justifying the imposition of *Francovich* liability upon the Member State. However, the Court in *Köbler* repeatedly stressed that its ruling applied only to national judges acting at last instance, who carry a particular responsibility both for ensuring the effective enjoyment by individuals of their treaty rights, and for making preliminary references to the Court under Article 234 EC. It remains to be seen whether there might ever be circumstances in which infringements of the Treaty perpetrated via decisions delivered by lower courts and tribunals will furnish the basis for Member State liability under *Francovich*.[15]

II. Effective Judicial Protection Against Community Institutions

Article 300(7) EC provides that agreements concluded between the Community and third countries shall be binding on the institutions of the Community and on Member States; but the Court held in *Demirel* that the effects of an international agreement within the Community legal order must be determined in the light of its nature and purpose.[16] Against that background, the Court had already reached the conclusion that World Trade Organization (WTO) agreements are not capable of providing the basis for reviewing the legality of Community measures: first, the global trading rules place considerable emphasis on political negotiation as a means of resolving disputes between contracting parties; second, some of the Community's most important trading partners – or rather rivals – did not treat the WTO agreements as a direct grounds for invalidating their own internal acts. The Court conceded that the situation would be different only where the Community institutions intended to implement a particular obligation assumed in the context of the WTO; or where the relevant Community act expressly refers to precise provisions of the WTO agreements.[17]

That case-law concerned the situation which exists *before* binding decisions are adopted by the WTO's Dispute Settlement Body. *Biret International* raised the question whether the legal framework should differ *after* the Dispute Settlement Body has found the Community in breach of its WTO obligations and obliged to remedy the situation. Here, the Community's prohibition on the importation of hormone-treated beef and veal contravened the Agreement

---

[15] Especially bearing in mind the duty to exhaust available remedies (such as rights of appeal). Cf. Case C-129/00 *Commission* v. *Italy* (judgment of 9 December 2003).

[16] Case 12/86 *Demirel* [1987] ECR 3719.

[17] E.g. Case C-149/96 *Portugal* v. *Council* [1999] ECR I-8395.

on the Application of Sanitary and Phytosanitary Measures. The Community was given until 13 May 1999 to comply with its WTO obligations. No action had been taken by June 2000, when Biret International (a French meat trading company which was subject to judicial liquidation proceedings) sought damages under Articles 235 and 288(2) EC in respect of losses allegedly incurred through the ban on importing hormone-treated meats. The Court of First Instance found against the claimant on the simple grounds that the Community prohibition predated the Agreement on the Application of Sanitary and Phytosanitary Measures, and therefore the Community could neither have intended to implement nor expressly referred to that Agreement.[18]

But on appeal, Advocate General Alber argued that the Dispute Settlement Body's decision was in itself capable of providing the basis for reviewing the legality of Community measures: the Community was under an obligation to comply with that decision, even if it had discretion about exactly how to comply; if the deadline for action had passed and the Community institutions had taken no action, there was no good reason to deny the possibility of compensation for affected individuals. The Court found that, as regards the period prior to 13 May 1999, there could be no basis for judicial review against the Community institutions, since the deadline for complying with the decision of the Dispute Settlement Body had not yet expired. However, the Court conveniently avoided having to resolve the vital issue of whether judicial review was possible after expiry of the May 1999 deadline: the date for cessation of payments under the French judicial liquidation proceedings against Biret International had been set at 28 February 1995, so there could in any case be no possibility of damages liability being incurred by the Community after that date.[19] One could almost hear the sigh of relief all the way from Luxembourg. But we can be sure that it will not be too long before the potential legal effects of the WTO agreements within the Community legal order – with all that implies as regards the institution's room for political manœuvre on the international stage, the commercial position of Community undertakings *vis-à-vis* their foreign rivals, and the social rights and cultural choices of European citizens and consumers – return to the judicial arena.

III. Free Movement of Goods: Peaceful Protests

The rules on free movement of goods under Articles 28–30 EC are directly binding on the Member State *stricto sensu*, as well as on certain bodies whose actions are controlled or underpinned by the Member State.[20] However, the

---

[18] Case T-174/00 *Biret International* [2002] ECR II-17.
[19] Case C-94/02 *Biret International* (judgment of 30 September 2003).
[20] E.g. Case 249/81 *Commission* v. *Ireland* [1982] ECR 4005; Case C-292/92 *Hünermund* [1993] ECR I-6787.

Court established in Case C-265/95 *Commission* v. *France,* that Article 28 EC requires Member States not merely themselves to abstain from adopting measures liable to constitute an obstacle to trade but also, when read with the duty of loyal co-operation contained in Article 10 EC, to take all necessary and appropriate measures to ensure that free movement is respected on their territory, in particular in the face of obstacles created by the actions of private individuals. The case itself concerned a widespread campaign of often violent protests by French farmers specifically targeting foreign imports. The campaign was conducted on a regular basis over a ten-year period, and the authorities had taken little action either to prevent attacks or prosecute those responsible. In those circumstances, the Court held that France had manifestly exceeded its margin of discretion in determining which measures were most appropriate to eliminate private barriers to free movement.[21]

Commission v. *France* raised the question: what about non-violent and/or lawful conduct (such as peaceful protests or organized boycotts) which disrupts free trade? Would this be caught by the Treaty, and what 'appropriate measures' would Member States be required to adopt against it? These issues were addressed in *Schmidberger.* The case concerned the Brenner Corridor through the Austrian Alps, which constitutes the primary transport route linking Northern Italy to Southern Germany. Environmentalists organized a demonstration on the motorway, peacefully and with the consent of local police, to demand greater traffic restrictions in an effort to cut pollution. The demonstration resulted in the total closure of the Brenner Corridor to heavy goods vehicles for almost 30 hours. Schmidberger, a German company which used the Brenner Corridor to transport its goods to Italy, brought an action in the Austrian courts claiming *Francovich* damages for the profits it had lost as a result of this state-sanctioned obstacle to free movement. The Court of Justice recalled the principle in *Commission* v. *France* that, where national authorities are faced with restrictions on the free movement of goods which result from actions taken by individuals, they are required to take adequate steps to ensure that freedom within the national territory. That obligation is all the more important where the case concerns a major transit route such as the Brenner motorway. Without drawing any distinction between violent/unlawful and peaceful/lawful protest, the Court held that for Austria not to have banned the demonstration amounted to a restriction on intra-Community trade which had to be objectively justified. For these purposes, Austria relied on respect for the freedoms of expression and assembly (as guaranteed by its own constitution and the European Convention on Human Rights). The Court was therefore called upon to reconcile the protection of fundamental rights with a fundamental freedom enshrined

---

[21] Case C-265/95 *Commission* v. *France* [1997] ECR I-6959. Cf. Regulation 2679/98, OJ 1998 L 337, p. 8.

in the Treaty. Neither imperative was absolute, since each could be subject to restrictions relating to the public interest. It was therefore necessary to weigh the interests involved, having regard to all the circumstances of the case, to determine whether a fair balance had been struck. In this regard, the facts of *Schmidberger* were clearly different from the facts of *Commission* v. *France*, and it could not be said that Austria had committed a breach of Community law such as to give rise to liability under *Francovich*.[22]

There was never seriously any doubt that the Court would reject this claim. And given that even the facts of *Schmidberger* were fairly unique, in terms of the importance of the Brenner motorway within the trans-European transport network, it is clearly not the case that any protest which closes down a road and disrupts the transportation of goods will cause the Member State to breach Article 28 EC, or that private campaigns to promote domestic goods or boycott the purchase of certain imported goods will require any particular response from the national authorities. Nevertheless, the fact that the Court has chosen to pursue a very broad interpretation of the types of situation which are caught by the principle in *Commission* v. *France*, and must therefore be justified under Community law, does in itself have significant conceptual implications. In particular, the result of *Schmidberger* is that fundamental rights go 'on the defensive': it is no longer up to the Member State to prove *why* it restricted the individual's liberty of expression or assembly; it is now for the national authorities to prove *why they did not* restrict the citizen's fundamental freedoms. This is not necessarily to criticize the Court. *Schmidberger* should in fact be seen as a valuable contribution to theoretical debate about the relationship between traditional civil and political rights and more recent economic and social rights, set against the background of the Nice Charter of Fundamental Rights, which proclaims all such liberties to be indivisible and refrains from establishing any order of precedence between them.[23]

IV. Free Movement of Services: Cross-border Healthcare

The liberalizing impact of the treaty rules on free movement of services on the cross-border provision of non-emergency healthcare was addressed by the Court in 2001 in its groundbreaking judgment in *Smits and Peerbooms*.[24] Some commentators have feared that more generous rights to seek medical treatment abroad at the expense of one's own social security system will threaten the financial balance of the national welfare budget, and breach the principle of solidarity upon which essential public services are organized and delivered.

[22] Case C-112/00 *Schmidberger* [2003] ECR I-5659.
[23] Charter of Fundamental Rights of the European Union, OJ 2000 C 364, p. 1.
[24] Case C-157/99 *Smits and Peerbooms* [2001] ECR I-5473.

Other commentators see such rights as a valuable means of achieving a more efficient co-ordination between supply and demand in the healthcare sector viewed from a wider European perspective, whereby the Community's aggregate resources are collectively mobilized in an effort to prevent unnecessary suffering and increase patient choice. The dispute in *Müller-Fauré and van Riet* gave the Court an important opportunity to develop its jurisprudence on this issue, and the judgment suggests that the Court tends towards the latter viewpoint.[25]

Both *Smits and Peerbooms* and *Müller-Fauré and van Riet* concerned the Dutch sickness insurance scheme. Sickness funds entered into contracts with authorized healthcare providers, who agreed to supply care to insured persons in return for reimbursement at flat rate fees. Insured persons themselves were entitled to treatment provided free at the point of delivery, so long as they were treated by a contracted healthcare provider. Sickness funds granted authorization for insured persons to seek treatment from a non-contracted healthcare provider when two conditions were satisfied: first, the treatment was regarded as normal in Dutch professional circles; and second, it could not be provided at a contracted institution without undue delay. Both cases concerned insured persons who obtained medical treatment from non-contracted healthcare providers established in other Member States, at their own initiative, and then sought reimbursement of their costs from the sickness funds, arguing that the requirement of (and conditions for) prior authorization under national law constituted a hindrance to their freedom to receive medical services under Article 49 EC. *Müller-Fauré and van Riet* builds on the legal framework for dealing with this issue in three main ways.

The first concerns the issue of whether medical treatment provided free at the point of delivery amounts to an *economic service* under Article 49 EC. The Court in *Smits and Peerbooms* decided – perhaps surprisingly – that it does. As regards the essential requirement of 'remuneration' for the service provided, the Court identified two relevant economic transactions: the insured person paid the foreign hospital directly for its medical services; the sickness fund paid its contracted healthcare providers for the medical treatment supplied to insured persons. *Smits and Peerbooms* appeared to suggest that these two transactions were cumulative in establishing the presence of a remunerated service under Article 49 EC. As such, it was assumed that the Court's approach would not apply to systems where the Member State itself delivers medical treatment directly and without the intermediary of a contracted healthcare provider. However, the judgment in *Müller-Fauré and van Riet* suggests that the absence of the second transaction is not decisive, since the first transaction

---

[25] Case C-385/99 *Müller-Fauré and van Riet* [2003] ECR I-4509. Note also, Case C-56/01 *Inizan* (judgment of 23 October 2003).

in itself furnishes a sufficient economic service on to which the Treaty can bite. Indeed, the Court stated expressly that a medical service does not cease to fall within Article 49 EC just because it is paid for through a national health service or from the national budget. So, whatever doubts might have lingered before, the Court's case-law now clearly applies also to systems such as the UK's National Health Service.

The second issue concerns the finding in *Smits and Peerbooms* that the requirement of prior authorization, before seeking reimbursement for *hospital treatment* with a non-contracted healthcare provider, constituted an obstacle to the insured person's freedom to receive services; but this obstacle could be justified by the concern to ensure careful forward planning of the hospital infrastructure, to maintain sufficient and permanent access to a balanced range of high-quality treatment, and to control costs and minimize wastage. However, it remained necessary to ensure that the Dutch conditions for obtaining such prior authorization were proportionate to their objectives. In this regard, *Smits and Peerbooms* upheld the requirement of 'undue delay', but left open the basis on which it was to be calculated. Important clarification was offered in *Müller-Fauré and van Riet*: the national authorities must have regard to all the circumstances of each specific case, taking into account the patient's medical history as well as his/her current condition; but cannot refuse authorization simply on the grounds that there are waiting lists for the relevant hospital treatment within the Member State. So, just because it usually takes 12 months to have a given operation on the National Health Service cannot mean that the claimant who is prepared to travel abroad to have that operation much sooner should pay for it him/herself. The Court clearly considered that Member State fears about 'queue jumping' were based essentially on economic factors – without considering the possibility that notions of social solidarity could play any legitimate role, particularly if those individuals more likely to benefit from the right to move are relatively better educated and more affluent than those citizens left behind to wait.

The third issue concerns the lawfulness under Community law of a requirement of prior authorization, before seeking reimbursement for *non-hospital treatment* with a non-contracted healthcare provider. The Court in *Müller-Fauré and van Riet* again identified an obstacle to the insured person's freedom to receive services; but this time, the obstacle could *not* be justified by concerns about forward planning and controlled spending. The existence of barriers such as physical distance, linguistic differences, the costs of staying abroad and the relationship of trust between patient and doctor made it unlikely that removing the requirement of prior authorization altogether would result in sufficient uptake by insured persons as to upset seriously the Dutch social security and public health systems. Moreover, Community law does not affect the basic right of Member States to limit the types of treatment covered by their sickness insurance scheme, to impose a ceiling on maximum recoverable costs, or to insist that patients fulfil certain objective conditions before benefits are made available (for example, to consult a GP before seeing a specialist). Nevertheless, the overall effect of *Müller-Fauré and van Riet* is further liberalization of the legal framework governing cross-border access to healthcare at the home state's expense.

V. Free Movement of Goods and Services: The Internet

2003 saw several judgments in which the Court considered the implications of the internet for the internal market – both its unparalleled capacity to integrate the Community market in goods and services, and its far-reaching potential to question the legitimacy of national regulations which create obstacles to trade.

For example, *Gambelli* concerned Italian legislation making it a criminal offence to provide betting services in relation to sporting events without authorization from the national authorities. Stanley (a bookmakers registered and regulated in the UK) sought to evade this restriction by organizing a network of Italian agencies to take requests for bets on sporting events from individuals, and transmit those requests via the internet to Stanley's offices in Liverpool. Stanley processed the requests and confirmed the bets, again through the internet, at which point the punters would pay the appropriate sum to Stanley's Italian agents. When the latter were prosecuted for fraud against the Italian state by unlawfully organizing clandestine bets, they argued that the national legislation was incompatible (*inter alia*) with Article 49 EC. The Court held that the activity of enabling Italian nationals to engage in betting organized in the UK was a service for the purposes of Article 49 EC (even though the sporting events in question took place in Italy). Moreover, Article 49 EC applies to situations where the provider offers its services from one Member State via the internet to recipients established in another Member State, so that any restriction on those activities constitutes an infringement of the free movement rules which must be justified under Community law. In that regard, the Court accepted that restrictions on betting were motivated by concerns about consumer protection and the prevention of fraud. However, insofar as Italy was in fact substantially expanding gambling within its territory with a view to generating revenue for the public purse, it could not simultaneously argue that its restrictions on betting were necessary to protect the general interest.[26]

---

[26] Case C-243/01 *Gambelli* (judgment of 6 November 2003).

Deutscher Apothekerverband concerned German rules restricting the sale by mail order of any medicinal product which, in accordance with national legislation, could be sold only in dispensing pharmacies. DocMorris was a company established in the Netherlands which, under licence from the Dutch authorities, sold prescription and non-prescription medicinal products by mail order via its internet site – including to customers living in Germany. The Court held that, as regards medicines which had not yet been authorized for the German market, Community secondary legislation clearly permitted that Member State to restrict their sale without risk of infringing Article 28 EC. But the situation was different as regards medicines which had already been authorized in Germany. In that context, a prohibition on the sale of certain goods by mail order is *prima facie* a selling arrangement falling outside the scope of Article 28 EC in accordance with the judgment in *Keck and Mithouard*.[27] However, the Court noted that the emergence of the internet as a method of cross-border sale requires the scope and effect of such a rule to be examined within its broader context. It was clear that the German rules created more of an obstacle to trade for pharmacies established outside the national territory than for pharmacies established within the Member State: the latter were still able to sell medicinal products through their dispensaries, whereas the former were deprived of a significant means of gaining direct access to the German market. The disputed restrictions therefore discriminated in practice against the sale of imported medicinal products, and constituted a measure having equivalent effect to a quantitative restriction within the meaning of Article 28 EC. The Court continued to find that there was no good reason for an absolute prohibition on the sale by mail order of non-prescription medicines; but that the greater risks associated with prescription medicines could justify limitations on their sale other than over the dispensing counter.[28]

VI. Free Movement of Workers: Family Members

Article 39 EC and Regulation 1612/68 give migrant workers the right to bring certain family members, including their spouse, to live with them in the host state, even if those family members are not themselves Community nationals.[29] The Court established in *Surinder Singh* that such treaty-based family rights also benefit own nationals returning to their state of origin having exercised their right to live and work in another Member State. However, the Court did point out that there are limits on the extent to which own nationals can rely

---

[27] Cases C-267 and 268/91 *Keck and Mithouard* [1993] ECR I-6097.
[28] Case C-322/01 *Deutscher Apothekerverband* (judgment of 11 December 2003).
[29] Regulation 1612/68, OJ 1968 L 257, p. 2.

on a past exercise of their right to free movement, so as to claim the benefit of Community law against their state of origin, in particular, where this would allow the Treaty to be abused so as to evade national immigration legislation.[30]

The issue of what constitutes an abuse, and the legal situation of third-country national family members more generally, was addressed by the Court in *Akrich*. The case concerned a Moroccan man who (it seemed) was residing unlawfully in the UK when he married an English woman. The couple went to live in Dublin, where Mrs Akrich worked for several months, before returning to the UK. Mr Akrich applied for a residence permit on the basis that Mrs Akrich had exercised her right to free movement in another Member State under Article 39 EC and, on the basis of *Surinder Singh*, was entitled to bring along her spouse. The problem was that the couple actually told immigration officials they 'had heard about EU rights, staying six months and then going back to the UK' – on which basis the authorities believed that their sojourn in Ireland was deliberately designed to manufacture a right to residence for Mr Akrich and thereby evade British immigration restrictions, amounting to an abuse of the Treaty which could not warrant a residence permit.

The first point identified by the Court constitutes a new development in free movement law: if Mr Akrich could not prove that he was lawfully resident within a Member State, at the time Mrs Akrich wished to exercise her rights to free movement, he would be unable to benefit from the rights of entry and residence available to spouses under Regulation 1612/68. The purpose of giving a right of residency to the third-country national spouse of a Community worker is to ensure that the worker's decision to move to another Member State does not result in any loss of opportunity for the couple lawfully to live together. But if the third-country national spouse had no right to live in the home state anyway, the worker's decision to move to another Member State cannot in itself result in any loss of opportunity for the couple lawfully to live together. The only concession the Court was prepared to make in this situation was that the national authorities must nevertheless respect the fundamental right to respect for family and private life as enshrined in Article 8 ECHR and protected as a general principle of Community law. This aspect of *Akrich* is therefore of fundamental significance for all third-country nationals who are or become married to Union citizens: the mere fact of movement between Member States, or of residence within another Member State, will not of itself regularize the spouse's immigration status.[31]

If Mr Akrich could indeed prove that he was lawfully present within the Community territory, the second issue arose: had the couple abused their free movement rights so as to evade UK immigration rules? The ECJ held that they

[30] Case C-370/90 *Surinder Singh* [1992] ECR I-4265.
[31] Cf. Case C-459/99 *MRAX* [2002] ECR I-6591.

© Blackwell Publishing Ltd 2004

had not: the motives of a Community worker in exercising his/her rights to free movement are irrelevant, in assessing whether his/her conduct is to be treated as abusive. Provided the marriage itself was genuine, a British national returning to the UK having worked abroad was entitled to bring along her third-country national spouse, even though the British national had only worked abroad so as to trigger the application Article 39 EC, and thereby acquire a more secure right of residence for that spouse than was available under purely domestic rules.[32] The Court in *Akrich* has therefore adopted a very narrow interpretation of the concept of abuse referred to in *Surinder Singh*. But the judgment is consistent with the Court's broader case-law: after all, if companies can exercise their freedom of establishment by incorporating in one Member State with lower regulatory standards, for the sole purpose of avoiding the more stringent rules applicable in another Member State where they wish to conduct their entire economic activity,[33] why should individuals not be entitled to exercise their right to free movement under the Treaty by working in one Member State, for the sole purpose of uniting their family in their country of origin, despite the latter having a stricter immigration regime?

VII. Police and Judicial Co-operation in Criminal Matters

The disputes in *Gözütok and Brügge* provided the Court of Justice with its very first opportunity to rule on the interpretation of the Convention implementing the Schengen agreement.

Acting in accordance with the protocol integrating the Schengen *acquis* into the framework of the European Union (as agreed at Amsterdam), the Council determined that the third pillar should furnish the legal basis for Article 54 of the Convention. That provision sets out the *ne bis in idem* principle, i.e. that a person whose trial has been finally disposed of in one Member State may not be prosecuted in another Member State for the same acts; provided that, if a penalty has been imposed, it has been enforced, is actually in the process of being enforced, or can no longer be enforced under the laws of the sentencing state. This principle is intended to ensure that individuals are not prosecuted on the same facts in several Member States, on account of having exercised their right to free movement across the Community. Indeed, Advocate General Ruiz-Jarabo Colomer observed that it would be 'inherently unfair and contrary to the principles on which the construction of a United Europe rests if … a person could be punished in several Member States for committing the same

---

[32] Case C-109/01 *Akrich* (judgment of 23 September 2003).
[33] E.g. Case C-212/97 *Centros* [1999] ECR I-1459; Case C-208/00 *Überseering* [2002] ECR I-9919; Case C-167/01 *Inspire Art* (judgment of 30 September 2003).

acts'.[34] *Gözütok and Brügge* concerned the situation of individuals suspected of committing a criminal offence, where proceedings in the relevant Member State were discontinued, in accordance with national law, after the accused agreed to pay fines under an agreement reached with the public prosecutor. The issue arose whether such procedures, which barred further prosecution in the relevant Member State, could activate the principle contained in Article 54 as regards other Member States.

The Court held that where, following such a procedure, further prosecution was definitively barred, the individual's case should be considered 'finally disposed of'; and that where the fine has been paid (or other conditions fulfilled), the penalty imposed should be considered 'enforced'. It is irrelevant for these purposes that no court was involved, and that the final decision was not judicial in nature. After all, no provision of the third pillar makes application of Article 54 of the Convention implementing the Schengen agreement conditional on the harmonization of national criminal laws – which necessarily implies that Member States have mutual trust in their criminal justice systems, and will recognize the criminal law in force in other countries, even if their own national rules would reach a different outcome. This emphasis on the principles of mutual trust and mutual recognition is perhaps the most striking element of the judgment in *Gözütok and Brügge*: after all, it hints at the same powerful dynamic which fuelled integration in the field of free movement law following judgments such as *Cassis de Dijon*;[35] and indeed, it creates a powerful incentive for Member States, some perhaps uneasy at the idea of having extensive obligations of mutual recognition in this field, to agree harmonized (procedural and substantive) standards of criminal justice.[36]

The Court reinforced its findings by reference to other more fundamental considerations, again indicating the sort of attitude it is likely to adopt as regards future references under the third pillar. First, the Union has set itself the objective of creating an area of freedom, security and justice; and has integrated the Schengen *acquis* with a view to developing that area more rapidly. Article 54 of the Convention cannot play a useful role in attaining those goals unless it is also found to apply to procedures definitively discontinuing prosecutions in the relevant Member State, even without the involvement of a court or adoption of a judicial decision. Second, national legal systems which provide for procedures for barring further prosecution generally do so only in respect of offences which are not considered serious and are punishable only by relatively light penalties. If Article 54 of the Convention were to apply only to

---

[34] At para. 58 Opinion.
[35] Case 120/78 *'Cassis de Dijon'* [1979] ECR 649.
[36] Cf. the proposals for greater harmonizing powers in this field contained in the Convention's draft Constitutional Treaty, OJ 2003 C 169, p. 1.

procedures involving a court or to decisions of a judicial nature, that provision (and the underlying right to free movement it is intended to promote) would benefit only defendants guilty of relatively serious offences.[37]

VIII. Equal Treatment for Men and Women: Compulsory Military Service

The Court established in judgments such as *Sirdar* and *Kreil* that Directive 76/207,[38] guaranteeing equal treatment between men and women as regards employment, applies to posts within the armed forces – thus preventing Member States from engaging in unjustified discrimination (for example) against female applicants seeking access to remunerated work.[39] After that, it was only a matter of time before the Court was asked to assess the legality of compulsory military service as practised by certain Member States. The applicant in *Dory* duly obliged.

The case concerned the requirement under German law for all male (but not female) nationals who attain the age of 18 to perform military service. When Mr Dory's application for exemption from call-up was rejected, he argued that the German rules constituted a breach of the principle of equal treatment between men and women: even if compulsory military service cannot in itself be considered 'employment' for the purposes of defining the scope of application of the principle of equal treatment under Community law, it nevertheless has the effect of denying access to employment for men subject to call-up and of thereby delaying their career progress as compared to women of the same age, which should be enough to justify applying Directive 76/207.

The Court recalled that decisions of the Member States concerning the organization of their armed forces are not completely excluded from the application of Community law, especially as regards access to employment in military posts. But it does not follow that Community law governs the Member State's choices about military organization for the defence of its territory or other essential interests. The obligation under German law for young men to perform military service is the expression of a choice about military organization – inspired by concerns such as the democratic transparency of the army, and the mobilization of sufficient manpower in the event of conflict – to which Community law is not applicable. Even if that choice had inevitable adverse consequences for the labour market participation and career progression of the young men involved, Community law could not encroach on the Member State's competences by insisting that compulsory military service either be

---

[37] Cases C-187 and 385/01 *Gözütok and Brügge* [2003] ECR I-1345.
[38] Directive 76/207, OJ 1976 L 39, p. 40.
[39] Case C-273/97 *Sirdar* [1999] ECR I-7403; Case C-285/98 *Kreil* [2000] ECR I-69.

extended also to women or simply abolished altogether.[40] And it would have taken a very brave Court indeed to say anything else.

IX. Payment of Public Subsidies for the Provision of Public Services

Altmark Trans raised questions about the range of public subsidies which should be classified as state aid falling within the scope of Article 87(1) EC, and which therefore require justification under Article 87(2) or (3) EC, in accordance with the rigorous procedural regime established under Article 88 EC.

The case concerned the compatibility with Community law of the grant by the Magdeburg Regional Government of licences for scheduled local bus services, together with public subsidies for operating those services, to Altmark Trans. Insofar as Germany had made proper use of its right to derogate from the common rules on public service obligations in the field of transport, attention focused on the potential application of Articles 87-88 EC.

The Court recalled the constituent elements of the concept of state aid contained in Article 87(1) EC. For these purposes, questions first arose about whether public subsidies for the provision of local transport services could have the required effect on trade between Member States. The Court held that they could: such subsidies could still maintain or increase the supply of services by the recipient undertaking, so that undertakings established in other Member States find it more difficult to penetrate the domestic market. Questions then arose about whether the German measure could be regarded as an economic advantage conferred on the recipient undertaking which it would not have obtained under normal market conditions. In this regard, the Court held that, where a national measure acts as compensation for the discharge of public service obligations by the recipient undertaking, which does not therefore enjoy a real financial advantage and is not put in a more favourable competitive position than its rivals, such a measure escapes definition as state aid and falls outside Article 87(1) EC altogether – provided that certain conditions are fulfilled. For example, there must actually be clearly defined public service obligations to discharge; the basis for calculating the compensation must be established in advance in an objective and transparent manner; and compensation must not go beyond what is necessary to cover the costs incurred in discharge of the public service obligation (taking into account a reasonable profit).[41]

Altmark Trans affirms the Court's basic approach in its earlier judgment in *Ferring*,[42] whilst incorporating some of the refinements suggested by Advocate

---

[40] Case C-186/01 *Dory* [2003] ECR I-2479.
[41] Case C-280/00 *Altmark Trans* [2003] ECR I-7747.
[42] Case C-53/00 *Ferring* [2001] ECR I-9067.

General Jacobs in the recent *GEMO* dispute.[43] Some commentators will no doubt query whether the Court's test is really supported by the conceptual framework for analysing state aid cases intended by the treaty drafters. But it will surely be greeted by public authorities across Europe which have entrusted the performance of important public services to private undertakings without notifying any subsidies involved to the Commission under Article 88 EC – a procedural default which could in itself have rendered those subsidies unlawful, and entitled third parties to seek orders for their repayment.[44] By incorporating more of a balancing act between the provision of public subsidies and the discharge of public service obligations into the very definition of state aid under Article 87(1), the Court has avoided those drastic consequences. Incidentally, *Altmark Trans* also promotes an increased role for the national courts in settling state aids disputes – for better or worse, without directly involving the Commission – despite the limited direct effect of Community rules in this sector.

X. Inter-Institutional Balance: Second Comitology Decision

Comitology continues to provide a source of litigation between the institutions about the constitutional balance of power. Case C-378/00 *Commission* v. *Parliament and Council* involved the Commission's action for annulment of Regulation 1655/2000 concerning the financial instrument for the environment, insofar as it made the adoption of measures necessary for implementing its programme of financial assistance in respect of qualifying projects subject to the regulatory committee procedure.[45] The Commission argued that, according to the criteria for selecting an appropriate procedure for the adoption of implementing measures contained in Article 2 of the Second Comitology Decision, the Council and Parliament should have agreed to apply the (relatively less intrusive) management committee procedure, which is meant to be used for the implementation of programmes with substantial budgetary implications.[46]

The Court held that Article 202 EC empowers the Council to lay down principles and rules, not only establishing the types of procedure to which exercise of the Commission's implementing powers may be subject, but also as regards the choice to be made between those various procedures. However, Article 202 EC leaves the Council free to decide whether those principles and rules will be binding upon the Community legislature when adopting basic instruments conferring implementing powers, or will instead be limited to setting

---

[43] Case C-126/01 *GEMO* (judgment of 20 November 2003).
[44] E.g. Case C-354/90 *FNCE* [1991] ECR I-5505; Case C-39/94 *SFEI* [1996] ECR I-3547.
[45] Regulation 1655/2000, OJ 2000 L 192, p. 1.
[46] Decision 1999/468, OJ 1999 L 184, p. 23.

out criteria for guidance. In that regard, it was clear from its very wording that the Second Comitology Decision did not intend to make the criteria contained in Article 2 binding in character. The Community legislature could therefore determine the choice of committee procedure on a case-by-case basis, and do so in a manner which (as here) was at variance with the criteria contained in Article 2. However, the Commission did win a more limited victory. Even though Article 2 merely lays down a rule of conduct indicating the practice to be followed, the same considerations of consistency and predictability which persuaded the Council to adopt the Second Comitology Decision in the first place now required that the Community legislature should not depart from the Article 2 criteria without stating its reasons for doing so. Regulation 1655/2000 did not contain any such statement of reasons, and was therefore annulled for infringement of an essential procedural requirement, though (at the Commission's request) its legal effects were upheld pending imminent amendment.[47]

XI. Protection of the Community's Financial Interests

The dispute in Case C-11/00 *Commission* v. *European Central Bank* raised several important issues, not least the scope of the Community institutions' obligation under Article 108 EC to respect the independence of the European Central Bank.

Regulation 1073/1999 empowered the European Anti-Fraud Office (OLAF) to carry out administrative investigations, with a view to fighting illegal activity affecting the Community's financial interests, within all the institutions, bodies, offices and agencies.[48] Not long after, however, the European Central Bank adopted Decision 1999/726, purporting to entrust its own Directorate for Internal Audit with sole responsibility for conducting anti-fraud investigations within the ECB.[49] The Commission sought annulment of the decision on the grounds that, not only was it incompatible with the investigative powers conferred upon OLAF under the regulation, but indeed amounted to an outright rejection of the regulation's applicability to the ECB.

The ECB argued in its defence that, for several reasons, the regulation itself was unlawful under Community law. For example, the ECB claimed that Article 280 EC – the legal basis for the regulation – is concerned only with protection of the Community's budget, whereas the ECB has its own separate budget. However, the Court replied that the ECB owes its existence to the EC Treaty, contributes to achievement of the Community's objectives, and falls squarely within the Community framework. The resources at the ECB's dis-

---

[47] Case C-378/00 *Commission* v. *Parliament and Council* [2003] ECR I-937.
[48] Regulation 1073/1999, OJ 1999 L 136, p. 1.
[49] Decision 1999/726, OJ 1999 L 291, p. 36.

posal therefore have a direct financial interest for the Community within the meaning of Article 280 EC. The ECB also argued that the powers conferred under Article 280 EC are restricted to measures for combating fraud at the level of the Member States. But the Court rejected that interpretation not only for lack of any convincing textual basis, but also as incompatible with the Treaty's underlying objective of fighting financial irregularities more effectively.

Perhaps the ECB's most important ground of defence was that the regulation was unlawful because OLAF's powers of investigation would conflict with the ECB's independence as guaranteed under Article 108 EC. However, the Court remained unconvinced, and essentially adopted the 'functional approach' to Article 108 EC suggested by the Commission. The purpose of Article 108 EC is to shield the ECB from all political pressure likely to interfere with the performance of its specific tasks (maintaining price stability and otherwise supporting the Community's economic policies). But this does not have the consequence of separating the ECB entirely from the Community, or exempting it from every rule of Community law. Indeed, there are no grounds for finding that the Community legislature is *in principle* precluded from adopting measures capable of applying to the ECB. Moreover, the ECB had failed to demonstrate how the regulation's application could *in practice* undermine its ability to perform its tasks independently. OLAF's functioning and powers are subject to strict guarantees of complete independence, as well as extensive legal and judicial controls. Its investigations are to be carried out under the specific conditions laid down in decisions adopted by each Community institution or body, and may thus be tailored to meet any necessary restrictions identified by the ECB itself. And the fact that certain economic operators on the international financial markets might, through a failure to appreciate the true picture of OLAF's functioning and powers, fear that the Commission was actually in a position to influence the ECB's decisions, could not justify finding that the regulation actually undermined the latter's independence. In the end, the Court found that there were no grounds for questioning the regulation's legality. Turning to the substance of the Commission's complaint, it was clear that the contested decision reflected a decision by the ECB to regard itself as exempt from the regulation and assume for itself sole responsibility for combating internal fraud, and should be annulled.[50]

---

[50] Case C-11/00 *Commission* v. *European Central Bank* [2003] ECR I-7147. Cf. the parallel proceedings in Case C-15/00 *Commission* v. *European Investment Bank* [2003] ECR I-7281.

External Policy Developments

DAVID ALLEN AND MICHAEL SMITH
Loughborough University

I. General Themes

2003 marked a low point in the external relations of the EU with the significant divisions that arose between the Member States over the events in Iraq. Nevertheless advances were also made and the draft Constitutional Treaty produced by the Convention on the Future of the European Union in mid-2003 made a number of radical suggestions about how future EU external policies might be developed and managed. The year was of course dominated by the conflict in Iraq and by the divisions that this caused both within the European Union and between the European Union and the United States.

The Commission continued the administrative reform of its external service (which the draft Treaty proposed to develop into a broader and more extensive EU external service). In 2003 new delegations were opened in Cuba, Ecuador, Laos and Malaysia, and a Commission Economic and Trade Office was opened in Taiwan. By the end of the year the Commission had 130 delegations represented by 105 heads.

Foreign and Security Policy

2003 was a momentous year for the common foreign and security policy (CFSP) and for the evolution of the European security and defence policy (ESDP). The Greek Presidency and Javier Solana, the High Representative, faced the difficult task, in the first half of the year, of attempting to preserve the semblance of unity. This was in spite of the fact that the Member States of the EU (along with the ten applicant states) were deeply divided over the issue of military intervention in Iraq. In the months before the US-led invasion of Iraq, Solana's attempts to preserve unity by brokering innocuous common statements were undermined by the determination of the larger Member States to pursue their own policies regardless of their impact on an EU common position. As Britain strove to make the case for armed intervention alongside the United States,

Germany and France made it clear that they opposed such action. The latter two felt that the UN resolutions in place did not provide the basis for intervention, and they advocated giving the weapons inspectors, acting on behalf of the UN, more time to complete their investigations.

Attempts at holding a common EU line were made more difficult by the deliberately unhelpful intervention of US Defense Secretary, Donald Rumsfeld, who referred to France and Germany as the 'old Europe', and intimated that there were other EU Member States who were more sympathetic to the US. As if summoned by the US, eight present and prospective EU members produced a letter (that many in the EU institutions felt broke the provisions of the Treaty on European Union (TEU)) supporting the US line. Shortly after this, ten more applicant and potential applicant states published their own letter (the 'Vilnius 10'), along similar lines. The hostile response from French President Chirac, who went so far as to suggest that France might reconsider its support for further enlargement, indicated that there was no prospect that the EU could produce a common stance on Iraq that had any meaning. The Greek Presidency valiantly stage-managed an emergency European Council in February as well as the routine spring Council in March. At both meetings, the leaders of the major EU countries could barely bring themselves to speak to one another. EU unity was preserved at the lowest possible level by agreement on the fundamental role of the UN in resolving the Iraq crisis – the fact that individual EU Member States were pursuing fundamentally different and opposed policies at the UN was overlooked. One consequence of these divisions was that Solana's role during the Iraq crisis was almost entirely marginalized although he continued to play a significant part in EU efforts to remind the US of the ongoing importance of the wider Middle East peace process.

Once the immediate hostilities in Iraq were concluded, the EU embarked on a determined effort to repair the damage to the CFSP caused by internal division as well as to the EU–US relationship. Whilst some might see the Iraq conflict as demonstrating the utter hopelessness of any ambition to construct a meaningful CFSP, others drew some solace from the collaborative achievements in the second part of the year. In Brussels in December, the European Council was able to reach agreement for the first time on a European security strategy drawn up by Solana (albeit one that had been significantly sanitized by France and Germany of its initial British-inspired reference to the possibility of the pre-emptive use of force). Earlier the EU had reached agreement on a strategy and action plan for dealing with the problem of weapons of mass destruction and the Commission developed a non-proliferation conditionality clause for EU agreements with third countries. These two developments were designed to assure the US of the EU's serious focus on global foreign and security issues, and in this context were well received. The US was less enthusiastic about, although eventually compliant with, EU plans to create a European Armaments Agency, designed to improve and rationalize European arms procurement and manufacture. The US was also cautious towards the EU decision to establish, under ESDP, a headquarters facility for planning and controlling any EU military activity that might take place without either Nato participation or the agreed use of Nato assets. Agreement on the latter brought to an end a long-running dispute with the US and within the EU about the relationship between the EU and Nato. During 2003, France, Germany, Belgium and Luxembourg irritated Britain in particular by meeting with the avowed intention of unilaterally establishing a separate EU military headquarters. In the end the 'Big Three' (Britain, France and Germany) got together to sort this out amongst themselves and with the US. There was further evidence of a potential CFSP *directoire* at work when the Big Three travelled together to Tehran. They brokered a solution (and thus preserved the EU's dialogue with Iran) to the dispute between Iran and the International Atomic Energy Agency that the US was anxious to exploit in a more hostile manner.

The EU did manage to give some substance to the ESDP in 2003 with three successful civil–military actions. In Macedonia the EU-led military operation (Concordia) replaced the Nato force in March until it in turn was replaced in December by a European Union police mission (Operation Proxima). In Bosnia and Herzogovina the EU monitoring mission continued, and an EU police mission (EUPM) began work at the start of the year. In December the European Council announced that the EU was ready to consider an ESDP military mission to Bosnia to replace the existing Nato stabilization force making use of the 'Berlin Plus' arrangements as in Macedonia. Finally, in mid-2003, the EU launched and successfully concluded 'Operation Artemis' – an ESDP military intervention to stabilize the situation in the Democratic Republic of the Congo.

At the height of the Iraq crisis, when the CFSP was being effectively humiliated, the Convention on the Future of Europe was of course putting the finishing touches to the draft Constitutional Treaty that Giscard d'Estaing presented to the European Council at Thessaloniki. The CFSP/ESDP provisions of this draft Treaty proposed some fairly radical changes to the EU's institutional arrangements. Although the IGC did not succeed in agreeing on a new Treaty in December, it would seem to be the case that the Member States have by and large accepted the recommendations relating to external relations laid down in the draft Treaty. There is therefore a reasonable expectation that any Treaty agreed in 2004 will include the following: arrangements for the election of a President of the European Council to replace the current rotating Presidency; the creation of the post of European Foreign Minister to be taken up by an individual who will combine the present role and responsibilities of the CFSP High Representative (currently Javier Solana) and the Commissioner for External Relations (currently Chris Patten); and the establishment of a legal identity for the European Union. We should also see the formation of an EU external action service which will convert the present external delegations of the European Commission into EU delegations, and involve the establishment of an EU diplomatic staff drawn from the Commission, the Council Secretariat and the diplomatic services of the Member States. It is also expected that the Treaty will envisage an extension of the Petersberg tasks and arrangements for enhanced structural co-operation in defence matters. The European Defence Agency that was mentioned in the draft Treaty is to be established in advance of any new Treaty and the provisions in the draft Treaty for a mutual solidarity defence clause remain the subject of debate between the Member States.

During 2003, the EU adopted seven new joint actions and defined ten common positions. The mandate of the special representatives in Afghanistan, the African Great Lakes region, Macedonia and to the Middle East peace process and the stability pact for south-eastern Europe were all extended. Marc Otte was appointed to replace Miguel Moratinos as EU special representative to the Middle East peace process and Heikki Talvitie was appointed as EU special representative for the southern Caucasus. The EU and the Presidency issued 147 declarations listed in the European Commission's 2003 General Report on the Activities of the European Union (point 764, Table 15).

External Trade and the Common Commercial Policy

As in previous years, during 2003 the EU's attention to external trade issues was essentially split between areas that had a strong element of the routine – or at least the pre-programmed – and those that involved much more fundamental issues relating to the framework of trade and related policies. In the former area, work continued on the development of customs procedures and customs co-operation, with the initiation of the new 'Customs 2007' long-term programme. The Commission also produced a Green Paper dealing with the application of rules of origin in the context of preferential trading agreements, and paid continuing attention to the regulation of the arms trade, particularly the trade in so-called 'dual use' weapons. At the same time, the Community's Generalized Scheme of Preferences (GSP) was extended for a further year (until the end of 2005) in October. On a key issue of Community competence, that of negotiations on air routes, the Commission was finally entrusted with a mandate in the summer, with the aim of negotiating major agreements with both the USA and other partner countries (see below).

In the specific context of enlargement, there was a good deal of work to be done on the reframing of bilateral investment treaties. The incoming new members had a variety of such arrangements with the United States in particular, and a memorandum of understanding was signed in September to remove the incompatibilities between these treaties and Community law. The Commission also paid attention to the increasing problem of the trade in counterfeit goods. Whereas previously this had been seen largely as a problem with luxury items, it had become clear that many more mundane products were now subject to serious counterfeiting problems. Agreement was reached during July on new measures, incorporated in a regulation that is due to enter into force in July 2004. Linked to this concern is the continuing EU activity in the field of anti-dumping: during the year the Community imposed definitive duties in three new cases, and confirmed or amended definitive duties in 33 proceedings after review. At the same time, 18 proceedings were closed without renewal of duties, whilst 7 new investigations and 20 new reviews were initiated. Anti-subsidy duties were confirmed in two cases. But this was in many ways a quiet year on the anti-dumping front.

This work on longer-term or pre-programmed issues has to be seen in parallel with more unexpected and novel developments, often in seemingly mundane areas. Thus the extension of the GSP had to cater for problems with special preferences extended to Pakistan in the context of the 'war on terror' and conflict in Afghanistan, and about which India had complained. Customs co-operation was given new dimensions by the fact that maritime and aviation security has become a matter of the highest politics: thus issues about the sharing of information and the searching of cargoes are now key in negotiations between the EU and the USA. In the same way, the initiation of discussions about air routes was surrounded by a range of other issues about transfer of passenger data and other matters embedded in the broader international security system. In a very different area, the year also saw a major innovation in the management of international anti-trust policies, with a joint action by the EU, the US and Japan to break up a cartel dealing with the raw materials for PVC production.

At a broader international level, the EU had to cope with a variety of challenges in the international trading regime. The Community was as always embroiled in a range of disputes, some of which are referred to in the appropriate sections below; as always, most of these involved the USA. In a throwback to the GATT Uruguay round, provision had to be made for the phasing-out of quota arrangements in the field of textiles: this was the result of agreements reached almost ten years earlier. Other changes were more the reflection of potential future developments: the EU supported World Trade Organization (WTO) entry for Russia – a matter complicated by the difficulties of agreement on the energy trade – and for Saudi Arabia, with whom a new trade deal was agreed. The Union also pursued negotiations with a variety of regional groupings within the international arena, including Mercosur in South America, the Gulf Co-operation Council and ASEAN (see below). In the context of the Cotonou agreement between the EU and African, Caribbean and Pacific (ACP) countries, a start was made on the negotiation of what will be a vast network of bilateral 'economic partnership' agreements. This is a major task of commercial diplomacy, and one about which some ACP countries are suspicious, seeing the possibility of divide and rule effects.

One of the reasons for the bilateral/multilateral tension is to be found in the process that dominated EU external trade policies during 2003: the Doha development round of negotiations within the WTO. The Community had strongly supported the initiation of this round and had placed great emphasis on it as a means for dealing with the problems of developing countries. But 2003 saw an inevitable and growing tension between this worthy aim and the Community's own negotiating interests. Most obvious was the tension between the demands of agricultural producing countries (not all of them developing countries) for the end of export subsidies and the Community's continuing difficulties over the reform of the common agricultural policy (CAP). Despite an apparent breakthrough in the middle of the year on CAP planning, with the breaking of the link between payments and production, the Community was unable to contemplate any real concessions on export subsidies. At the same time, the Community and its chief negotiator, Trade Commissioner Pascal Lamy, placed great importance on the gaining of concessions in the areas of tariffs on industrial goods and on the so-called 'Singapore issues' dealing with investment, competition, public procurement and trade facilitation. In contrast to previous rounds, there did appear to be an effort to co-ordinate policy with the USA, for example on agriculture and industrial tariffs. But the USA was far less willing to support the Community on the 'Singapore issues'. Not only this, the EU–US agriculture proposals engendered immense suspicion among agricultural producers because they did not deal definitively with the issue of export supports. Another area on which the Community placed enormous emphasis was that of so-called 'geographical indicators'. There had been disputes in the EU itself about this, for example, over the right to name feta cheese as feta cheese if it came from Denmark rather than Greece, and the Community's efforts to export this problem and stake its claims on a wide range of products came up against enormous suspicion.

Thus, when the negotiators arrived in Cancún, Mexico, for the crunch negotiations in September, there was very little on which agreement had been reached. The talks turned into a major stand-off between the EU, the US and the so-called Group of Twenty-One (now more often the G-20) led by India, Brazil, China and South Africa. The result was what appeared to be an almost complete failure, with the talks collapsing amid mutual recriminations and allocation of blame. Within the Community, opinions differed as to who was responsible, although it was clear that Lamy had not made any concessions (for example, on the 'Singapore issues') until it was far too late to affect the outcome. Not surprisingly, there was a period of some reflection in the Commission after this. By December, the Commission felt able to re-enter the fray, issuing a new strategy paper: in this, significantly, there was an emphasis on new flexibility, both on agricultural export supports and on the 'Singapore issues' – but this flexibility was explicitly linked to flexibility from others. Although some hoped for a meaningful resumption of talks in 2004, it was not clear in a US election year (and the year of a new Commission) what substantive progress might be made. Meanwhile, there was a temptation to turn to bilateral or inter-regional deals as a substitute for the global regime. Finally, concern was apparent in the Commission at what might happen when the ten-year 'peace clause' in agriculture expired during 2004: would the Community be targeted by a range of countries aiming to embarrass or to punish it for its past behaviour? If there was no progress in the Doha round, this might be the key area of new problems for Brussels.

Development Co-operation Policy and Humanitarian Aid

Fears were expressed during the year about several aspects of the EU's development policy efforts. Firstly, there was concern that foreign and security priorities would come to play a greater role in aid and development policies than in the past, with the result that countries would be selected to receive aid based on the role that their governments chose to play either in the fight against terrorism or against the proliferation of weapons of mass destruction. The case of Pakistan was frequently cited as a country that was now receiving EU aid because of its prominent role in the fight against terror. This was in spite of the fact that its government had come to power via a military coup and seemed to pay little regard to the human rights of its citizens. It was also noted, by those who worried about the changing nature of EU development policies, that in the decade since 1990, EU aid to the very poorest countries had fallen from 76 per cent of total EU aid to just 36 per cent. The major beneficiaries were the states of the EU's 'near abroad' in the western Balkans, the Mediterranean and the former Soviet Union, despite the fact that poverty reduction remains the core stated EU development objective.

In September, EuropeAid's second annual report was published recording the fact that, in 2002, the EU committed €6.5 billion and spent €5.2 billion in development aid. The report highlighted the fact that the EU was beginning to make progress towards the objectives it had set itself of consistency, co-ordination and complementarity with other major aid donors. The Commission identified water management as the most important remaining challenge. In May, the Council gave its backing to a €1 billion European water fund for the ACP countries to be financed from the ninth European development fund managed by the European Investment Bank.

In 2003 the European Community Humanitarian Office (ECHO) allocated €600 million in humanitarian aid. The bulk of this aid went to Africa where the Horn of Africa experienced both severe drought and flooding, and where the Great Lakes region continued to suffer from military conflict. A considerable sum (€52 million) was allocated towards assisting with the ongoing HIV/AIDS pandemic in southern Africa. In Chechnya the EU spent an additional €26 million and, in the Middle East, over €100 million went to Iraq, along with €38 million to Palestinian refugees in the Lebanon. In Afghanistan €55 million was spent, and in North Korea, where the EU is the only significant donor, some €17 million was devoted to a number of health projects. The Commission provided €370 million in food aid and food security programmes. The Court of Auditors, reporting on the distribution of food aid in the period between 1997 and 2001, was critical of the lengthy delays in distributing food that it identified, along with poor financial controls and weak co-ordination with other aid agencies. Finally in 2003, the EU committed €200 million to aid to refugees and €257 million to rehabilitation aid which included €124 million for the reconstruction of Afghanistan.

II. Regional Themes

The European Economic Area and EFTA

The European Economic Area Council held meetings in April and October, in line with established patterns. During 2003, the EEA agreement had to be adjusted to cater for the ten new Member States. This gave Poland the opportunity in April to threaten a veto of the revisions if their demands on fisheries were not met. Although this was defused, the October meeting had to identify who would pay for the administration of the new agreement. An agreement was reached whereby the three EEA non-EU members, Iceland, Liechtenstein and Norway, would greatly increase their contributions from €24 million a year to €233 million. The increased costs would be met largely by Norway.

Work continued on implementing the bilateral agreements reached to regulate relations between Switzerland and the EU, which also had to be adjusted for the newly enlarged EU. In elections held during October, support for the far-right parties in Switzerland increased radically. As a result, it was clear that no progress would be made on Switzerland's application for EU membership, which remained technically on the table; indeed, the application might well be withdrawn altogether.

Western Balkans

As eastern enlargement approached in 2004, pressure from the western Balkan would-be EU applicants inevitably increased. In the margins of the Thessaloniki European Council in June, an EU–western Balkans summit was held. The latter produced a joint declaration confirming the EU's commitment to the eventual admission of the western Balkan states to the EU, and confirming also the stabilization and association process (SAP) as the agreed method for achieving this. Some progress was recorded in 2003 with regard to the development of stabilization and association agreements (SAA), but by the end of the year the EU had not managed to add to the SAAs signed with Croatia and Macedonia in 2001. Negotiations with Albania began in January, but preliminary negotiations with Bosnia were delayed by the failure of the Bosnian government to deliver either fundamental reforms or war criminals to the International Criminal Tribunal for the former Yugoslavia (ICTY).

Within the framework of the SAP and community action for the reconstruction, development and stabilization (CARDS), the EU continued to offer significant aid to the western Balkan countries. In 2003 this amounted to a total of €865 million, with a significant sum (€32.5 million) being allocated for the support of regional co-operation between the western Balkan countries themselves. During its Presidency, the Greek government pressed for even more sums to be allocated and for some of the pressure on western Balkan governments to hand over war criminals to be eased. However, the other Member States (in particular the UK) resisted this attempt to speed up the process of association.

We have already noted above the success of the ESDP military operation and police mission in Macedonia and the EUPM in Bosnia. It remains to be seen whether or not the EU is able to mount a more challenging ESDP military operation in Bosnia in 2004. In February Croatia applied to join the EU, and the Council requested the Commission to deliver an opinion which should be ready in 2004. This is likely to be positive provided that Croatia can meet the Copenhagen criteria. In Serbia and Montenegro, where the Serbian Prime Minister, Zoran Zivkovic, was assassinated in March, Javier Solana worked hard to maintain a process designed to keep Serbia and Montenegro together, and to maintain a dialogue between Serbia and Kosovo. No wonder then that the negotiations for a SAA have yet to start.

In June the mandate of Erhard Busek, the EU's special representative to the western Balkans, was extended to make him also the special co-ordinator of the stability pact for south-eastern Europe. It was also proposed that, in 2004, Lord (Paddy) Ashdown, the UN High Representative in Bosnia and Herzegovina, be appointed to a similar position for the EU.

Russia and the Soviet Successor States

This section concentrates on the former Soviet states and the next section on the Mediterranean. Yet, it should be noted that, in 2003, the Commission proposed that a new framework be developed for relations between the enlarged EU and the countries located on its land and sea frontiers (Russia, Ukraine, Moldova, Belarus, Algeria, Egypt, Israel, Jordan, Lebanon, Libya, Morocco, the Palestinian Authority, Syria and Tunisia). If Turkey were to join the EU, then there would also be a case for allowing Georgia, Armenia and Azerbaijan into what the Commission hopes will become known as the 'wider neighbourhood policy' designed to maintain good relations between the EU and its 'ring of friends'. The Commission is also keen to create a 'new neighbourhood instrument' first to co-ordinate, and then replace, the current instruments (Phare, Interreg, Tacis, CARDS, MEDA). To date the Member States have expressed only cautious enthusiasm for this ambitious new external relations framework.

For Russia and a number of the successor states, the forthcoming enlargement of the EU has dominated their own relationship with the EU in recent years. There were two EU–Russia summits in 2003; at the first in St Petersburg it was agreed that the Co-operation Council would become a Permanent Partnership Council. Under the partnership and co-operation agreement, the EU and Russia are committed to making progress within the framework of four 'spaces' covering the economy, justice and internal security, external security, and research, education and culture. Russia's concern with enlargement is focused both on the increased trade relationship (the EU will become Russia's major trading partner taking 50 per cent of its exports after enlargement) and on the close attention that the new EU Member States are likely to give to the EU–Russia relationship. At the second summit, the EU was put on the back foot by the extraordinary behaviour of the Council President and host, Silvio Berlusconi. The Italian Prime Minister took it upon himself to protect President Vladmimir Putin from any attempt by the Commission or other EU Member States to raise the question of Chechnya, Moldova, the treatment of a number of wealthy Russian entrepreneurs, or Russia's approach to the question of climate change.

The EU also held a summit with the Ukraine in 2003. Ukraine is unhappy about being grouped with others in the EU's prospective neighbourhood policy. It would prefer, but will not get, a stabilization and association agreement along the lines currently on offer to the western Balkan potential applicants. At present, membership is clearly out of the question for any more of the Soviet successor states, and this fact may well force some of them to move more closely to Russia. The EU examined the potential in 2003 for a more active engagement (possibly via an ESDP military operation) in the conflict in Transnistria in Moldova. No decisions have been made, but any such action would require close co-operation between the EU and Russia. A not dissimilar situation exists in Georgia, where the EU is concerned about the conflict in South Ossetia and in the country as whole following the political crisis that saw the departure of Eduard Shevardnadze. Here the EU will need to tread a delicate path between the competing interests of the US and Russia if it is to make any progress of its own.

In 2003 the EU extended €483 million in aid to the individual states of the region. Heikki Talvitie was appointed in July to be the EU special representative for the southern Caucasus.

The Mediterranean and the Middle East

The EU's relations with this part of the world were, of course, dominated by the conflict in Iraq that is dealt with elsewhere in this chapter and in the keynote article. Although not directly involved in the invasion of Iraq, the EU was always destined to intervene in the aftermath either by providing aid for reconstruction or by a formal participation in any UN follow-up force. Towards the end of 2003 the EU and its Member States pledged a total of €700 million for the reconstruction of Iraq. Apart from handling its own divisions the EU was anxious in 2003 that the US obsession with Iraq (and perhaps also Iran and North Korea) did not cause it to lose sight of the importance of continuing to work for the resolution of the Arab–Israeli conflict. Here the EU, under the able direction of Javier Solana, had begun to play an important role as a member of the Quartet (along with the US, Russia and the UN). Solana was sidelined over Iraq, but continued to play a significant part in attempts to keep the Middle East peace process on track during this turbulent period. The EU is a firm supporter of the 'road map' approach to a 'two-state' solution to the Arab–Israeli conflict and continues to support the Palestinian Authority with significant quantities of aid.

Notwithstanding its new enthusiasm for a wider 'neighbourhood policy', the EU continued to work within the multilateral framework of the Euro–Mediterranean partnership (the Barcelona process). In 2003 the Commission allocated €600 million for the MEDA programme, as well as €100 million to deal with the situation on the West Bank and Gaza. Foreign ministers met in Naples in December for a meeting that was notable for the return of Syria, Lebanon and Israel to the Mediterranean side, as well as the full participation of the ten applicant states alongside the current 15 EU Member States. For once perhaps, the fact that the procedures attracted full participation was significant, despite the lack of any substantive progress. In any case some progress was made during the year in sectoral meetings of the Euro–Mediterranean partnership covering fisheries, energy and trade.

Relations between the EU and Syria (the only participant in the Barcelona process yet to sign a Mediterranean association agreement) were a source of ongoing friction with the US. The EU, seeking to build on the success that had been obtained in relations with Libya and Iran, may well choose in future to explore an improved relationship with Syria via the good offices of the Big Three. In October the foreign ministers of Britain, France and Germany flew to Tehran to broker an agreement with Iran over its nuclear weapons programme. This was designed to preserve the EU–Iran relationship in the face of US insistence that firmer methods be used to deal with Iran's potential development of weapons of mass destruction. The result of the visit was that Iran agreed to submit to International Atomic Energy Agency questions and inspections and to sign the Additional Protocol to the Non-Proliferation Treaty.

The Israeli government, already unhappy at the EU's role in the Middle East peace process, were further dismayed in 2003 to discover that, according to a poll of 7,500 people in the 15 EU Member States, 59 per cent felt that Israel posed the greatest threat to world peace. On the other hand, the Saudi Arabian government was delighted to obtain the support of the EU for its application to the WTO. In July the EU special representative for the Middle East, Miguel Moratinos, whose mandate was extended to include security issues, was replaced by Marc Otte.

Africa

In 2003 the Cotonou Agreement entered into force, and negotiations began to bring about the anticipated regional economic partnership agreements that the EU is keen on, but which the African countries would prefer to ignore. Nevertheless in October, negotiations with the central African region began in Brazzaville and with the west African region in Cotonou. The African states were also dismayed at the Commission's expressed desire to integrate the European development fund into the Union's general budget. In both cases the African countries fear that their special status will be further diminished.

In April, the second EU–Africa summit, due to be held in Lisbon, was postponed. Nevertheless, the EU troika held several meetings during the year with the African Union troika (an interesting institutional development if nothing else). In November the EU Council approved in principle the creation of a support facility (€250 million) for peace operations in Africa to be funded from the European development fund. In the Democratic Republic of the Congo, the EU military force (Operation Artemis) consisting of 1,500 troops under French leadership successfully stabilized the security and humanitarian situation in the Ituri region and were withdrawn. The operation was a success for the ESDP, although the problems that arose in moving troops over 6,500 kilometres highlighted the EU's lack of military transport aircraft (the EU has just 4 and the US has 350!).

Under Article 96 of the Cotonou Agreement, the EU suspended its dealings or extended previous suspensions with a number of African states in 2003. Action was taken against Zimbabwe, the Central African Republic, Guinea, Guinea-Bassau, Liberia and Somalia.

In 2003 African countries received a total of €2458 million directly from the European development fund plus a share of €1018 million EDF money allocated to non-geographic programmes. The mandate of the EU special representative for the Great Lakes region, Aldo Ajello was renewed and extended into 2004.

Asia

During 2003, there were several ministerial meetings in the context of the Asia–Europe Meeting (ASEM) involving foreign ministers, economics ministers and finance ministers, and culture ministers met in Beijing during December. The Fourteenth Ministerial Meeting between the EU and the Association of Southeast Asian Nations (ASEAN) took place in January. Pascal Lamy participated in a meeting of ASEAN economy and trade ministers during April; this conference focused on trade reform, and Lamy's presence if nothing else was related to the build-up to the Cancún WTO meeting (see above). The EU troika also attended the meeting of the ASEAN Regional Forum in July, as usual. A new Commission communication published in July set out a new framework for relations with Southeast Asia, with multilateral principles accompanied by the desire for more specific bilateral trade and co-operation agreements. These bilateral agreements would be pursued within the context of what were termed TREATI (trans-regional EU–ASEAN trade initiatives).

At the bilateral level, EU relations with Asia were as usual highly diverse and differentiated. Continuing involvement in the post-war effort in Afghanistan – alongside the transfer of the mandate for the international stabilization force to Nato – meant that the EU and its Member States were deeply concerned with issues of reconstruction. The EU's representative in Afghanistan, Fancesc Vendrell, had his mandate extended in both June and December 2003.

Relations with the countries of South Asia during 2003 were less fraught than in 2002. Apart from India's concern with trade preferences given to Pakistan (see above), there was a broad move towards the intensification of contacts with New Delhi. The Third EU–India summit took place in November, and among other things saw an agreement on potential Indian use of the Galileo satellite system. The EU also played an increasing role in the politics of Sri Lanka, chairing a donor conference in Tokyo that saw pledges of $4.5 billion for post-conflict reconstruction. Late in the year Chris Patten, the Commissioner for External Relations, visited Sri Lanka and amongst others met leaders of the Tamil Tigers' organization; this raised some eyebrows in Europe and elsewhere, but was justified by Brussels on grounds of contacts with all those involved in the peace process. Elsewhere, new EU delegations were established in Laos and Malaysia, in pursuit of an established programme. There was some friction over developments in the province of Aceh with the Indonesian government, and relations with Myanmar (Burma) continued to be relatively distant as sanctions were renewed. The confinement – again – of Aung San Suu Kyi, the opposition leader led to protests and calls for her release during the summer.

The Commission produced a new policy paper on EU–China relations during September, and this was matched by the first ever Chinese strategy paper on relations with the EU. This placed strong emphasis on non-intervention in Chinese affairs and such issues as Tibet. In general, however, relations were intensified during 2003, and this was symbolized by the visits of several Commissioners as well as by the annual summit held in Beijing at the end of October. This meeting covered a variety of key areas – trade, finance, investment the war on terrorism – and also saw an agreement on Chinese participation in the Galileo project (see above). China is to contribute €230 million to the project and to participate in training activities – no doubt a matter on which the Pentagon in Washington will keep a close watching brief. The USA was also concerned by a Franco–German proposal during December for lifting the arms embargo placed on China in the early 1990s. During the year there were also more intense contacts with Taiwan, although these were kept strictly under the umbrella of the EU's 'One China' policy. A trade office was opened in Taipei, but when the European Parliament wished to entertain the President of Taiwan this was blocked.

During 2003, the EU committed €413 million (including funds for Afghanistan and East Timor) under financial and technical co-operation programmes in Asia; €102 million were committed for political, economic and cultural co-operation, and €23 million for displaced persons and refugees. Measures against terrorism included the funding of initiatives in Indonesia and the Philippines. Some tension was caused in late 2003 by attempts in the European Parliament to reduce the overall aid allocation for Asia by €247 million and to reallocate the money to Latin America.

Latin America

During 2003 the EU made continuing efforts to develop the 'strategic partnership' that had flowed in general terms from the Rio and Madrid conferences held in 2000 and 2002 respectively. Two 'political development and co-operation' agreements were signed in Rome during December 2003: one with the Central American countries of the San José Group, and a second with the Andean Community. At the same time, inter-regional negotiations proceeded on other fronts. Most notable was the renewed attempt to conclude a trade and co-operation/association agreement with the Mercosur countries (Brazil, Argentina, Uruguay, Paraguay). This was given added momentum by the economic recovery of key countries in the region, and by resolving some issues relating to reform of the common agricultural policy during the year. An added impetus was given by the US-sponsored efforts to push forward the plan for a free trade area of the Americas (FTAA).

Bilateral relations were further developed with Chile (especially through implementation of parts of the free trade agreement signed in 2002, and the first meeting of the Association Council) and Mexico, with the third session of the Joint Council established under the free trade agreement, which took place in Athens during March. New delegations were opened in Cuba (subordinate to the existing delegation in the Dominican Republic) and Ecuador. During the spring, under cover of the world's focus on Iraq, the Cuban authorities mounted a crackdown on political dissidents. As a result, the negotiations over Cuba's possible alignment with the Cotonou convention were suspended, and indeed the Cuban application was withdrawn later in the year. Other bilateral contacts included some rather tense exchanges with Colombia over the EU's plans to withdraw trade preferences for fruit and flowers, and over the Colombians' desire to gain some EU military support for their political stabilization and reconstruction plans – a desire resisted by Brussels.

During 2003, the EU committed €318 million for geographical co-operation in Latin America; €248.5 million for financial and technical co-operation with developing countries; €10.5 million for aid to uprooted populations; and €13 million for rehabilitation and reconstruction measures in developing countries.

The United States, Japan and other Industrial Countries

John Peterson's keynote article has covered much of the 'big picture' in EU–US relations, so the reader is referred there for discussion of the 'war on terror', Iraq and related issues.

Outside the war on terror and Iraq, a strongly related issue that persisted throughout 2003 was that of the International Criminal Court (ICC). The EU and its Member States have consistently supported this UN body, and had ratified the relevant treaties. When the ICC came into existence during 2003, the US still had not accepted it, and devoted time and effort to seeking bilateral agreements with countries including prospective EU members exempting them from the Court's provisions. This divide and rule strategy paid off to a degree in the form of agreements with Romania, Albania, Macedonia, and this undoubtedly increased pressure on the EU as a whole to accord the USA some concessions. At the same time, the USA was outraged by Belgian attempts to use their domestic legislation in indicting US military leaders for war crimes. In the UN Security Council, France and Germany abstained (along with Syria) on the vote to extend an exemption from ICC jurisdiction for UN peace-keepers (including most importantly US peace-keepers in the Balkans and elsewhere).

As Peterson notes, the tangled and ultimately desperate story of the Doha development round saw the EU and the US actually co-operating more than before, for example on agriculture. Ironically, this may have been too much co-operation at the wrong time for other WTO members, creating suspicion of and resistance to the EU–US position. Both the US and the EU found themselves bewildered by the emergence of a resistant caucus in the shape of the Group of 20/21. Elsewhere, however, the grand tradition of EU–US recriminations was upheld. It appeared at times as if the US had made a strategic decision to go after the EU's regulatory policies and attack the 'precautionary principle' that lies at the heart of many of them. Thus, during the year, there were strong attacks on the EU's stance on genetically modified organisms (GMOs), leading to a US-led complaint to the WTO. Ironically, in this case the Commission badly wanted to do something in response, yet was thwarted by the inability or unwillingness of Member States to agree with any of its proposals for GMO approvals. There was also strong US resistance (but this was matched by EU firms) to radical EU proposals for an extension of approvals processes for many chemicals. In addition, there was a robust rejection of EU claims that they had provided evidence in justification of their position on hormones in beef, on which the WTO had authorized sanctions against the EU from a variety of injured parties.

Added to this set of frictions were others growing out of US extra-territoriality, most notable of which were conflicts over implementation of the Sarbanes-Oxley Bill in the USA. This legislation – passed in the aftermath of the Enron and WorldCom collapses – demanded that accountancy firms in the EU register with the US authorities and adhere to US standards even where it might be argued that EU standards were higher. The Internal Market Commissioner, Frits Bolkestein, spent much of the year threatening counter-legislation in the EU and demanding exemptions for EU companies, with some limited success. Other US legislation was more venerable: the EU had complained in 2000 to the WTO about the use of the 1916 anti-dumping legislation, and the WTO had supported Brussels. But the US refused to yield, despite the threat of sanctions. During the year, there was also friction over the Byrd Amendment (by which US firms receive the proceeds of fines levied on foreign companies for unfair trading practices).

There was thus a good deal of rancour in many EU–US commercial exchanges during 2003. By the end of the year, the EU was on the point of imposing large-scale sanctions in respect of the US foreign sales corporations legislation, which had still not been modified despite WTO findings in favour of the EU and others. Indeed, there was every prospect of continued commercial friction and even escalation. Although the US administration had eventually yielded to WTO rulings in respect of its illegal tariffs on steel imports, and had dropped them in late 2003 (some would say, after they had ceased to be useful anyway), the atmosphere was definitely sour.

Some relief was provided in the autumn by the opening of talks about the creation of an Atlantic 'open skies' regime – for which the Commission had received its mandate in the summer. Nevertheless, there were clear differences between the position of the US and some Member States on the one side favouring rapid progress on a limited agenda, and that of the Commission that seemed to favour a sweeping global negotiation. More 'cement' for the EU–US relationship also seemed to be provided by evidence of intensifying exchanges and co-operation in the field of competition policy, where there were moves to increase the sharing of data and where the possible transatlantic frictions over the Commission's pursuit of Microsoft were well muted – not least by the fact that most of the companies complaining to the Commission about Microsoft were themselves American. In a year which saw the 50th anniversary of the establishment of relations between the US and the European Coal and Steel Community (ECSC), there was still no shortage of issues on which the trade diplomats and others could exercise their skills.

As was inevitable in such a year, other industrial countries took a back seat to EU–US dealings. The EU–Japan summit in May dealt with a range of industrial and commercial issues, and the groundwork was laid for major advances in competition policy co-operation as well as scientific and technical collaboration. Relations with South Korea continued to be dominated by EU efforts to pin down and counter unfair practices in the shipbuilding industry; but also by the continuing efforts to deal with North Korea's nuclear provocations, which were somewhat muted but not resolved during the year. With Canada, largely warm feelings were expressed in the EU–Canada summit (also in May). The summit planned for a new bilateral co-operation agreement and frictions over the use of 'geographical indicators' to describe products were largely resolved. Yet, the latter re-emerged on the much bigger stage of the Doha round negotiations (see above). Some tensions emerged with Australia over the country's use of its food import quarantine system, and at the end of the year over an Australian–Thai–Brazilian complaint to the WTO about the EU's sugar regime. A significant development in EU–New Zealand relations was the plan to open a delegation in Wellington (as opposed to serving New Zealand via Canberra).

JCMS 2004 Volume 42. Annual Review pp. 113–16

Enlarging the European Union

JULIE SMITH
University of Cambridge

The signing of the Accession Treaty in Athens on 16 April 2003 effectively marked the culmination of the accession process for ten states that were to join the Union on 1 May 2004. From then on Cyprus, the Czech Republic, Estonia, Hungary, Latvia, Lithuania, Malta, Poland, Slovakia and Slovenia were effectively members of the club. True, the Commission was still monitoring the new members' adherence to the *acquis*, a process that continues even after accession; true that there was still a difficult ratification process to go through – each candidate state had to ratify its membership and, as outlined by Henderson elsewhere in this volume, all bar Cyprus chose to do so by referendum. Each of the current Member States also had to ratify the Accession Treaty, as did the European Parliament. In theory this should not have been difficult. Yet, there were some scares along the way, not least when French President Chirac reminded those would-be EU members supporting intervention in Iraq that France had a veto over enlargement.

In the event, ratification was a smooth process. Despite concerns about each of the ten raised in the Commission's 2003 Regular Reports, frequently relating to corruption (see Commission Regular Reports; European Parliament, 2004a), there was little to deter the first wave of post-communist enlargement. Although not formally EU members, the ten began to participate actively in EU affairs throughout 2003, most visibly in the Intergovernmental Conference, in which perhaps prefiguring the nature of decision-making in an enlarged Union, Poland worked with Spain to thwart the Italian Presidency's hopes of agreeing a new Treaty by the end of December 2003. By the March 2004 European Council meeting, it seemed that 'enlargement is now an established reality, absorbed into EU awareness as a fact, rather than reflected on as a hypothesis' (Commission, 2004a).

If enlargement was 'an established reality' for the EU-25, the enlargement process was far from over. The December 2002 Copenhagen Council had recognized the commitment of Bulgaria and Romania to join the EU by 2007 and had also agreed to review Turkey's position in December 2004. In order to expedite the situation, the Commission had proposed 'road maps' for Bulgaria and Romania, which indicated short- and medium-term issues that the countries needed to address in their preparations for membership. These 'road maps' were supplemented in May 2003 by revised accession partnerships, which outlined in greater detail 'principles, priorities, intermediate objectives and conditions' (European Council, 2003a, b). In addition to assessing the countries' progress in meeting the Copenhagen criteria, in its regular reports for 2003, the European Commission also reviewed Bulgaria and Romania's progress in terms of the priorities set out in their respective accession partnerships.

The Commission found that both Bulgaria and Romania had begun to address the priorities set, although much remained to be done to complete the commitments for 2003–04 (Commission 2003b, c). In particular, the Commission noted that Bulgaria had continued its reforms in public adminis-tration and judiciary but the former stipulated that further work was needed on matters of implementation. It was deemed to be making good progress in the economic sphere, although work remained to be done on regulatory matters. The Commission felt that Romania continued to fulfil the political criteria for membership and that, with sustained progress, it could be deemed to have a functioning market economy, although 'vigorous and sustained implementation of its structural reform programme is required in order for Romania to be able to cope with competitive pressure and market forces within the Union in the near term' (Commission, 2003c, p. 121).

By the end of 2003, Romania had opened 30 of the 31 negotiating chapters and provisionally closed 22. Bulgaria was further advanced, having opened 30 chapters and provisionally closed 26, leaving only the four chapters with financial implications, as well as the 'Other' chapter. The Commission's pro-posal for a financial package for the accession negotiations with Bulgaria and Romania (Commission, 2004b) paved the way for Bulgaria to complete its negotiations in 2004, putting it in a good position to meet its objective of ac-ceding in 2007. Romania's progress remained weaker, leading the European Parliament to assert in March 2004 that Bulgaria's progress should not be held up by Romania (European Parliament, 2004b).

Like Romania and Bulgaria, Turkey made considerable progress in 2003 in terms of adapting its legislation (Commission, 2003d). Nonetheless, as in so many would-be Member States, its record on implementation lagged behind somewhat, leading Commissioner Verheugen to assert, 'I am impressed by the determination of the Turkish Government to accelerate the pace of reforms in view of achieving compliance with the EU political criteria. The adoption of the last two reform packages has led to substantial legislative progress. However, when it comes to implementation, the practical effects of several of the reforms still remain to be seen' (Commission, 2003a). The European Parliament remained unconvinced that Turkey had made significant progress, arguing that it still did not meet the political criteria, thereby failing a requirement for Turkey to be given a date to begin negotiations (Euractiv, 2004; see also Commission 2003c). While Turkey still had nine months to prove its political credentials, one other issue about enlargement still stood in the way of its longed-for accession negotiations: Cyprus.

While the European Council had agreed at the 2002 Copenhagen summit to accept Cyprus regardless of whether or not it was united, the European Council was firmly in favour of the whole island acceding on 1 May 2004 if at all possible. The role of Turkey in impeding previous unification talks was not forgotten and Turkey was told in no uncertain terms that failure of unification talks would make its own accession impossible. The Turkish government heeded the warning. Nevertheless, the Turkish Cypriot government proved less amenable to negotiations. Thus by early 2004 it remained unclear whether Turkey would be given a date that year. However, the moves made by the Turkish government, coupled with support from leaders such as Blair and Schröder meant that the chances of Turkey beginning negotiations were brighter at the end of 2003 than at the start.

References

Commission of the European Communities (2003a) 'Bulgaria, Romania and Turkey make significant progress towards accession criteria'. *Press Release* (IP/03/1499, 05-11-03), available at «http://www.europa.eu.int/rapid/start/cgi».

Commission of the European Communities (2003b) *2003 Regular Report on Bulgaria's progress towards accession.*

Commission of the European Communities (2003c) *2003 Regular Report on Romania's progress towards accession.*

Commission of the European Communities (2003d) *2003 Regular Report on Turkey's progress towards accession.*

Commission of the European Communities (2004a) *Enlargement Weekly – 30 March 2004*, available at «http://europa.eu.int/comm/enlargement/docs/newsletter/latest_weekly.htm».

Commission of the European Communities (2004b) 'Communication from the Commission – A financial package for the accession negotiations with Bulgaria and Romania'. SEC(2004) 160 final, Brussels, 10 February.

Euractiv (2004) 'Parliament: Turkey not ready for EU entry yet'. Euractiv.com, available at «http://www.euractiv.com».

European Council (2003a) Council Decision 2003/396/EC of 19 May 2003 on the priorities, intermediate objectives and conditions contained in the Accession Partnership with Bulgaria (OJ L 145, 12.6.2003, p. 1).

European Council (2003b) Council Decision 2003/397/EC of 19 May 2003 on the priorities, intermediate objectives and conditions contained in the Accession Partnership with Romania (OJ L 145, 12.6.2003, p. 21).

European Council (2003c) *Presidency Conclusions,* Thessaloniki European Council, 19 and 20 June.

European Council (2003d) *Presidency Conclusions,* Brussels European Council, 12 December.

European Parliament (2004a) 'Ten new Member States urged to keep up their efforts'. *News Report,* 20 February, available at« http://www2.europarl.eu.int».

European Parliament (2004b) 'Bulgaria: on track for accession'. *Daily Notebook,* 11 March, available at« http://www2.europarl.eu.int».

JCMS 2004 Volume 42. Annual Review pp. 117–33

Justice and Home Affairs

JÖRG MONAR
University of Sussex

Introduction

The Union's 'area of freedom, security and justice' (AFSJ) evolved substantially during 2003. Although the aim of a genuine common asylum system was not fulfilled, significant progress was made in this field. Some steps forward were taken in the area of legal immigration, and projects on practical co-operation at external borders proliferated. Important legal acts were also adopted in the fields of civil and criminal law, with some new elements of minimum harmonization. Before the backdrop of a huge increase in the texts adopted by the Justice and Home Affairs (JHA) Council since 1999, the European Convention's draft Constitutional Treaty opened up the perspective of new major reform of the JHA domain, parts of which remained controversial at the end of the year.

I. Developments in Individual Policy Areas

Asylum

After a year which – to the great frustration of the Commission – had seen hardly any substantial developments in the asylum domain, 2003 saw significant steps towards the creation of the 'common asylum system' which the Tampere European Council of 1999 had defined as one of the central objectives of the area of freedom, security and justice. The year started on a positive note with the Eurodac system becoming fully operational on 15 January. This enables Member States to identify asylum-seekers and persons who have illegally crossed an external EU border by comparing fingerprints. Eurodac allows Member States to determine whether an asylum-seeker or a foreign national found illegally within a Member State has previously claimed asylum in another Member State, and so it plays a key role in the practical application of the Dublin Convention principles on the determination of the Member States responsible for processing an asylum application. The Eurodac system is based on a central unit within the Commission for comparing the fingerprints of asylum applicants and electronic data links between this unit and the responsible authorities in the Member States.

An important new legal element of the common asylum system was put into place with the adoption on 27 January of the Council directive laying down minimum standards for the reception of asylum-seekers (2003/9/EC). This directive defines common minimum conditions to be guaranteed to asylum-seekers in all Member States while their application is being processed. It covers the issuing of documents certifying their status, the provision of adequate information, conditions of residence and freedom of movement, the safeguarding of family unity, access to health care, education, vocational training and employment, as well as modalities for material reception conditions which are aimed at ensuring an 'adequate standard of living'. While defining only minimum standards, the directive leaves, for instance, the granting of access to employment largely to the conditions applicable under national legislation. This legal instrument also provides a barrier against a continuing 'race to the bottom' between Member States lowering their reception standards in order to avoid becoming more attractive as a destination than other Member States. When it comes fully into force in 2005, it is expected, firstly, to compel some Member States with under-resourced asylum systems to make additional efforts (this is likely also to apply to some of the new Member States); and, secondly, to ease pressure on those Member States with relatively more generous reception conditions. Yet the directive could also lead to a reducing of reception conditions, with some Member States lowering their more generous standards to the directive's minimum requirements. Germany insisted on the possibility of restricting the freedom of movement of asylum-seekers within the country of reception, a procedure currently only applied in Germany, but which could also be adopted by other Member States.

On 18 February the Council finally agreed on the so-called Dublin II regulation (EC 343/2003), intended to address some of the flaws of the original Dublin convention which was replaced by the new regulation. It introduced a complex but clearer system for determining which Member State is responsible for processing an asylum application. Responsibility is assigned, in the first place, to the Member State where a member of the family of the asylum-seeker is already settled as a refugee. Priority is also given to the family reunification principle in the case of unaccompanied minors. If the family reunification criterion is not applicable, responsibility is attributed to the Member State who had granted a valid residence permit to the asylum-seeker or – as a third criterion – to the one who granted a visa to the asylum-seeker. If none of these criteria can be applied, responsibility lies with the Member State whose territory was first entered illegally by the asylum-seeker. As this applies to the greatest number of asylum applications, the provision clearly reinforces the importance of effective external border controls. Yet the Dublin II regulation also states that this responsibility is limited to 12 months. After that, responsibility passes to the Member State where the asylum-seeker has stayed illegally for over five months which, in turn, means that pressure is placed on Member States not to tolerate illegal residents. The regulation also provides for shorter delays for the transfer of asylum-seekers between Member States. Requests for another Member State to take charge have to be made within three months, and the transfers have then to be completed within the next six months. This is intended to accelerate the processing of applications, and to reduce the uncertainty for asylum-seekers who in the past have often been left in limbo for well over a year.

The strong emphasis on family reunification and less uncertainty for asylum-seekers was broadly welcomed by NGOs defending asylum-seekers' rights. Concern was expressed, however, about the fact that as long as basic asylum law provisions continue to differ from one Member State to another, refugees still risk ending up in a Member State giving them a lower chance of protection. The British Refugee Council even called this a 'dangerous lottery' (Refugee Council, 2004). The Dublin II regulation might also push Member States to even tighter external border controls, making it even more difficult for refugees to reach EU territory.

The major agreements reached on reception conditions and the reform of the Dublin system were slightly overshadowed, however, by the Council's failure to meet its second deadline for the adoption of the 'qualifications directive' (intended to provide a common definition of who is a refugee and who is otherwise in need of protection), and the directive on minimum standards for granting and withdrawing refugee status. By the end of the year, Member States were still struggling with a number of substantial points of difference such as the necessary common approach on safe countries of origin and safe third countries. Widespread concern within human rights organizations (and even some third countries) was created by the British proposal to create 'zones of protection' in third countries for the processing of asylum applications outside the EU. While this did not gain sufficient support in the Council to become part of a common EU approach, it seemed likely at the end of the year that the directive would leave the option to individual Member States.

Immigration

In the area of legal immigration, traditionally one of the most difficult areas for common action, substantial progress was achieved through the adoption of two major legal instruments.

On 22 September 2003 the Council adopted Directive 2003/86/EC on the right to family reunification. It entitles third-country nationals who hold a residence permit valid for at least one year, as well as recognized refugees, to be reunited with their families through the family reunification procedure. Those eligible under this procedure are primarily the applicant's spouse and the legitimate, natural and adopted children of the couple, but Member States may, in addition, authorize the reunification of an unmarried partner, or adult dependent children, as well as dependent ascendants depending on their national rules. There are, however, a number of restrictions. The right to family reunification is subject to public order and public security exemptions, and Member States can impose other conditions such as to require the third-country national to have adequate accommodation, stable and regular resources and sickness insurance, and to comply with integration measures as provided for by national law. Also, polygamous marriages are not recognized, so that only one spouse and his or her children can benefit from the right to family reunification. Applications for entry, residence and renewal, or renewal of a residence permit can be refused in the event of fraud or marriages of convenience. While these are clearly major restrictions, the directive – on the positive side – makes reunited family members entitled to access to education, employment and self-employed activity, and access to vocational training, and – after a minimum of five years – to an automatic residence permit.

On 25 November, the Council adopted Directive 2003/109/EC on the status of third-country nationals who are long-term residents. It provides that third-country nationals may acquire the status if they have been legally resident for an uninterrupted period of five years, if they have stable and regular resources to maintain themselves and their families, adequate sickness insurance, and if they do not constitute a threat to public order. As an additional condition, Member States may also require the long-term resident to comply with specific integration conditions as defined by the respective national law. These persons will receive permanent status in the form of an automatically renewable 'long-term EC residence permit' valid for at least five years. This permit is in the first place only valid for the territory of the issuing Member State, but the directive also sets out conditions under which the long-term resident will be allowed to settle in another Member State in order to work, carry out self-employed activities or study, an important step towards greater flexibility of non-EU work forces within the EU. The holders of long-term EC residence status will enjoy treatment equal to nationals as regards access to employment and self-employed activity, education and vocational training, recognition of professional diplomas and other qualifications, social security and protection, tax benefits, free access to goods and services and freedom of association. This brings the status of long-term non-EU residents into line with EU nationals, a position which the Commission has been strongly advocating for several years.

With their reserves, exceptions and minimum standards, the two directives are a good example of the minimum rather than comprehensive harmonization approach pursued by Member States. Yet, in spite of their limitations, the two directives represent significant steps towards a common EU approach to legal immigration. Some progress was also made in negotiations on the Council directive on the conditions of entry and residence of third-country nationals for the purpose of paid employment and self-employed economic activities (proposed by the Commission in July 2001). There was also some movement on the directive dealing with the conditions of entry and residence of third-country nationals for the purpose of studies or vocational training (proposed by the Commission in October 2002). However, the Member States failed to reach a compromise before the end of the year on these other two legal instruments essential for a common approach to legal immigration.

Co-operation with countries of origin continued to be a key element of the Union's strategy in the fight against illegal immigration. The Union expanded its efforts aimed at negotiating a comprehensive range of readmission agreements with major countries of origin. Agreements were signed with Macao in October and Albania in November, and an agreement with Sri Lanka was close to being finalized at the end of the year. Significant progress was made regarding China, one of the main countries of origin of illegal immigration into the EU, when both sides agreed during the EU–China summit on 30 October on a Memorandum of Understanding on Agreed Destination Status which was widely regarded as a stepping stone towards a comprehensive readmission agreement. This memorandum, which is intended to facilitate Chinese group tourism into Europe, obliges China to take back those who overstay, and includes provisions for the rapid repatriation of overstayers. Negotiations on readmission agreements with Morocco, Russia and the Ukraine continued at the end of the year.

While the Union is not averse to exercising political pressure on countries of origin over their co-operation in controlling and reducing migration to the EU, it has also recognized that those countries might need help and additional incentives. As a follow-up to its communication on 'Integrating migration issues into the EU's external relations' of December 2002, the Commission adopted on 11 June 2003 a proposal for a regulation establishing a programme for financial and technical assistance to third countries in the area of migration and asylum (COM(2003)355). With a projected overall expenditure of €250 million for a multi-annual programme for 2004–08, this proposal is aimed at a significant expansion of the aid provided to countries of origin. Although specific aid projects had already been approved before, these had been limited to countries and regions for which the Council had agreed special action plans on migration such as the return plan for which €7 million were earmarked in 2003. The Commission's proposal provides for a broader legal framework and substantial appropriations. Although to a large extent designed to compensate third countries for the signing of readmission agreements, the Commission withstood pressure from some Member States to make this financial instrument exclusively a means of funding the implementation of readmission agreements. The proposed regulation, on which good progress was made in the Council until the end of the year, is aimed at supporting institution-building in the third countries for the successful management of migratory flows, such as border controls and guaranteeing the security of travel documents, and includes action on international protection and human trafficking issues. It would also fund information and awareness-raising campaigns to acquaint third-country citizens with the procedures for legally gaining access to the European Union and the consequences of illegal immigration and clandestine work.

External Border Management

During the year, substantial parts of the June 2002 Council Action Plan on the management of external borders were implemented. Progress was made in both the development of a common integrated risk analysis model (CIRAM) and a common core curriculum programme for border guard training. CIRAM was based on a matrix structure and systematic information processing designed to produce problem-oriented external border risk analyses as a basis for decisions on joint operational measures. The core curriculum programme identified eight training fields (including applied working methods, information technology and criminology) for border guard officers which should become part of the national training programmes (Council Document 8285/1/03 REV 1).

Several 'ad hoc' centres for co-operation on external border controls became operational. The most important of those was the Centre for Land Borders in Berlin, with the primary task of serving as a co-ordinating body for joint operations at external borders aimed at improving surveillance and control, creating more effective standards, deterring illegal immigration and preparing new Member States for their adaptation to Schengen standards. The Centre carried out, *inter alia*, four joint operations at the Polish–German, Slovakian–Austrian, Czech–German and Slovenian–Italian borders, each of which involved the participation of border control officers from other Member States. While these were regarded as largely successful, some limitations have also become apparent. The legal basis for deploying guest officers (Articles 7 and 47 of the Schengen Implementing Convention) was seen as inadequate for operational purposes, as it does not allow the conferring of any executive powers to guest officers, who are therefore restricted to adviser or observer status (Council Document 10058/1/03 REV 1).

Another 'ad hoc' centre is the Risk Analysis Centre (RAC) which started work in Helsinki in April 2003, and is managed by the Finnish Border Guard. Its task is to produce annual tailored external border risk analyses based on CIRAM. Yet only ten Member States actively participated in the work on CIRAM, and the RAC also has to struggle with late and/or incomplete submissions of national data necessary for its analysis work, a problem which has also affected the development of Europol.

Progress was also made in the context of a number of pilot projects aimed at improving current operational standards (Council Document 10058/1/03 REV 1). France led a project to facilitate the organization of joint repatriation operations, particularly through the adoption of common security standards and the organization of group flights for the return of illegal immigrants. Italy led on the 'International Airports Plan', involving ten Member States. This focused on the development of standardized airport control procedures that should ultimately be implemented throughout the EU.

The UK initiated two further pilot projects: 'Deniz' on proactive enforcement action with Turkish authorities against illegal maritime migration and 'Immpact [sic] 2' to provide specialist immigration training and advice to reconstituted border guards within the Republics of Serbia and Montenegro. Both projects received clear support from the respective targeted third countries, but the interest that other EU Member States had expressed in 'Deniz" was not met by offers of practical support or corresponding EU funding. In the case of "Immpact 2', only four Member States (France, Greece, Italy and the Netherlands) offered practical support.

Joint operations at external borders were identified as a priority in the June 2002 plan, and quite a number were implemented during 2003. Probably the most widely reported was 'Operation Ulysses', carried out under Spanish leadership on the basis of 80 per cent EU funding in two phases (25 January–8 February and 27 May–2 June). Its aim was to develop new forms of co-operation at external sea borders with a focus on the fight against trafficking in illegal immigrants. The first phase centred on joint patrolling of the Mediterranean Sea from the southern Spanish coast to the Italian coast of Sicily, the second on the control of coastal waters around the Canary Islands. 'Ulysses' involved patrol-boats, aeroplanes and helicopters from France, Italy, Portugal, Spain, and – as the only 'non-regional' participant – the UK. Although the operation's effectiveness was reduced by language difficulties and problems of equipment inter-operability, it led to the arrest of 454 illegal immigrants and the interception of 15 boats, providing additional lessons on the challenge of this type of joint sea border patrols (Council Document 10058/1/03 REV 1).

Greece took the lead in 'Operation Triton', aimed at simultaneous controlling and monitoring operations of illegal immigration in selected territorial waters. 'Triton' was carried out (4–7 March) with the active participation of France, Greece, Italy and Spain, and led to the apprehending of 226 illegal immigrants and six facilitators, as well as the confiscation of ships. The operation also provided valuable evidence on illegal immigration by sea, but was too short to allow the full evaluation of difficulties in co-operation between sea border authorities (Council Document 10058/1/03).

Spain led a similar operation (5–11 May) with the focus on illegal immigration by sea, although this time centring on controls in ports. 'Operation Rio IV' involved simultaneous reinforced controls in a total of 20 ports in Finland, France, Germany, Italy, the Netherlands, Spain and the UK. The operation led to the apprehending of 279 illegal immigrants and six people smugglers, revealing also the use of false documents as the main *modus operandi*. Yet the operation also showed problems of communication between the Member States and Europol, and inconsistencies in reporting (Council Document 8783/03 ADD 2).

In the case of land borders, four Member States (Finland, Germany, Greece and Italy), as well as Norway, engaged under Greek leadership in a joint control operation aimed at testing the effectiveness of border control procedures and communicating EU practices to candidate countries. Nine external land borders were targeted by the 'land borders project': Norway–Russia, Germany–Poland, Germany–Czech Republic, Italy–Slovenia, Greece–Albania, Greece–Bulgaria, Greece–Former Yugoslav Republic of Macedonia and Greece–Turkey. A total of 3,793 aliens were intercepted in the participating countries during the three 10-day phases of the project, and conclusions were drawn on the use of false documents and land borders for illegal immigration. Nevertheless, the project was affected by a 'low level of commitment' by some participants who failed to forward essential data on time (Council Document 10058/1/03 REV 1).

While the number of joint projects was quite impressive, at least four major problems also became apparent. The first was the absence of a uniform level of commitment by Member States: in most cases only some participated in a given project, often some only declared an interest, or even did not fully deliver what they had promised. The second was that the projects were carried out very much on an ad hoc basis with no strategic plan or effective co-ordination. More often than not, individual Member States took the lead in a project and carried it out together with interested partners without paying much attention to overlap or potential synergy with other projects. The third problem was the absence of a proper legal framework for seconding border guard officers to other Member States. In most cases it limited their role in common operations to mere observer status. The fourth problem was funding. In many cases the availability of EU funding for co-operation projects had a major impact on the degree of success. Yet these funding problems remained limited to a small number of EU programmes subject to restrictive conditions and cumbersome procedures.

In order to enhance operational co-operation and co-ordination between national border guard forces and common training, on 11 November the Commission proposed the creation of an External Border Management Agency (COM (2003) 687 final/2). The Council agreed on 27 November on the main elements for the Agency, which will take over some of the tasks of the existing non-permanent Council 'common unit' of external borders practitioners. It should come into operation on 1 January 2005.

Judicial Co-operation

Increasing European citizens' access to justice is part of the central objectives of judicial co-operation. Progress was made in this domain with the adoption on 27 January of Council Directive 2003/8/EC on legal aid in cross-border disputes in civil and commercial matters. It applies to persons living in a Member State other than the one in which their case is to be heard, or where a decision affecting them is to be enforced and who do not have sufficient resources to defend their legal rights. The directive defines the conditions relating to the applicant's financial resources and the substance of the dispute under which legal aid is to be awarded. It covers access to pre-litigation advice, legal assistance and representation in court, and exemption from or assistance with the cost of proceedings, including the costs connected with the cross-border nature of the case, including translation costs. Some of those have to be borne by the Member State in which the court is sitting, others by the Member State of domicile or habitual residence. The directive also provides for the possibility for a person to submit an application in his or her country of residence which then has to transmit it to the authorities of the country which is to grant the aid.

On 27 November the Council adopted a new regulation on parental responsibility (EC 2201/2003) which extended the provisions on mutual recognition and enforcement of the 2000 Brussels II regulation to all decisions on parental responsibility. It also reinforced the right of children to maintain contact with both parents by ensuring that decisions on access rights are automatically enforceable in other Member States and the obligation for courts to order the prompt return of a child in cases of child abduction within the EU.

In the field of judicial co-operation in criminal matters, a step forward was taken with the adoption by the Council on 22 July of the framework decision (2003/577/JHA) on the execution of orders freezing property or evidence in the framework of criminal proceedings. It provides that the requested state must execute the order, which is forwarded by the requesting judicial authority of the other Member State in the form of a harmonized certificate, immediately and with no further formality. The grounds for non-recognition and non-execution are strictly limited. While the principle of double criminality (that the offence on which the freezing order is based must also be punishable under the laws of the requesting state) has generally been maintained, it does not apply to offences relating to taxes or duties. The framework decision, which is also of importance in the fight against terrorism, represented a further important application of the mutual recognition principle to the criminal justice domain in its most far-reaching form – the automatic execution of judicial decisions in another Member State.

Police Co-operation and the Fight against Crime

After the progress achieved in 2002 with various measures in the fight against crime, 2003 was mainly a year of implementation. The Commission closely monitored national implementation measures of agreed EU action in the fight against money-laundering and terrorism. At its meeting on 27–28 November, the Council finally adopted the protocol amending the Europol Convention (Council Document 13650/03), most of which had been negotiated during 2002 (see the previous *Annual Review*). Once ratified (amendments to the Europol Convention need to go through the time-consuming national ratification process), it will enable Europol to act on mere suspicion and not only a factual indication of organized international crime. It should extend Europol's advisory and research functions to training, equipment, crime prevention and investigation methods, and provide for the Council of Europol to set priorities for its steadily widening field of activities. The protocol will also allow designated national authorities (for instance, individual police forces) other than the Europol national units, to have direct contact with Europol. This is, however, with the proviso that the national units are kept fully informed. Provision is also made for the European Parliament's increased rights of consultation and information.

On 27 February, the Council adopted a decision (2003/170/JHA) on the common use of liaison officers posted abroad. According to the decision, liaison officers posted to the same country or international organization shall constitute 'liaison officers networks' providing each other with information and mutual assistance. Officers are allowed to pass on information relating to serious criminal threats to other Member States directly to the liaison officers of the Member State in question. A Member State not represented by a liaison officer can also address requests for information on such threats to officers of other Member States. This decision not only marked a step forward in police co-operation, but also for solidarity between Member States.

On the legal side, progress was achieved with the adoption on 22 July of the framework decision (2003/568/JHA) on combating corruption in the private sector. By providing a common and fairly detailed definition of corrupt business practices, as well as a maximum criminal penalty of at least one to three years of imprisonment and disqualification from commercial activities, this framework decision constitutes one of the still rare examples of minimum harmonization in the fight against crime. The same applies to the framework decision on attacks against information systems, on which political agreement was reached in February, but which was delayed by parliamentary scrutiny. This framework decision is aimed at a minimum level of approximation of criminal law for illegal access to and interference with information systems and computer data, including intentional hacking and distribution of viruses. Agreement was reached on a maximum penalty of between one and three years' imprisonment for offences involving interference with information systems and computer data, and a maximum penalty of between two and five years' imprisonment when the offences are committed in the framework of a criminal organization.

II. Development Perspectives

The Area of Freedom, Security and Justice (AFSJ) in its Fifth Year

During the reporting period, the 'area of freedom, security and justice' entered its fifth year and was nearing the end of the transitional period established by the Treaty of Amsterdam in 1999. This seems an appropriate time to look briefly at the action taken by the Council in its construction. Table 1 shows the overall number of the different types of texts adopted by the JHA Council from the date of entry into force of the Treaty of Amsterdam (1 May 1999) to the end of 2003. Although not all of the original objectives of the Treaty of Amsterdam had been achieved by the end of 2003 – this is especially true for asylum and immigration policy – the overall 'output' of the Council has clearly been impressive. Over the 53 months of this period, the Council adopted a total of 500 texts (nearly 10 per month), compared to only 324 during the 67 months (just under 5 per month) of the life of the 'old' (Maastricht) third pillar from 1993 to 1999. While this is a clear indication of the considerable growth in EU action in this area, a perhaps even more significant development has been the increased used of legally binding texts. During the period of the 'old' third pillar, only close to 10 per cent of the acts adopted by the Council were legally binding. Since the entry into force of the Treaty of Amsterdam, the figure has increased to over 36 per cent (including the first six categories of texts listed in the table, from conventions to directives). This marks a clear shift towards legal codification and the consolidation of common measures in

Table 1: Decisions Taken in the JHA Area, 1 May 1999–31 December 2003[a]

	Conventions[b]	Framework Decisions Art. 34 TEU	Decisions/ Common Positions Art. 34 TEU	Decisions Other[c]	Regulations	Directives	Resolutions	Recommendations	Conclusions	Other[d]	Total
Asylum, immigration, frontiers				27	16	8	2		24	30	107
Civil law				17	9	1				4	31
Criminal law	4	15	9 (3 common positions)	8			1		3	16	56
Police co-operation	3		8	13			6	8	3	83	124
Customs co-operation (third pillar)	1						1			8	10
Horizontal issues: title VI (police and criminal, drugs, organized crime)			11	6			12	7	9	38	83
Horizontal issues: titles IV and VI (Schengen, enlargement, etc.)			1	23	1				3	61	89
Total	8	15	29	94	26	9	22	15	42	240	500

Notes: [a] This table has been kindly made available to the author by Hans G. Nilsson, Head of the Judicial Co-operation Unit of the General Secretariat of the Council of the EU.
[b] Including agreements under Articles 24 and 38 TEU.
[c] Negotiation mandates, authorization, etc.
[d] Action plans, reports, administrative decisions (budget, etc.).

the JHA domain.[1] The statistics also reveal – unsurprisingly – the Council's strong focus on law enforcement and internal security issues which not only comprise police and criminal law co-operation and the horizontal issues under Title VI TEU, but also most of the 'cross-pillar' horizontal issues (Titles IV TEC and VI TEU).

The AFSJ in the Draft Constitutional Treaty

Having regard to the major extension of the EU's agenda in the JHA domain over the last few years – reflected in the figures analysed above – it is hardly surprising that the European Convention devoted a significant part of its work to this area. The reforms proposed in the draft Constitutional Treaty adopted in July 2003 were substantial enough to regard them as indeed creating a new basis and framework for EU justice and home affairs.

The proposed formal abolition of the three 'pillars' is one of the most important elements of reform. It would put an end to the need to adopt 'parallel' legislative acts under the different pillars in domains of cross-pillar implications (such as money-laundering). Furthermore, it should reduce the potential for controversy over the appropriate legal basis, contribute to legal coherence and facilitate the negotiation and conclusion of agreements with third countries on 'cross-pillar' matters.

The proposed incorporation of the Charter of Fundamental Rights would create a better basis for comprehensive fundamental rights protection in the JHA domain on sensitive issues such as the right to the protection of personal data which – having regard to the proliferation of databases and exchange systems in the context of the AFSJ (SIS, Europol, Eurodac, etc.) and the rapidly developing co-operation with third countries – is of increasing importance. Of considerable relevance for the AFSJ are also the judicial rights laid down in Title VI of the Charter. With the inclusion of the right to legal aid, the principle of proportionality of offence and penalty, and the right not to be tried or punished twice for the same criminal offence (*ne bis in idem* principle) these judicial rights go beyond mere minimum guarantees. Taken together, they define important elements of a common approach by the Member States to criminal justice and could well serve as important corner stones for the gradual creation of an EU criminal justice system.

The draft Treaty also provides for partly new and more ambitious policy-making objectives. This applies, in particular, to the formal provision for an integrated management system for external borders, a 'common asylum policy' including a 'uniform status of asylum' and a 'common policy' in the

---

[1] Author's own calculations based on the annual lists of texts published by the Council, available at «http://www.ue.eu.int/jai/default.asp?lang=en», and the analysis of the pre-Amsterdam situation in de Lobkowicz (2002, pp. 85–6).

immigration domain (excluding volumes of admission, however). The new objectives also open the possibility of adopting framework laws on minimum rules regarding the mutual admissibility of evidence, the rights of individuals in criminal procedure, the rights of victims of crime and other 'specific aspects' of criminal procedure, authorization for EU action in the field of crime prevention, and the possibility of the establishment of a European Public Prosecutor's Office. They may also facilitate the adoption of legally binding rules on the conditions and limitations under which national law enforcement authorities may operate in the territory of another Member State – a notoriously difficult issue since the very start of JHA co-operation.

A further innovative element was the provision of an explicit solidarity principle (including its financial implications) in relation to the framing of a common policy on asylum, immigration and external border controls, measures for the benefit of Member States experiencing an emergency situation caused by a sudden inflow of third-country nationals, and the mobilization of all instruments at the Union's disposal to prevent terrorist threats, protect democratic institutions and the civilian population, and assist a Member State in the event of an attack. Although different meanings can obviously be given to the term 'solidarity', the formal introduction of the principle nevertheless marks a substantial step towards a system of support for common tasks and effective burden-sharing – with the significant inclusion of the use of EU budgetary means.

As regards decision-making, the draft Treaty provided a major breakthrough towards increased parliamentary control and qualified majority voting. Co-decision by the European Parliament with majority voting in the Council would also become the standard decision-making procedure for JHA co-operation. There would be only a limited number of exceptions. Unanimity would still apply to measures concerning family law with cross-border implications, the establishment of minimum rules concerning not explicitly mentioned aspects of criminal procedure, and the identification of new areas of serious crime for which minimum rules concerning the definition of criminal offences may be introduced. It would also apply to the adoption of the 'European law' on the establishment of the European Public Prosecutor's Office, legislative measures regarding operational co-operation between national law enforcement authorities, and the laying down of the conditions and limitations under which national law enforcement authorities may operate in the territory of another Member State.

While all these elements, taken together, would create significant potential for both substantial progress in the JHA domain and more guarantees for citizens in terms of protection of their rights and democratic control, the draft Treaty also had some serious flaws. The overall package of reforms clearly lacked balance. On the one hand, some of the proposed reforms appeared very daring indeed because of their likely consequences for still highly different national legal and public order systems. The rather broad remit for the European Public Prosecutor's Office and majority voting on harmonization measures in the criminal justice area are prominent examples in this respect. On the other hand, however, there are many issues on which the draft turned out to be extremely conservative, allowing for hardly any new development potential. The maintaining of unanimity for family law and the provisions on Europol are examples of that. Also, in far too many instances, the text of the draft Constitutional Treaty bore the hallmark of cumbersome compromises, making the JHA provisions in Part III of the draft even less accessible and transparent than the much maligned provisions of the Treaty of Amsterdam. In spite of the formal abolition of pillars, for instance, a number of special decision-making rules applying to the former third pillar areas would lend the pillars a sort of 'ghostly' after-life which overshadows and blurs the unity of the JHA policy-making domain. More general provisions in one paragraph are in many cases made subject to detailed special rules which partially restrict or change their meaning or obscure the general rationale of Union action. The exemption of immigration volumes from the 'common policy' in the immigration field, and the extraordinarily complex provisions on judicial co-operation in criminal matters were striking examples.

Most of the JHA provisions survived the first round of the IGC negotiations until the failed Brussels summit in December. Yet, the Convention's compromise package was 'unbundled' to a significant extent in the criminal justice field. Mainly because of the insistence of the UK government, the IGC agreed on the insertion of a specific clause protecting the differences between the legal traditions and systems of the Member States and 'in particular between the common-law systems and the others' in relation to any EU measures in the domain of criminal procedure (new Article III-171(2)). In addition, a sort of 'emergency break' procedure was designed. According to this, a Member State that considers that EU legislation in the domains of both criminal procedure and substantive criminal law infringes the fundamental principles of its legal system would be able to refer the draft law to the European Council, thereby 'suspending' its adoption according to the normal legislative procedure. The European Council would then have the possibility of either referring the draft law back to the Council for termination of the suspension, or request the Commission or the group of Member States who initiated the law to submit a new draft. This must be seen as a most peculiar innovation, as it would not only allow any Member State simply to interrupt an ongoing legislative process but also give the Heads of State and Government in the European Council a *de facto* legislative role which is clearly not in line with the institutional system of the EU. It shows the dangers of a selective 'opening' of the Convention draft in response to specific national interests.

It was hardly surprising that, in response to UK concerns, the Italian Presidency proposed to make any extension of the European Public Prosecutor's powers beyond the protection of the financial interests of the EU dependent on unanimity in the Council and national ratification by Member States. Yet at the Brussels summit, the Heads of State and Government failed to reach agreement on the introduction and the powers of a European Public Prosecutor, and on the question of majority voting in the criminal justice domain, so that all this remained open for renegotiation in a potential second round.

References

Commission of the European Communities (2003a) 'Proposal for a Regulation ... establishing a programme for financial and technical assistance to third countries in the area of migration and asylum'. COM(2003)355.

Commission of the European Communities (2003b) 'Proposal for a Council Regulation establishing a European Agency for the Management of Operational Co-operation at the External Borders'. COM (2003) 687 final/2, 20.11.2003.

Council of the European Union (2003a) 'Council Decision 2003/170/JHA ... on the common use of liaison officers posted abroad by the law enforcement agencies of the Member States'. OJ L 067, 12 March.

Council of the European Union (2003b) 'Council Directive 2003/86/EC ... on the right to family reunification'. OJ L 251, 3 October.

Council of the European Union (2003c) 'Council Directive 2003/9/EC ... laying down minimum standards for the reception of asylum-seekers'. OJ L 31, 6 February.

Council of the European Union (2003d) 'Council Directive 2003/109/EC ... concerning the status of third-country residents who are long-term residents'. OJ L 16, 23 January 2004.

Council of the European Union (2003e) 'Council Framework Decision ... on combating corruption in the private sector'. OJ L 192, 31 July.

Council of the European Union (2003f) 'Council Framework Decision 2003/568/JHA ... on the execution in the European Union of orders freezing property or evidence'. OJ L 196, 2 August.

Council of the European Union (2003g) 'Council Regulation (EC) No 343/2003 ... establishing the criteria and mechanisms for determining the Member State responsible for examining an asylum application lodged in one of the Member States by a third-country national'. OJ L 50, 25 February.

Council of the European Union (2003h) 'Council Regulation (EC) No 2201/2003 ... concerning jurisdiction and the recognition and enforcement of judgments in matrimonial matters and the matters of parental responsibility'. OJ L 338, 23 December.

de Lobkowicz, W. (2002) *L'Europe de la sécurité intérieure* (Paris: La documentation française), pp. 85–6.
Refugee Council (2004) 'Refugee Council briefing on the common European asylum system', available at «http://www.refugeecouncil.org.uk/downloads/briefings/intl/common_euro.pdf».

JCMS 2004 Volume 42. Annual Review pp. 135–51

Developments in the Member States

MICHAEL BRUTER
London School of Economics and Political Science

Introduction

The year 2002 proved critical for several of the most powerful states of the European Union (EU), including France and Germany. Amongst other things, new elections brought about very surprising results, substantial discussions on enlargement took place, and the euro came into use as a 'physical' currency in the 12 members of the euro area. The first part of the year was rich in elections that seemed to favour the extreme right, and show persistent erosion in the vote of traditional parties more generally and left-wing parties in particular. The second semester showed a return to more traditional politics, with a few set-backs for extreme right-wing parties and a limitation of the losses of the European left which managed, against all odds, to win the German general elections again.

In comparison, 2003 was expected to be a relatively calm year in electoral terms. None of the largest European Union Member States was expected to hold general elections, and public attention focused primarily on the Swedish referendum on the single currency, announced in the autumn of 2002 and to be held a year later. Perhaps yet more importantly, 2003 was permeated by political and public opinion discussions in the Member States about such topics as the proposed new draft Constitutional Treaty and the growing tension – and ultimately war – in Iraq.

I. Elections: Give us a Break?

While 2003 was by no means as important an electoral year in the European Union compared to the previous year, several Member States held general elections that give us an overview of the political *rapports-de-force* across European countries before the European Parliament (EP) direct elections of June 2004. First of all, the failure of the Dutch parliament to find a strong governing coalition led to new elections in January. Then, in March, Finland held legislative elections. In May, the Belgian general elections were to be disputed as the country reacted to the shock of the Dutroux affair. Finally, in November, Northern Ireland held long-postponed elections to its devolved assembly.

The Dutch General Elections: Forgetting the Fortuyn Phenomenon?

The Dutch 2002 elections took place only a few days after the assassination of right-wing populist leader Pim Fortuyn. The country, shocked by the murder of the politician apparently by a mentally unbalanced homophobic young man, gave the 'List Pim Fortuyn' a very high share of the votes and made it the second party in the Parliament. However, the refusal of the moderate right-wing parties to form a ruling coalition with the extremist right-wing party or – for that matter – the absence of an electoral agreement with any of the other major parties in the country, led to a dissolution of Parliament. New elections were scheduled for January 2003.

The campaign was far less passionate than in 2002. The main expectation of political commentators was that the List Pim Fortuyn, this time not benefiting from the shock assassination of its former leader, and having been unable to find a new charismatic replacement, would lose a large part of the ground it had gained in 2002. The elections of 22 January clearly confirmed this expectation. Indeed, the List Pim Fortuyn, which was the second Dutch main party in 2002 with 17 per cent of the vote, dropped to fifth place, with only 5.7 per cent of the votes and 8 seats in Parliament (as opposed to 26 previously). The Christian Democratic Appeal (CDA), the overwhelming winner of the 2002 elections with 27.9 per cent of the votes further reinforced its position in 2003, polling 28.6 per cent of the vote. However, their main traditional competitors, the left-wing Labour Party which had been overwhelmingly rejected by the voters in 2002 came in neck-and-neck with the Christian Democrats. The Labour Party obtained 27.3 per cent of the votes (15.1 per cent in 2002) and 42 seats against 44 for the Christian Democrats. The liberal Freedom Party (17.9 per cent and 28 seats; up 2.5 percentage points and four seats) and the Socialist Party (6.3 per cent; up 0.4 percentage points) both made small gains in the 2003 election. In contrast, the Greens, the centrist Democrats 66, and the Christian-right wing Christian Union all lost ground slightly.

As a result, the 2003 election showed a return for the Netherlands to a situation reminiscent of the pre-2002 period, with no clear majority in Parliament, and a variety of possibilities for the Christian Democrats to find a ruling coalition.

However, in line with what has happened since the late 1990s, the CDA chose to favour the bipolarization of Dutch political life. Ignoring the Labour Party, they formed an ideologically coherent majority with the liberals and

Table 1: Results of the 2003 Dutch Elections

Party	Votes 2003	2003/02	Seats 2003	2003/02
Christian Democratic Appeal (Centre Right)	28.6	+0.7	44	+1
Labour (Left)	27.3	+12.2	42	+19
People's Party for Freedom and Democracy (Liberal)	17.9	+2.5	28	+4
Socialist (Left)	6.3	+0.4	9	0
List Pim Fortuyn (Extreme Right)	5.7	−11.3	8	−18
Greens	5.1	−1.9	8	−2
Democrats 66 (Centre)	4.1	−1.0	6	−1
Christians' Union (Christian Populist)	2.1	−0.4	3	−1
Political Reformed Party (Protestant)	1.6	−0.1	2	0

the centrist Democrats 66. This action confirms recent trends in the evolution of Dutch politics. Once mostly split between Protestant and Catholic political movements, and then between religious and secular ones, the Netherlands has traditionally been one of the few examples in Europe where virtually all ideological coalitions were possible and usually followed months – and sometimes over a year – of negotiation. This phase now seems to have been replaced for good by an era of bipolar right–left opposition that may facilitate new multi-party system competition, as has been the case also, for example, in Italy and Austria since the 1990s.

The Finnish Elections of March: Calm Before the Storm?

If there is one country in the European Union where the domestic political scene is not well known to the mass public it is, without doubt, Finland. For years, Finnish politics has been dominated by three large parties – one social democrat, one conservative and one liberal agrarian. They obtain about the same share of the vote, and form various coalitions with each other and with some of the other minor parties represented in parliament. In 1999, the social democrats of Prime Minister, Paavo Lipponen had gained a slight edge over the agrarian liberal Centre Party (KESK) and the Conservative National Coalition Party (KOK) and therefore continued in office, leading a 'rainbow coalition' of parties from across the political spectrum.

The 2003 election campaigns were largely unexciting. Most attention focused on finding out whether it would be a social democratic-led coalition under Lipponen or the opposing Centre Party led by Anneli Jäätteenmäki that would have the chance to form a new government, since the conservatives had been losing ground in the polls and there was a close finish. There were also sporadic rounds of political fighting between Lipponen and Jäätteenmäki towards the end of the election campaigns. In particular, Lipponen was extensively criticized for leading and managing the country's response to the Iraq crisis. The Centre Party leader heavily criticized Lipponen for double standards in foreign policy and for officially stressing Finland's non-alignment at home, while giving informal support to US President Bush during an earlier state visit.

On election night, Lipponen's Social Democrats lost their status as the largest party in the Parliament to the Centre Party, opening yet another period of cohabitation in Finland between a President and a Prime Minister of different political parties. This situation, however, has traditionally provoked much less conflict than its more archetypical French equivalent.

Aside from the three leading parties, the small parties in Parliament did not see their representation alter in any significant way. The 2003 election itself seemed to confirm Finland's profile as one of 'calm' political stability which, among the three nations which joined the European Union in 1995, seems to have developed the highest level of support for the Union.

Yet, the fragility of this calm was to be shown by a political storm that blew up shortly after the election. The new Centre Party Prime Minister, Jäätteenmäki resigned after only 63 days in office (18 June 2003) due to her involvement in the so-called 'Iraq affair' in which she misled parliament and solicited the

Table 2: Results of the 2003 Finnish Elections

Party	Votes 2003	2003/02	Seats 2003	2003/02
Finnish Centre (KESK, Agrarian-Liberal)	24.7	+2.3	55	+7
Finish Social Democrats (SDP)	24.5	+1.6	53	+2
National Coalition Party (KOK, Conservative)	18.5	−2.5	40	−6
Left Alliance (VAS, Socialist)	9.9	−1.0	19	−1
Green Alliance (VIHR)	8.0	+0.5	14	+3
Finnish Christian Democrats (KD)	5.3	+1.1	7	−3
Swedish People's Party (SFP)	4.6	−0.5	8	−3
True Finns (PS, Nationalist)	1.6	+0.6	3	+2
Aland Representative	–	–	1	0

leaking of official secret documents. The impact of a more assertive US foreign policy has ramifications for the Nordics as everywhere else in Europe.

Belgium: Under the Shadow of a Monster?

In the last general elections of 1999, Belgium had experienced a mini-revolution. The traditional predominance of the Christian Democrats and Socialists, usually allied in coalition government, had been ended. A new majority appeared in which the liberals and the Greens, representing political change, had won the right to determine the political destiny of the government led by Prime Minister Guy Verhofstadt. This change had undoubtedly signified a profound crisis in the relationship between the Belgian people and their governing politicians and administrators. In 1999, the country was already facing the trauma of the disturbing Dutroux affair, as well as a continuing clash between the French and Flemish-speaking communities in a country that had never fully come to terms with its various disparities and political differences.

The Dutroux affair is the case of a serial paedophile rapist and murderer who had been known to the police long before his arrest in August 1996. The exact number of victims of the Walloon paedophile is still uncertain. Yet, the tragic episode of his failed evasion attempt in April 1998 sealed the divorce between Belgian public opinion and its political leaders, its police, and its justice system. In the late 1990s, less than 20 per cent of Belgian public opinion trusted the government. While 52 per cent of the Belgian public approved the way democracy worked in 1995, this figure had been halved by 2003. Perhaps more significantly, more than 50 per cent of the Belgian public believed that Dutroux had been protected by the highest echelons of the state. The public had consequently lost confidence not only in Belgian politicians, but also the country's gendarmerie, police, and even judges by the time of the 2003 elections, one year before the Dutroux trial was due to start.

As for the growing tension between Belgium's communities, it was primarily marked by the seemingly unstoppable progress of the Flemish extreme right-wing independence movement, the Vlaams Blok, as illustrated in Figure 1. Indeed, the party which started with 1.1 per cent of the votes nationwide in 1981 had progressed to 6.6 per cent of the votes in 1991, and 9.9 per cent of the votes in 1999, giving it about one-sixth of the votes in Flanders. Simultaneously, annoyance at Flemish nationalism was starting to grow in Wallonia and Brussels.

In this context, very little was clear before the 2003 elections. Certainly, the government in office had failed to convince the sceptical Belgian public fully. Yet, the conservative opposition seemed as weak as ever. Within the governing coalition, experts expected a progress of the dominant liberals, particularly in Wallonia where they were traditionally weak. In fact, some expected such

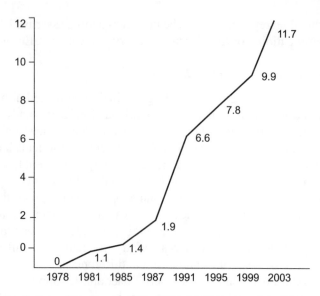

Figure 1: Evolution of the Score of the Flemish Extreme-right Vlaams Blok, 1978–2003

strong progress by the 'Mouvement Reformateur' (MR), that they envisaged the possibility that, for the first time in years, a French-speaking party might become the largest party in the Belgian Parliament, and that Foreign Minister, Louis Michel, might become the first Walloon Prime Minister of Belgium for many years. The other clear expectation was that Vlaams Blok would continue its progress and, some believed, could for the first time become the leading party in Flanders if voters' dissatisfaction with more moderate parties was again confirmed.

In fact, the election proved rather less surprising. By and large, most of the parties in the ruling coalition had their existing strength reconfirmed and some even slightly improved, with one notable exception. The ecologists, the second pillars of the 1999 coalition, saw their vote completely collapse, and the Flemish Greens fell below the necessary threshold of votes even to be able to send a single representative to Parliament. While the Flemish liberals of the VLD with their Walloon allies of the MR remained the largest party in Parliament, the Socialists were the big winners in the elections, gaining 15 seats (the Belgian Parliament has 150) between its Flemish and Walloon components. The change was particularly sensitive in Flanders where the Socialists have traditionally been a relatively weak party, overshadowed by their French-speaking counterparts. For the first time, votes for the Parti Socialiste increased. The vote of the Christian Democrats decreased even further in both parts of the country, and the vote for the extremes rose. The Walloon National Front obtained 2 per cent

Table 3: Results of the 2003 Belgian Elections

Party	Vote 2003	2003/02	Seats 2003	2003/02
VLD (Flemish Liberal)	15.4	+1.1	25	+2
SPA-SPIRIT (Flemish Socialist)	14.9	+5.3	23	+9
CD&V (Flemish Christian Democrats)	13.3	−0.8	21	−1
PS (Walloon Socialists)	13.0	+2.9	25	+6
Vlaams Blok (Extreme Right Separatist)	11.6	+1.7	18	+3
MR (Walloon Liberal)	11.4	+1.3	24	+6
CDH (Walloon Christian Democrats)	5.5	−0.4	8	−2
ECOLO (Walloon Greens)	3.1	−4.2	4	−7
N–VA (Flemish Separatist)	3.1	+2.5	1	−7
AGALEV (Flemish Green)	2.5	+5.5	0	−9
FN (Walloon Extreme Right)	2.0	+0.5	1	−

of the votes (up 0.5 percentage points) and the Flemish Vlaams Blok registered 11.6 per cent of the national vote (a rise of 1.7 percentage points).

A new coalition government of Flemish and Walloon liberals and socialists, once again led by Guy Verhofstadt, came into office, although this time leaving out their former Green allies. The new government, with two fewer partners, managed to secure an even larger majority in Parliament with 97 of the 150 seats (against 93 with six parties previously). However, this apparent success should not hide the continuing dissatisfaction of the Belgian public with its political leaders. According to the *Eurobarometer* survey (No. 60), covering autumn 2003, only 22 per cent of the Belgians trusted their political parties, and 38 per cent their government (by contrast, 45 per cent trusted the European Union). Only 34 per cent trusted their national justice system, the lowest score across the European Union (average 47 per cent), even after the previously deteriorating ratings of the police had finally come to an end.

Elections in Northern Ireland: Now ... or Later?

The Good Friday Agreement signed on 10 April 1998 between the United Kingdom and the Republic of Ireland represented a new step in the Northern Irish peace process and its future sovereignty. The referendum on the Agreement that followed saw a 'yes' vote of 71.1 per cent (94.4 per cent in the Republic of Ireland), and led to the first elections to the Northern Irish Assembly in 1998. At these elections, the social democratic SDLP, the moderate unionist UUP, the nationalist unionist DUP, and Sinn Fein all obtained a large share of the vote. In the months and years that followed, the Agreement and the peace process in general experienced some difficult moments as the IRA refused to dismantle its military capacity, and as part of the Protestant population became more radical. The Good Friday Agreement and the Northern Irish institutions were suspended for three months in February 2000, and then again on two occasions in 2001. However, the biggest institutional crisis in Northern Ireland happened when the Assembly was suspended and elections postponed between 14 October 2002 and 26 November 2003. When they finally took place in 2003, it was in an atmosphere of extreme tension and political uncertainty.

The suspension was largely caused by continuing problems with the IRA and a growing tension between the Catholic and Protestant camps. Tony Blair was clearly worried that elections would be held in a context of heightened tension, which would be favourable to the extremists. When he finally decided in favour of holding the elections, the predictions of the main survey institutes were that, indeed, the extremists were likely to gain ground from the pivotal Protestant UUP and the Catholic social democrats of the SDLP.

As expected, the elections in November consolidated the power of the two more extreme partners within the governing coalition: the Protestant and

Table 4: Results of the 2003 Northern Irish Elections

Party	Vote 2003	2003/02	Seats 2003	2003/02
Democratic Unionist Party (DUP, Protestant)	25.7	+7.7	30	+10
Sinn Fein (Socialist Separatist, Catholic)	23.5	+5.8	24	+6
Ulster Unionist Party (UUP, Protestant)	22.7	+1.4	27	−1
Social Democratic Labour Party (SDLP, Catholic)	17.0	−5.0	28	−6
Alliance Party of Northern Ireland (APNI, Liberal)	3.7	−2.8	6	−
Progressive Unionist Party (PUP, Protestant)	1.2	−1.4	1	−1
UK Unionist Party (UKUP, Nationalist Protestant)	0.8	−3.7	1	−4
Northern Ireland Women's Coalition (NIWC)	0.8	+0.8	0	−2

Unionist Democratic Unionist Party (DUP) and the Catholic and Republican Sinn Fein. The two moderate partners, the Protestant UUP of Prime Minister David Trimble, and the Catholic SDLP were correspondingly weakened. The two extreme parties accounted for almost 50 per cent of the votes in 2003, against only 35 per cent in 1998. It should also be noted that at 63.1 per cent, the turnout was relatively low for such a close and consequential election.

Despite the result, David Trimble remained Prime Minister of Northern Ireland, and the coalition formed by the Democratic Unionist Party, Sinn Fein, the Ulster Unionist Party, and the Social Democratic and Labour Party remained unchanged.

II. Public Opinion in the Member States

The Swedish Euro Referendum

Euro coins and banknotes started to be used by the citizens of 12 EU Member States on 1 January 2002. By and large, commentators were largely surprised by the initial rise in public support for the single currency – following several difficult years – after the arrival of the new currency in citizens' wallets. Pessimistic fears about citizens finding it difficult to understand and grasp the value of the new currency were quickly dismissed. This even encompassed those countries where the exchange rate did not make conversion easy (in France, one euro is worth 6.55957 former French francs). Moreover, many countries, including Germany and the Netherlands, saw such a rapid acceptance by citizens of the exclusive use of the new currency that demands were even made for an early end to the period of double circulation (in which the national currency and the euro were simultaneously legal tender).

Nevertheless, despite these positive elements, many citizens expressed the opinion that – contrary to official statistics– the adoption of the euro had resulted in a hidden increase in the level of prices of many daily goods. This impression was further inflated by the very bad weather of winter 2002, which led to an increase in the prices of fresh fruit and vegetables, and persisted at the beginning of 2003. In the run-up to the Swedish referendum (scheduled for 14 September 2003), the inflationary argument featured prominently. Fears of higher prices were particularly used by the 'no' camp in a country which had experienced a large devaluation a decade earlier. During the referendum campaigns, the 'no' camp also focused on the fear that participation in the euro implied a loss of yet more sovereignty and, in particular, an independent monetary policy. In addition, the anti-EMU campaigners argued that the dominant policy line of the euro area system was too 'neo-liberal' when compared to the Swedish model of state intervention and welfare nationalism. Finally, they focused on the persistent fluctuations of the external value of the euro *vis-à-vis* the American dollar around the time the referendum took place.

Throughout the year, Swedish discussions on the euro seemed rather flat and uninspiring, with almost all of mainstream Swedish parties supporting a 'yes' vote in the referendum, but not getting too involved in the campaign. Opinion polls showed, for the most part, a persistent lead for the 'no' camp from March to September 2003. The 'no' camp ran a significantly more effective campaign while, in contrast, the 'yes' campaign seemed to be largely ineffectual. However, it was commonly perceived that the final outcome would largely depend on the level of participation that many expected to be at an historic low, probably below 50 per cent, in a way that was likely to benefit the more mobilized anti-euro camp.

However, a few days before the vote, the campaign took a tragic and unexpected turn with the brutal assassination of the country's Foreign Minister, Anna Lindh, in a large department store in Stockholm's city centre. The most prominent woman in the social democratic government, she was primarily known for her direct style and strong opinions. She was considered to be one of the most effective campaigners in the 'yes' camp, having claimed that, if Sweden rejected the single currency, it would be likely to retain lower levels of economic growth and foreign direct investment when compared to its neighbours in the euro area.

Her murder – the second assassination of a top politician in Sweden in the past 20 or so years after that of Olaf Palme – was unanimously condemned in the country and abroad. The 'no' camp denied any connection, in any form, with her death, while the 'yes' camp emphasized its desire not to exploit the event politically and to stop campaigning immediately. Soon afterwards, a mentally unstable young man was suspected of killing the minister. With no further official campaigning by either camp, it was understood that the first clear result of the assassination would be an increase in turnout. However, a significant part of the Swedish media suggested that the tragic events might also lead to a paradoxical inflation of the pro-euro vote as a result of the killing of the 'yes' camp leader in a passionate and irrational response by part of the public to the political crime.

Perhaps in part because of these paradoxical predictions that the murder of Anna Lindh would save the 'yes' camp, a majority of the mobilized voters chose to vote 'no'. The anti-euro victory was in fact much larger than predicted by exit polls on the day of the referendum, with a majority of 55.9 per cent against joining the euro, and 42 per cent in favour. The 'no' result was largely a result of the anti-euro support of the countryside and of part of the older suburban working class, while a majority of the urban working class and the young supported the adoption of the single currency. Stockholm, for example, voted in favour of the euro by 56.1 per cent with 41.7 per cent against, and Malmö by 53.5 for, 44.5 per cent against. In contrast, the very rural county of Jämtland voted against the single currency by 77.2 per cent with 21.4 per cent for, and Västerbotten by 72.3 per cent against the euro with only 26.1 per cent in favour.

The impact on other Member States was largely predictable. Pro-euro supporters regretted the failure of the referendum and the negative economic and political impact they predicted it would have on Swedish growth, foreign direct investment, and the quality and adaptation of the social welfare system so central to Swedish society. At the same time, the 'no' camp's victory warmed the hearts of eurosceptics, especially in Denmark and the United Kingdom.

In Denmark, the Swedish result was closely monitored by the right-wing government before deciding whether or not to organize a referendum on the euro in 2004. While Danish opinion polls were moderately favourable to the single currency, the government was afraid of a 'Swedish contagion' effect and decided to postpone the holding of a referendum.

In Britain, the 'Save the Pound' camp became yet more vocal following the 'no' victory in Sweden. eurosceptic campaigners claimed that if such a small country as Sweden could decide to stay out of the European single currency, then the same should happen in a larger country such as the UK. They rejected the claims that the 'no' result would penalize the Swedish economy and its social security system and argued that the Swedish rejection reinforced the sceptical line of the UK Chancellor of the Exchequer, Gordon Brown, towards British participation in the single currency.

Member States, Public Opinions and the Debate on Iraq

At the beginning of 2003, it became clear that the United States intended to increase pressure on the Iraqi government of Saddam Hussein over the United States' and United Nations' fear that the country might possess weapons of mass destruction. The US government's communication campaign confirmed their desire to go to war with Iraq if they did not obtain full satisfaction, and the Americans started to discuss with their traditional partners obtaining the backing of the United Nations for such a policy line. However, they faced opposition from several of their partners, including Germany and France, who did not approve of the foreign policy stance of George W. Bush in his growing conflict with Iraq. In particular, during early 2003, the Americans wanted explicitly to threaten Saddam Hussein with possible military action if the Iraqi government did not comply with US demands. By contrast, most other countries, including those in Europe, were not in favour of military intervention in Iraq at that time, believing that Iraq was co-operating sufficiently for a diplomatic solution to be pursued further.

The conflict between those who supported the American leadership in the Iraq crisis and those who did not believe America's policy stance was the most suitable grew in the first months of 2003. It escalated in March when the Americans tried to push through a United Nations resolution, supported by the UK, but opposed by several countries, including Russia, China, France and Germany. Matters came to a head on 20 March when the Americans, backed by countries that included the UK, Spain, Poland and Australia, decided to lead a military action into Iraq to find any allegedly hidden weapons of mass destruction and overthrow the regime of Saddam Hussein. Those countries that had long opposed the intervention condemned it, and refused to support the 'coalition of the willing' either militarily or financially.

Across Europe, the conflict between the members of the 'coalition of the willing' and those who opposed the American line on Iraq threatened to become much deeper than a simple diplomatic disagreement. European nations – with so many opposed to military intervention – seemed to be splitting into two camps. On the one hand was what the American leadership hastily labelled the 'old Europe' (the anti-war camp, led by Germany and France and allied to Russia). On the other, lay the so-called 'new Europe' (the pro-intervention camp led by Spain, Britain and Poland, as well as a few other eastern European nations).

More than any other previous crisis, the Iraq debate underlined the difficulty in finding common positions between the Member States. However, the debate it generated in the various European countries varied from case to case. In Britain in particular, it reinforced existing doubts expressed by some leading politicians, particularly in the Conservative Party, that a European common foreign and security policy (CFSP) was utopian, and was likely to go against what was branded Britain's 'special relationship' with the United States. In most other countries, however, it prompted politicians to consider new ways to reinvigorate the CFSP and avoid the humiliating disagreements of the Yugoslavian – and now as well the Iraq – crises.

In several Member States, the Iraq debate generated substantial domestic debates between political parties, particularly in Spain and Italy where the parties in power defended the intervention, while opposition parties opposed it. The disagreement took on particular significance in Spain. General elections were to follow in 2004, and the popularity rating of José Maria Aznar and his government started to be undermined by the overwhelming (90 per cent to 10 per cent) opposition of Spanish public opinion to military intervention in Iraq. In Italy, no forthcoming election was so close. Yet here too, an overwhelming majority of Italians opposed the stance of a still popular Silvio Berlusconi in the Middle East conflict. The apartments of Rome, Milan and Venice became more numerous in displaying 'Pace' ('peace') rainbow signs registering opposition to the involvement of their country's military alongside American troops.

In Britain, the Conservative opposition backed the Labour government over military intervention in Iraq, making the internal debate in Parliament mostly an issue of opposition between the government and anti-war Labour backbenchers, supported by a majority of Liberal Democrats. Public opinion, originally favourable to intervention, gradually turned to being almost equally shared between pro- and anti-war supporters, the latter even reaching a small majority towards the end of the year. Poland faced a relatively similar situation, albeit with Polish public opinion being much more clearly opposed to its country's stance in the conflict.

In most other countries, however, the Iraq crisis led to very little internal debate due to a fairly cohesive public opinion that opposed intervention. This was the case in France, Germany, Belgium, Greece and Scandinavia where anti-war figures approached plebiscite levels. Interestingly enough, however, the congruent preferences of public opinion and governments on the issue of Iraq in these countries very rarely resulted in a raised level of public approval of national governments and governing parties.

In most EU Member States, the question of the Iraq conflict took precedence in the public debate over the other issue that was expected to shape, very significantly, the longer-term future of European populations: that of an emerging European Constitution.

Member States, Public Opinion, and the Debate on the Constitutional Treaty

The year 2003 also saw the continuation of the debate on a forthcoming European Constitution in the Member States and public opinion. Gradually the Convention, presided over by Valéry Giscard d'Estaing, started to outline the thrust of the document it was preparing and discussing.

In autumn 2002, the United Kingdom started the psychological war when British Foreign Minister, Jack Straw, published an editorial in *The Economist* claiming that he preferred a short Constitution that would fit into his back pocket. This demand was quickly described as unrealistic by British and foreign constitutional experts. They claimed that such a short document would simply be impossible to negotiate, given the breadth and complexity of European Union law. They even feared that such a brief version could even be dangerous in that it would give substantial power of interpretation to the European Court of Justice, comparable only to that of the US Supreme Court. However, the length of the negotiated document was a relatively minor feature in the EU-related debates of several European societies.

In the small EU countries, first, several parties – and often national governments – attempted to focus the debate on the size of the future European

Commission, and their right to keep one 'national' Commissioner with voting powers in each serving Commission. The draft Constitutional Treaty proposed by the Convention favoured a formula whereby the Commission would be limited to 20 members. In effect, this ensured that only the largest countries of the EU would keep one – as opposed to two currently – Commissioners in each Commission, while the other countries would be given a Commissioner on a rota system.

In Poland, Spain, and Italy, representatives of the Catholic Church, led by Pope Jean Paul II also tried to involve public opinion in a debate on a reference to the Christian (or the Judo-Christian) heritage of Europe in the preamble of the Constitution. The Polish and Spanish governments strongly backed these demands and, in the Polish case, received the overwhelming backing of national public opinion. However, in countries like France, the UK and Belgium, national governments and domestic public opinion strongly rejected the suggestion of such an inclusion.

In Poland and Spain, the governments expressed strong hostility towards the principle of a new qualified double majority of votes and countries to avoid the risk of repeated decision-making deadlocks in an enlarged European Union. The Convention's draft proposed that, for each vote to be held under qualified majority rule, a majority of at least 50 per cent of the Member States, representing at least 60 per cent of the total population of the EU would be needed for a decision to be adopted. This proposal was judged unacceptable by the Spanish and Polish governments, with the Polish leader famously promoting the slogan 'Nice or death', and travelling to a summit of Heads of State and Government to defend ferociously an anti-double majority stance.

In a way, these differences were not necessarily as significant when seen from the point of view of public opinion as they were amongst the national governments. *Eurobarometer* (No. 60, Autumn 2003) showed, for example, clear support for the principle of a European Constitution across the Member States, as shown in Table 5.

At the same time, specific questions indicated that a majority of citizens in EU countries favoured certain features, such as a President of the European Commission directly elected by citizens (35 per cent for, out of four possible answers), as well as an extended term for the presidency of the Council of Ministers as suggested by the Convention's proposal (49 per cent against the existing six-month rotating term and 27 per cent in favour of it, with 24 per cent registering they do not know).

However, this apparent unanimity barely concealed some important tensions within individual Member States. Rather than focusing on the actual contents of the future proposed Constitution, these tensions often concerned the likely method of ratification of the future Constitutional Treaty. By the end of 2003,

Table 5: Support for a European Constitution

Country	In Favour	Don't Know	Against
Italy	74	21	5
Greece	74	16	10
Belgium	68	18	15
Netherlands	67	17	16
Luxembourg	66	25	9
Spain	65	27	8
Austria	64	29	6
Sweden	63	25	13
Germany	63	28	9
European Union	62	28	10
France	60	32	8
Portugal	55	36	9
Ireland	53	40	6
Finland	49	19	33
United Kingdom	48	38	14
Denmark	46	21	33

that is, before any Constitutional Treaty was actually adopted by the Heads of State and Government, either because of their legal obligation or by government choice, several countries had already decided in favour of parliamentary ratification. They include Germany, Greece, Belgium, Sweden, Finland, Estonia, Cyprus and Malta. Other countries, still either by choice or by obligation, had already announced that a referendum would be held on the forthcoming Constitution. They include Denmark, Ireland, Luxembourg, Portugal and the Netherlands. Other countries such as France, Germany and Austria were still undecided and, by the end of 2003, several of their prominent leaders, such as French Foreign Minister, Dominique de Villepin and several Italian ministers, had expressed their preference for an EU-wide referendum, which could symbolically complement individual countries' ratification. By the end of 2003, however, the prospects for an agreement on a European Constitutional Treaty looked so bleak as a result of the strong Spanish and Dutch opposition to the proposals of the other countries, that these questions had become, once again, slightly less secondary.

Conclusion: Impossible Reforms? Governmental Challenges and Public Opinion Mobilization

Other events throughout 2003 initiated some discussion and/or hostility towards governments in some of the Member States. They created tense internal situations in several countries prior to the 2004 European Parliament elections which were likely to be used by many voters as an opportunity to sanction their governments.

In Britain, the attacks on Tony Blair's government following the Iraq conflict were further compounded by accusations from the Conservative opposition and the mass media. They accused the British government of manipulating public opinion and more specifically, civil servant David Kelly, before sacrificing his name to the BBC, prompting him to commit suicide. A long-awaited report of the investigation commission led by Lord Hutton, a senior judge reputed for his stern attitude and integrity, resulted in the government being totally cleared of any wrongdoing. At the same time, the BBC was severely criticized in the Judge's report, plunging the public television and radio broadcasting service into its biggest ever crisis, and leading to the resignation of several leaders of the corporation. Several members of the Conservative opposition – now with a new leader, Michael Howard, following their own leadership crisis in the autumn – and journalists, particularly from the tabloids, questioned the integrity of the Judge's report despite earlier unanimity on the honesty and integrity of Lord Hutton and his team. The same week, the Blair government and the Prime Minister individually managed to survive another significant challenge by securing support in the House of Commons for a reform of undergraduate university tuition fees. This positive vote was obtained despite the opposition of a large section of the public, the students' unions, and a substantial number of Labour backbenchers as well as Liberal Democrat MPs. All in all, these victories did not leave the government's popularity totally undamaged. By the end of 2003, the Labour government, after several years in power, was anticipating a fraught end to its second term in office.

In France, social conflict accumulated throughout the year. The government proposed a series of radical social reforms of the retirement system, the unemployment system, and the unemployment benefits of several social categories, particularly artists. The latter caused a series of radical strikes and demonstrations throughout the country leading, among other things, to the unprecedented cancellation of several of the country's leading festivals. Tempest was also threatening to come from the medical profession, trying to direct public attention towards the deterioration of the French health system and of their own living and working conditions. There were storms also in the research sector, upset by the decline in the standing of France as a world class research centre, and among students, unhappy about a proposed reform of the university system, as well as numerous other groups. By the end of 2003, the popularity of President Chirac and Prime Minister Raffarin reached an all-time low, barely a few months before a series of regional elections which then looked very undecided. Only the Interior Minister, Nicolas Sarkozy, seemed to be able to maintain his popularity among the mass public, causing great anger in presidential circles.

In Austria, another retirement reform caused the first large strikes in the country in years to be held in the spring. The image of the once popular ÖVP–FPÖ government was further damaged in the eyes of the public. Similar problems were discernible in other EU countries such as Germany, Belgium and Italy, and even in the traditionally peaceful Scandinavian countries.

By the end of 2003, most national governments in the European Union Member States were facing a grave crisis of confidence and the risk of being challenged by their national publics following contested reforms over social issues and taxation systems. While the electoral year was less busy and/or surprising than the first semester of 2002, it was clear, for the most part, that the year 2004 was likely to result in a series of new governmental upsets in many a European country. What was less obvious was whether such dramatic winds would profit moderate opposition parties, as was the case until the early 1990s in most Member States, or those on the political extremes which, from their peak in spring 2002, seemed finally to have reached the height of their political ascension.

Developments in the Applicant States

KAREN HENDERSON
University of Leicester

Introduction

In 2003, ballot boxes in the applicant states were dominated by the EU issue as never before, as nine of the ten states due to join the EU on 1 May 2004 held referendums on accession. Successfully guiding their countries on the final stretch of the road to accession with a strong 'yes' in a referendum became a major government priority throughout eastern and central Europe.

The timing of the various referendums was not a random matter depending merely on the exigencies of domestic politics. Both the Visegrád Four (Hungary, Slovakia, Poland and the Czech Republic) and the Baltic states (Lithuania, Estonia and Latvia) voted in order, with the most pro-EU states going first. There was an expectation that the move 'back to Europe' would gain a strong international momentum as the referendums progressed, which would help avert any nasty accidents among possible waverers. Malta, the only accession state with an electorally strong eurosceptic party, confirmed its position as the outsider in a group of predominantly post-communist states by breaking this pattern and holding the first referendum of the year. Meanwhile Cyprus, still preoccupied with trying to settle the problems of its division, did not hold a referendum at all. Here, alone, joining the EU was not the overriding issue determining the country's future.

I. Referendums (and Some Elections) in the Applicant States

The EU accession referendums were in most cases very different from elections since they were marked by a high degree of consensus, and often characterized by the unusual sight of traditional political rivals having to make common cause in public. Referendums can be a heavily contested process, with arguments about whether or not they should be held, but in this case consensus had started early with widespread agreement that the citizens should be given a voice. Because of the length of the accession procedure, which averaged nearly a decade from the original application to join, several alternating governments had usually played a role in it, so joining the EU was rarely a partisan issue. Almost all significant political parties were in favour of membership and they did not feel threatened by a referendum they were confident would endorse and legitimize their decision to 'return to Europe'. The 'no' camp also had no reason to oppose holding a referendum since the alternative – simple ratification of the EU Accession Treaty by the national parliament – would mean inevitable defeat. A popular referendum, on the other hand, gave them one last chance to promote the eurosceptic view, and at least a tiny glimmer of hope that they might avert EU membership.

The general consensus on the need to join the EU meant that a major preoccupation of the referendum campaigns was ensuring a good turnout. This was particularly important in countries where referendums were valid only if 50 per cent of registered voters participated, and where the result was binding. As can be seen from Table 1, there was an intrinsic problem as turnout tended to be higher where there was a significant 'no' camp for citizens to vote against. There was also an uneasy awareness, partly from the Irish experience, that government complacency and low turnout together can unexpectedly produce the 'wrong' result. This motivated all governments to try to run an effective campaign in support of EU membership. The precise dynamics were everywhere different, but the outcome was always positive.[1]

Table 1: EU Accession Referendums 2003

Applicant State	'Yes' Vote (% of Valid Votes)	Turnout (% of Registered Voters)	'Yes' Vote (% of Registered Voters)	Referendum Date
Slovakia	93.7	52.2	48.2	16–17 May
Lithuania	91.0	63.4	57.0	10–11 May
Slovenia	89.6	60.4	53.9	23 March
Hungary	83.8	45.6	38.0	12 April
Poland	77.4	58.9	45.3	7–8 June
Czech Republic	77.3	55.2	41.7	13–14 June
Latvia	67.5	72.5	48.6	20 September
Estonia	66.8	64.1	42.6	14 September
Malta	53.6	90.9	48.0	10 March

[1] Further details of the EU accession referendums can be found in the comprehensive set of briefing papers assembled by the European Parties Elections and Referendums Network based at the Sussex European Institute and available at «http://www.sussex.ac.uk/sei/1-4-2-11.html». The author thanks other members of the network for the material on which much of this chapter is based.

Malta

The first of the year's accession referendums took place in Malta on 10 March, and was the exception that proved some of the 'rules'. It was the only state holding a referendum that had not once been communist, and also the only case where striving for EU membership had been a partisan affair. Its membership application, submitted in 1990, had been frozen by the Malta Labour Party when it won the 1996 election, and was only resurrected when the government changed after new elections in September 1998. This enabled Malta to start negotiating accession together with the 'second group' of post-communist states in spring 2000. Malta was also exceptional for two other reasons that affected the referendum campaign and result. Firstly, it was a highly polarized political community, and a nearly pure example of a two-party system, where the Labour Party and the Nationalist Party could between them take almost 100 per cent of votes and all seats in parliament. The party divide corresponded largely (but not entirely) with pro and anti-EU sentiment. Secondly, high electoral turnouts were the norm, as on a small island with an electorate of less than 300,000, citizens knew that every vote mattered in the bitterly contested political arena. Consequently, the highest 'no' vote of 2003, with 46.35 per cent of participants rejecting accession, was matched by an exceptionally high turnout of 90.9 per cent.

It was also important that Malta had to hold another general election by January 2004 and the prime minister, Eddie Fenech Adami of the Nationalist Party, called the election the day after the referendum for the earliest possible date, 12 April. He clearly hoped to win while buoyed by the referendum success but, in the Maltese political context, the parliamentary election amounted to a second referendum on EU membership. Since some Labour voters were pro-EU and had abandoned party allegiance to vote 'yes' in the referendum, it remained possible that Labour could win and derail the accession process. In the event, the election produced an identical parliament in terms of party composition to the one that had negotiated accession (see Table 2). Malta's path into the European Union had therefore finally been secured.

Table 2: Maltese Parliamentary Election, 12 April 2003

Party	Seats	% of Vote
Nationalist Party (PN)	35	51.8
Malta Labour Party (MLP)	30	47.5
Democratic Alternative (AD)	0	0.7

Slovenia

The EU accession referendum in Slovenia on 23 March was exceptional as a referendum on joining Nato was held on the same day. The only other post-communist state to have held a Nato referendum was Hungary, which joined during its first wave of eastern enlargement in 1999. As in most of the accession states, Nato membership was a far more contentious issue that joining the EU, and over one-third of those who participated in the referendum voted 'no' to Nato, as opposed to a mere 10 per cent who were against EU accession. Being aware of the greater vulnerability of the Nato vote, the government tended to concentrate more heavily on the campaign for Nato membership.

The referendum turnout of 53.9 per cent was disappointing, particularly compared with the 93 per cent turnout in the 1990 referendum on independ-ence, and it was also lower than in subsequent parliamentary and presidential elections since 1990. However, it was perfectly respectable compared with the referendums elsewhere later in the year, and might well have been lower if the EU referendum had not been held together with the more controversial Nato question. Low turnout was, in any case, compensated for by the 90 per cent 'yes' vote. Support for the EU increased as the vote approached, helped perhaps by the fact that the anti-Nato campaign emphasized the benefits of EU membership by claiming that this would provide sufficient guarantees of Slovenia's security. Opinion polls suggested that even among supporters of the small Slovene National Party – the only parliamentary party against mem-bership – three-quarters were in favour of membership, and among more highly educated people and, interestingly, the over-60s, almost no one voted 'no'.

Despite some worries over loss of sovereignty, the desire to 'return to Europe' had been a strong force behind Slovene politics when the country gained independence from Yugoslavia at the beginning of the 1990s, and the murder of Serbian Prime Minister Djindjić two weeks before the referendum took place can only have increased awareness of the nightmares that Slovenia was definitively leaving behind by joining the EU.

Hungary

The Hungarian referendum held on 12 April produced a very respectable 83.8 per cent in favour of EU accession, but with the lowest turnout of the year at 45.6 per cent. This was a cause of some alarm for Lithuania and Slovakia, both of which were holding referendums a month later in systems where a 50 per cent turnout was necessary for the result to be valid. However, low turn-outs were a long-standing Hungarian problem, and the exceptionally acerbic 2002 parliamentary election was the only occasion in its post-communist his-tory when participation at the ballot box had edged over 70 per cent. After

1989, every referendum failed to reach the 50 per cent mark, and in 1997 the requirement that 50 per cent of the electorate should vote was replaced by a stipulation that over 25 per cent of registered voters must say 'yes' in order for a referendum result to be valid. This change had averted disaster in november 1997, when only 48.6 per cent of the electorate participated in the referendum that overwhelmingly endorsed Nato membership.

Hungary had long been post-communist Europe's frontrunner for EU membership, and popular support for accession had been very high from the late 1990s onwards. The only party to oppose membership, the far-right Hungarian Justice and Life Party, had been eliminated from parliament by the 2002 election. There was consequently little chance of the referendum failing to endorse accession, which gave the major opposition party, Viktor Orbán's FIDESZ, some scope to politicize EU-related issues. With Orbán's 1998–2002 government having conducted most of the accession negotiations, he chose to attack the accession terms agreed by his Hungarian Socialist Party rivals during the final stages of negotiation in 2002.

While FIDESZ never opposed membership, the doubts it sowed about whether Hungarian nationalist interests (mainly in the economic sphere) were adequately protected in the deal negotiated by the Socialists led to a decrease in support for membership in the months prior to the referendum, and probably served to depress referendum turnout. There was opinion poll evidence that FIDESZ supporters were twice as likely not to have voted than Socialist supporters. Since there was never any doubt that the referendum would produce a 'yes' for membership, disaffected opposition supporters could abstain from participation in a symbolic act that risked looking like a triumph for the government they loathed.

Lithuania

Lithuania began 2003 with the second round of direct elections to the presidency, in which former Prime Minister Rolandas Paksas of the Liberal Democratic Party gained an unexpected victory over the incumbent President, Valdas Adamkus. Despite having trailed with 19.7 per cent against Adamkus's 35.5 per cent in the first round, he gained 54.7 per cent in the two-candidate runoff. Paksas, a professional pilot, supported his campaign by a demonstration of aerobatic flying in Vilnius, a feat which he was to repeat in the campaign before the EU referendum on 10–11 May. Unfortunately, his celebrity was to be short-lived, and by the end of the year he was embroiled in a corruption scandal and demands for his resignation, which led to impeachment proceedings early in 2004.

However, in the referendum Lithuania produced one of the year's most impressive results. The proportion of voters in favour of membership was the second highest of all nine states; the turnout was third highest; and the percentage of Lithuanians who actively said 'yes' to EU membership – 57 per cent – was higher than anywhere else. The country was not unique in having all relevant political parties, and an impressive array of present and past presidents, in favour of accession, but since popular Lithuanian support for EU membership had tended to be on the low side in successive *Eurobarometer* surveys, there is evidence of effective referendum campaigning.

Political attention to the referendum was focused by the fact that many previous referendums had failed, the EU referendum was binding, and it required a 50 per cent turnout. The Lithuanian referendum law had been amended to make the turnout requirement less stringent than previously, but it was still restrictive. Consequently, measures were introduced to help a high turnout, such as holding the referendum over two days instead of one, extending the voting hours at polling stations, and allowing political leaders to exhort the electorate to come out and vote throughout the polling period itself. Since turnout in recent parliamentary elections had been on the low side, these were wise precautions.

Turnout was lowest in areas with high concentrations of Russian and Polish speakers. There was also a relatively high 'no' vote in the vicinity of the Ignalina nuclear power station, whose future was jeopardized by EU regulations. Lithuania was helped, however, by the fact that, although citizens who were not ethnically Lithuanian were more inclined to abstain or vote against membership, the country was more ethnically homogeneous than the other Baltic states who were prone to the same phenomenon. It was, like Poland, a Catholic state, and one where the Catholic church gave strong support to the 'return to Europe'. Also, it was Lithuania that had led the exit of the smaller republics from the Soviet Union. It is therefore not altogether surprising that Lithuanians gave the strongest active endorsement of EU membership.

Slovakia

Slovakia succeeded in producing the highest vote for EU accession ever – 93.7 per cent – in its referendum on 16–17 May. This might appear surprising, since the Slovak government in power from 1994–98 had made so few domestic political concessions to the EU's requirements that in 1997 it had been excluded from the 'first group' of countries to negotiate EU accession because of its failure to meet the Copenhagen criteria on basic democratic standards.

However, the debacle of 1997, when Slovakia was also rejected by Nato, had reframed the whole European integration issue in Slovak domestic politics. The key question was not whether Slovakia wanted to join the EU, but whether the EU would accept it. The third Mečiar government had applied to join the EU in 1995 and been rejected, so when the opposition parties came to power in 1998 they never failed to remind the electorate of Mečiar's abject failure in this crucial policy area. Since Slovakia was a central European country with a capital city just 50 kilometres from Vienna, it had no real cultural and economic alternative to EU membership, and Mečiar strove for political rehabilitation on his opponent's terms – that is, by trying to prove his Europhile credentials.

Consequently, in 2003 all parliamentary parties supported a 'yes' vote in the referendum, and the 'no' campaign was completely non-existent. The battle revolved largely around turnout, since Slovak referendum law required 50 per cent participation by registered voters for the result to be valid, and none of the other four referendums held since Slovak independence at the beginning of 1993 had passed the barrier. This gave the 'no' camp a strong incentive to stay at home, which contributed both to the extremely high 'yes' vote, and to the second lowest turnout of the year, at 52.2 per cent. Domestic opinion polls had long shown that eurosceptics was more widespread amongst opposition parties, and that their voters – most particularly those of Mečiar's Movement for a Democratic Slovakia – were far less inclined to participate in the referendum. Their leaders' declared support for EU accession created a cross-pressure that produced political apathy.

In the end, the major effect of the referendum in Slovakia was that it marked the end of the extreme polarization of Slovak politics that had dominated most of the 1990s. A 'national interest' consensus existed on the EU issue, which led to government and opposition parties conducting more normal competitive relations with each other, thereby countering one of the major criticisms of Slovak political life made by the European Commission in 1997.

Poland

The Polish EU referendum on 7–8 June produced the median 'yes' vote of all nine 2003 referendums at 77.4 per cent, and a slightly low turnout of 58.9 per cent. This rather average outcome belies some of the more unusual features of Poland's relationship with the EU.

Poland is exceptional because its population, at nearly 39 million, exceeds that of all the other nine 2004 EU entrants put together. Its concerns with issues of national sovereignty are therefore of long-term import to the EU. It also has a strong agricultural lobby, with an informed concern about the implications of EU policy on subsidies to farmers, and a preoccupation with land sales to foreigners. Two of the six parties returned to parliament in the 2001 elections, the League of Polish Families and Self-Defence, were eurosceptic and supported a 'no' vote in the referendum, and popular support for EU membership had declined notably in the late 1990s (albeit from previously very high levels). To makes things worse, the Democratic Left Alliance government had become extremely unpopular, and was a minority government after ejecting its coalition partner, the Polish Peasant Party, in April 2003. The fact that Polish referendums require a 50 per cent turnout to be valid, together with generally low election turnouts (46 per cent in 2001), led to severe concerns about what would happen in the referendum. Voting was extended to last two days, and a new referendum law was passed which would have allowed parliament to approve EU accession by a two-thirds majority even if the referendum was invalidated by low turnout.

In the event, euroscepticism in Poland failed to become a significant force because it could not offer a realistic alternative to EU membership, while the 'yes' campaign was supported by the two most influential figures in Poland: Pope John Paul II, and President Kwaśniewski, who remained phenomenally popular despite coming from the same political camp as the government. Although, as elsewhere in the region, exit polls confirmed that EU accession was less popular with less educated and more rural voters, more voters from every social and demographic group said 'yes' than 'no'. Although Poles were prepared to argue about the specifics of EU membership conditions, the 'return to Europe' was still intrinsically linked with the Polish sense of national identity for which they had fought for decades under communism.

Czech Republic

The EU accession referendum on 13–14 June was the Czech Republic's first: not only had the Czechs avoided holding one when Czechoslovakia split but, unlike the Slovaks, they had also refrained from holding any since, and a special constitutional law was passed to permit one on joining the EU. Unfortunately, the referendum's novelty did nothing to encourage turnout though, at 55.2 per cent, it was only a few points below that in the 2002 parliamentary elections. The 77.3 per cent 'yes' vote was, however, perfectly respectable if compared to EU referendums in earlier waves of enlargement.

The Czech Republic had begun 2003 inauspiciously by failing to choose a president to replace the internationally revered (though domestically less popular) Václav Havel when his term in office expired at the beginning of February. A successful candidate required the votes of an absolute majority of all members of each of the two chambers of parliament, but Czech politicians lacked the will to compromise to meet this not overdemanding requirement. The largest opposition party, the rightist Civic Democratic Party, insisted on fielding its controversial ex-prime minister Václav Klaus, while the governing centre-left coalition was unable to agree a common candidate. After several votes with two sets of candidates, it looked as if the constitution would have to be changed to permit direct elections. However, on 28 February Klaus, standing against one other candidate, managed to win by a single vote, having gained support from both the Communist Party and some undisciplined members of the ruling Social Democrats.

President Klaus had long been renowned as a eurosceptic, or 'eurorealist' in Civic Democratic Party terminology, and although the presidential office is largely ceremonial in the Czech Republic, its new occupant was soon making high-profile political statements. The right-wing critique of the EU relates to its lack of economic liberalism, a dislike of ceding sovereignty, and a strong pro-US line that overlies a hostility to domination by their large German neighbour (shared, among others, by the Communist Party). However, there is a fundamental difference between criticizing the EU and not wanting to be a member. Klaus, as Prime Minister in 1996, had submitted the Czech Republic's application to join the EU, and supporters of his party, which tended to represent 'transition winners', had long shown nearly the highest levels of support for EU accession in the Czech Republic. The party could afford, therefore, to remain aloof from the official referendum campaign in the knowledge that membership would be approved anyway. President Klaus, alone of all presidents of accession states, failed to promote a 'yes' vote, and merely asked citizens to participate. He argued that his office required him to be politically neutral, while his counterparts elsewhere perceived EU membership to be a matter of 'national interest' above party politics.

The 'no' campaign in the Czech Republic was a good illustration of why there were solid grounds for refusing state funding to the opponents of accession. It was largely run by previously unknown right-wing groups who could claim to represent no one but themselves, and promoted nationalist arguments of little or no informational value. The Communists, who were the only parliamentary party opposed to entry, were internally divided because the choice between subordination to German or US capitalism was not an attractive one. Its campaign was thus weak and patchy, and exit polls indicated that more than one-third of its supporters eventually voted for membership. Long term, the EU is more likely to find the 'eurorealism' of the Civic Democratic Party a problem, since it has a strong chance of returning to power.

Estonia

Estonia was the only case apart from Malta where both a parliamentary election and an accession referendum were held in 2003. However, the two were clearly separated, with the election held on 2 March, and the referendum on 14 September.

Despite the importance of the country's accession to the EU, the election was dominated largely by domestic economic issues rather than foreign policy. The election result (see Table 3), and the creation of a three-party centre-right coalition government, represented both continuity and change. Although the

Table 3: Estonian Parliamentary Election, 2 March 2003

Party	Seats	% of Vote
Government coalition		
Res Publica (RP)	28	24.6
Estonian Reform Party (ER)	19	17.7
Estonian People's Union (ERL)	13	13.0
Total government coalition	60	55.3
Opposition		
Estonian Centre Party (EK)	28	25.4
Fatherland Union (IML)	7	7.3
Moderates (M)	6	7.0
Others	0	5.0
Total opposition	41	44.7

Reform Party remained in government, a new party, Res Publica, took almost one-quarter of the vote, and supplied the Prime Minister, Juhan Parts. It is also notable that no Russian party managed to enter parliament, although Russians made up some 30 per cent of the Estonian population and – even allowing for the large number of them still without citizenship – about 15 per cent of the electorate.

The new government had been in power for five months when the EU accession referendum took place. There was some unease about the possible outcome as EU membership had become an 'elite project' in Estonia even more than elsewhere in the post-communist world. Successive governments' economic reform efforts were rewarded by its starting accession negotiations with the four central European transition leaders, while society's 'transition losers' were left behind. In the event, the referendum produced a safe two-thirds majority in favour of membership, and a very respectable 64.1 per cent turnout that was higher than in the two previous parliamentary elections.

The relatively high turnout may be explained by both the fact that there was some level of contestation of the EU issue in Estonia, and that referendums were relatively rare, having previously been held only to decide on independence from the Soviet Union and to endorse the new constitution. This made it easier to project the idea that EU membership was a question of vital national inter-est. Although opponents of EU membership argued about loss of sovereignty, and the undesirability of joining another union so soon after escaping from the last one, the alternative of non-membership became increasingly infeasible as Lithuania and the rest of eastern and central Europe had already voted in favour of the EU.

Exit polling indicated that, as elsewhere, people with higher levels of education and living in cities were some 10 per cent more likely to have voted for EU membership, although the over-60s appeared to be the most pro-EU age group. The strongest correlation, however, was with party sympathies: while over 80 per cent of supporters of the two largest governing parties, Res Publica and the Reform Party, voted 'yes', this was true of only just over half the supporters of the opposition Centre Party. Russians, Belarusians and Ukrainians were also less likely to have supported membership than ethnic Estonians, although they were still narrowly in favour. This was a reversal of the earlier position, when Estonians lagged behind Russians in supporting EU membership. Russians were less concerned than Estonians about sovereignty-related issues, keen on the economic advantages of EU membership and migration opportunities, and had been helped by the EU on minority rights issues. However, the tendency of the 'yes' camp to promote EU membership as a defence against the threat from Russia alienated Estonian Russian voters. The vote for EU accession cemented Estonia's 'return to Europe' from the Russian orbit but, for the country's Russian speakers, a radical shift towards western culture that would cut their society off from Russia was not a welcome prospect.

Latvia

Latvia held the last accession referendum of 2003, and also achieved the highest turnout of all post-communist states at nearly 72.5 per cent. The 'yes' vote of 67.5 per cent was not particularly high, but very satisfactory as pro-EU sentiments in Latvia had consistently been some of the weakest in central and eastern Europe. The result therefore appeared to vindicate the government's decision to wait until last, in the hope that the electorate would be encouraged to vote by the knowledge that both its closest neighbours, Estonia and Lithuania, were joining the EU, and that a 'no' vote would leave the country isolated with its other neighbour, Russia. It was hoped that this would counteract Latvian reticence about joining another union so soon after seceding from the Soviet Union.

One of Latvia's major problems was that it had the highest ethnic minority population of any of the accession states, with over 40 per cent not having Latvian as their first language, and more than one-fifth of residents not having Latvian citizenship (though this meant that they could not vote in the referendum). As in Estonia, some of the referendum campaign arguments that emphasized Latvia's need to turn west rather than east alienated ethnic Russians, who were concerned about being cut off from family and contacts in Russia. The 'yes' vote was lowest in the east of the country, where in some places there were Russian majorities, and the economy was weakest. Geographical differentiation was stronger than in many countries, and some electoral districts actually had a majority of 'no' votes. Overall, however, the result was positive for a country that had long appeared one of the most lukewarm of the EU candidate states.

Some Concluding Comments on the Referendums

The major reason why the referendums gave such strong support to EU accession was that it was in the interests of the citizens concerned to join. With the exception of the Malta Labour Party, all medium-sized parties that had been in government realized this. Even where some euroscepticism remained, parties were loathe to campaign for a 'no' vote because identifying themselves with what was so clearly a lost cause might damage their image in the eyes of the voters. Opponents of membership tended therefore to be on the extremist fringes, and frequently pursued arguments about sovereignty, when the major concern of eurosceptic voters was that prices would go up.

The referendums generally performed a useful function in prompting government-led information campaigns familiarizing citizens with the details of EU membership. Since all sectors of society had to be encouraged to vote, it was necessary to counter previous perceptions of the EU as an economic project of benefit to 'transition winners', and more attention was at last paid to the advantages that a market economy and EU social protection measures could bring to the weaker members of society. Nevertheless, there was something inherently contradictory about government and EU-sponsored information campaigns led by bodies that were convinced of the merits of European integration. There were frequent complaints that there was too little discussion of the disadvantages of membership, and that insufficient (or no) public funds were made available to the 'no' campaigns. However, given the dearth of parliamentary parties opposed to membership, it was hard to identify legitimate recipients of funds.

In general, 'yes' votes predominated in all sectors of society, and the strongest correlation was with party support rather than demographic characteristics. While the right was more likely to be concerned about national sovereignty, centre-right reformist parties tended to have more strongly pro-EU supporters than centre-left parties that, although normally strongly in favour of accession (which they had frequently applied for or negotiated), were nevertheless likely to have more voters drawn from 'transition losers'. These people were more ambivalent about membership because of concerns about the economic effects of membership and continued change. Younger people, urban dwellers and the more highly educated were more enthusiastic about membership, although patterns were not uniform throughout the accession states. In some countries the over-60s produced very strong 'yes' votes. They may have heeded exhortations to vote for their grandchildren's future, and the fact that they alone had personal memories of the era before the iron curtain fell may also have strengthened the desire to 'return to Europe'.

II. Other Elections in Applicant States

Three other elections were held in the course of 2003 in applicant states that did not participate in the accession referendums. These deserve a separate mention because of their importance for the future shape of the EU.

Cyprus

The key question surrounding Cypriot elections was their impact on the negotiations of the Cyprus problem, and hence the likelihood that the Republic of Cyprus would take the entire island into the EU. The presidential election in the internationally recognized Greek part of the island took place on 16 February, and produced a first-round victory with 51.5 per cent for the opposition Democratic Party leader, Tassos Papadopoulos. Glafkos Clerides, who had been President since 1993 and was conducting the UN-brokered peace talks with the 'Turkish Republic of northern Cyprus', obtained only 38.3 per cent of the vote. The election result was not considered propitious for the talks, as Papadopoulos was expected to be more hard-line nationalist. However, when the talks collapsed in March it was largely because the Turkish Cypriot President Denktash had rejected the UN plan.

Although the easing of travel restrictions during the year reduced tension, most hope was vested in the prospect that Denktash's supporters would be defeated in parliamentary elections in the north in December. Popular demonstrations supporting the UN reunification plan by Turkish Cypriots who wished to join the EU made this prospect appear likely. However, the result of the election was inconclusive. The pro-unification Republican Turkish Party and the Peace and Democracy Party obtained a total of 25 seats with 48.3 per cent of the vote, while the Party of National Unity and the Democratic Party (led by Denktash's son) also won 25 seats, but with only 45.7 per cent of the vote. Judging the fairness of the electoral process is complicated since northern Cyprus's status meant that international observers were not present, and voters originating from mainland Turkey were easily induced to opt for parties opposing a reunification settlement that could jeopardize their position. Although talks on the island's future began again in 2004, the commitment of Turkish Cypriots voters to achieving speedy EU accession was not as clear as optimists had predicted before the election.

Croatia

Croatia applied to join the EU on 21 February, and thus became an applicant state although, unlike Turkey, it has yet to be accepted as a candidate state. It is a significant actor when discussing the next enlargement wave, since its level of economic development, as one of the more western Yugoslav successor states, is in many respects more advantageous than that of Bulgaria and Romania.

Domestic political developments in Croatia during 2003 are therefore significant. The country seriously began its 'return to Europe' with the death of President Tudjman in December 1999, and the subsequent election defeat of his Croatian Democratic Community (HZD), which had dominated Croatian politics for a decade. After nearly four years under a reformist President and parliament, voters disappointed by the hardships of economic reform used the parliamentary elections on 23 november to return the HZD to power in a minority government under Ivo Sanader. He assured the EU of Croatia's continued anxiety to join in 2007, and of its willingness to co-operate with the war crimes tribunal in the Hague. However, whether the party has really overcome its past to the extent that it can summon up enough reformist zeal to achieve these goals remains to be seen.

III. Public Opinion in the Applicant States

During 2003, public opinion on the EU in the applicant states began, for the first time, to become engaged in 'normal' debates on the future of the Union, instead of focusing solely on accession. Since the referendums were the only public opinion poll that mattered in terms of attitudes to membership, the final section of this chapter will look at views on the EU in the accession states that give some clues to the sort of members they will become.

Debates linked to the Convention on the Future of Europe and the draft Constitutional Treaty tend to be the preserve of the political elites, but they have to be responsive to the demands of public opinion. Post-communist countries have relatively fluid party systems, which means that smaller governing and opposition parties are rarely safe from the prospect of being ejected from parliament altogether, and even larger parties can find themselves outflanked by new parties appealing to populism. The new Member States may, therefore, show a tendency towards intransigence in intergovernmental negotiation because they genuinely have little domestic room for manœuvre. Parties and politicians do not enjoy a high level of trust, nor do they have a firm base of core voters whom they can persuade to accept unpopular measures. Their supporters are likely to defect to anyone who offers the hope of a better deal.

There are two areas where the views of citizens from accession states are particularly important. The first is their preoccupation with economic issues.

Eurobarometer surveys show that unemployment is considered particularly worrying, whereas issues such as terrorism and immigration cause less concern.[2] When offered different statements about the meaning of the EU and being an EU citizen, 'freedom of movement within the EU' and 'the right to work in any country of the EU' were most commonly put first by citizens of the accession states.[3] The failure of current Member States to open their labour markets is therefore a very sensitive issue, particularly since the opportunity to work and study abroad was promoted to citizens as a benefit of EU membership during the referendum campaigns. After May 2004, a major concern of the new Member States will be the proper completion of the accession process so that they are no longer feel like second-class citizens. not only transition periods restricting the free movement of labour, but also joining the Schengen area and the euro area will be a focus of attention.

Secondly, being predominantly small states and new states with a history of foreign domination, the accession countries are concerned about having an equal voice in the EU. When discussing the number of Commissioners or the duration of the Presidency, being fully-fledged members with equal access to power overshadows questions about the smooth functioning of EU decision-making procedures in an enlarged union. The demand that each country should have its 'own' Commissioner was one of the few issues that all accession states highlighted in their reactions to the draft Constitutional Treaty, and this stance is supported by public opinion.[4] Domestic politics gives governments limited room for manœuvre here. Because support for EU membership in the accession states is high, party political contestation in EU affairs frequently revolves around the government's efficacy in getting the best deal from Brussels. In December 2003, this meant that Poland's domestically unpopular government was not in a position to compromise on voting weights in the European Council. Although Poland is the only medium-sized new Member State, the most preoccupied with sovereignty and the most assertive, its stance does not bode well for the contribution of the new Member States as a whole to smooth decision-making in the enlarged Union.

[2] Commission, *Eurobarometer EB59 – CC-EB 2003.2. Comparative Highlights,* 2003, pp. 14–16. Data were collected in May 2003.
[3] Commission, *Eurobarometer 2003.4. Public Opinion in the Candidate Countries. Full Report,* 2003, pp. 115–18. Data were collected in October 2003.
[4] Commission, *Eurobarometer 2003.4. Public Opinion in the Candidate Countries. Full Report,* 2003, pp. 185–6.

Developments in the Economies of the European Union

NIGEL GRIMWADE
London South Bank University

I. Overview

Whereas 2003 proved to be a good year for the world economy as a whole, it turned out to be a disappointing year for the Member States of the European Union (EU). The OECD estimated real GDP growth at 2.9 per cent for the United States and 2.7 per cent for Japan, but only 0.7 per cent for the EU and 0.5 per cent for the euro area (OECD, 2003). The IMF estimated the growth of world GDP at 3.2 per cent, compared to the United States at 2.6 per cent, Japan at 2 per cent and developing Asia at 6.4 per cent. By way of contrast, growth in the EU was a mere 0.8 per cent and in the euro area only 0.5 per cent (IMF, 2003). The European Commission's Autumn Forecasts painted a similar picture, with world GDP growth at 3.3 per cent for the year as whole, but only 0.4 per cent in the euro area and 0.8 per cent in the EU (Commission, 2003). In the most recent Spring Forecast, the Commission lowered its estimate for world GDP growth to 3.2 per cent (Commission, 2004). Not only were the EU economies growing more slowly than in the dismal performance of 2002 (0.9 per cent for the euro area and 1.1 per cent for the EU), but the outcome was worse than the pessimistic forecasts of the Commission as recently as the spring of 2003. At a time when growth was picking up in the United States and Asia after the slowdown of the previous two years, there were few signs of any pickup in economic activity in the Member States of the EU.

The reasons for this have been the cause of much reflection both inside and outside the EU. Demand conditions were a major factor contributing to sluggish performance. Private domestic demand was depressed due to both low investment spending by companies and relatively weak spending on consumption by households. The latter was the result of a continuing low level of consumer confidence. In addition, external demand for EU goods and services was adversely affected by the appreciation of the euro. The European Commission estimated that the nominal effective exchange rate of the euro (i.e.

measured against a basket of major currencies in the world) rose by 11.8 per cent in 2003 (Commission, 2004). Although growth in the world economy as a whole benefited EU exports to the rest of the world, the substantial appreciation of the euro against other major currencies in the world over a period of two years served to erode export competitiveness.

Although automatic stabilizers operated to counteract the decline in demand, the ability of Member States to use discretionary fiscal policy to stimulate their economies was constrained by the large budget deficits that several EU countries faced. The need to fulfil the requirements of the Stability and Growth Pact (SGP) meant that some countries were forced to operate tighter rather than easier fiscal policies. During the year, both Germany and France received a warning from the European Commission for exceeding the 3 per cent limit for budget deficits expressed as a percentage of GDP under the terms of the Pact. Interest rates were lowered by the European Central Bank (ECB) in the course of the year, but the reduction was widely regarded as being too small to prevent an overall tightening of monetary conditions. One of the constraints on the ECB in making larger cuts in short-term interest rates was a continuing high rate of inflation. So-called 'headline inflation' as measured by the Harmonized Index of Consumer Prices (HICP) remained above the 2 per cent target for much of the year. The difficulty that the ECB faced was that, while inflation was well below the 2 per cent target in Germany, it was well above in Ireland, Greece and Spain. This has led to unfavourable comparisons with the United States, where interest rates have been cut by much more to give greater stimulus to demand. All in all, since the beginning of 2001, interest rates have fallen by 2.75 percentage points in the euro area, compared with 5.5 percentage points in the US (*Economist*, 2003).

II. Main Economic Indicators

Economic Growth

Quarterly growth rates (quarterly GDP compared with the previous quarter) show that the EU as a whole was stagnant during the first half of the year, with the euro area economies marginally declining. However, in the second half of the year, there were some signs of a recovery underway. In the EU as a whole, GDP grew by 0.4 per cent in the third and final quarters of the year, with growth of 0.4 per cent and 0.3 per cent respectively in the euro area. Table 1 sets out the percentage rate of increase in real GDP for the year as a whole in the individual Member States and for the EU and euro area as a whole for the period from 1961 to the present day. The last column shows the European Commission's most recent forecast for 2004.

Table 1: Annual Average % Change in Gross Domestic Product Measured in Volume Terms for Individual Member States 1961–2003

	1961 –90	1991 –5	1996 –2000	1999	2000	2001	2002	2003 Estimate	2004 Forecast
Belgium	3.4	1.6	2.7	3.2	3.8	0.6	0.7	1.1	2.0
Denmark	2.7	2.0	2.7	2.6	2.8	1.6	1.0	0.0	2.1
Germany	3.2	2.0	1.8	2.0	2.9	0.8	0.2	–0.1	1.5
Greece	4.5	1.2	3.4	3.4	4.4	4.0	3.9	4.2	4.0
Spain	4.6	1.5	3.8	4.2	4.2	2.8	2.0	2.4	2.8
France	3.8	1.1	2.7	3.2	3.8	2.1	1.2	0.2	1.7
Ireland	4.2	4.7	9.8	11.3	10.1	6.2	6.9	1.2	3.7
Italy	3.9	1.3	1.9	1.7	3.0	1.8	0.4	0.3	1.2
Luxembourg	3.7	4.0	7.1	7.8	9.1	1.2	1.3	1.8	2.4
Netherlands	3.4	2.1	3.7	4.0	3.5	1.2	0.2	–0.8	1.0
Austria	3.6	2.0	2.7	2.7	3.4	0.8	1.4	0.7	1.8
Portugal	4.8	1.7	3.9	3.8	3.4	1.7	0.4	–1.3	0.8
Finland	3.9	–0.9	4.7	3.4	5.1	1.1	2.3	1.9	2.6
Sweden	2.9	0.7	3.2	4.6	4.3	0.9	2.1	1.6	2.3
UK	2.5	1.7	3.1	2.8	3.8	2.1	1.6	2.2	3.0
EU–15	3.4	1.5	2.7	2.9	3.6	1.7	1.1	0.8	2.0
Euro area	3.6	1.5	2.6	2.8	3.5	1.6	0.9	0.4	1.7

Source: Commission (2003, 2004).

For both the euro area and the EU as a whole, the growth rate fell in 2003 compared with the previous year for the third year in succession. However, the picture was not a uniform one. Outside the euro area, the UK economy enjoyed faster growth in 2003, when compared with the previous two years. Inside the area, Greece, Spain, Belgium and Luxembourg all grew at a faster rate than in the previous year, although only Greece and Spain enjoyed strong growth. All other countries experienced slower growth. Worse still, Portugal, the Netherlands and Germany declined, while both France and Italy saw hardly any increase in output. If a recession is defined as two successive quarters of declining output, four countries – Germany, Italy, the Netherlands and Portugal – were all in recession for part of the year, while France narrowly escaped doing so.

The explanation for the somewhat better performance of the UK economy was that spending by households held up much better than in other Member

States. A high level of investment spending linked to preparations for the 2004 Olympic Games largely accounted for the continuing fast rate of output growth enjoyed by Greece. For Spain, a relatively fast rate of growth of exports combined with a supportive increase in government spending ensured sustained growth. For the rest of the EU, however, weak domestic demand, combined with disappointing export performance, resulted in slower growth in all countries and stagnation or even falling output in others. Rising unemployment, fears about the implications of the pensions crisis for households, and the slump in equity prices were the major reasons for the reluctance of households to spend. For companies, over-investment in the past, the collapse of the ICT bubble, a need to reduce over-leveraging of corporate balance sheets and weak demand were the major factors discouraging spending. In the third quarter of the year, however, output growth accelerated, driven mainly by exports which rose at an annual rate of 2.3 per cent. This followed two successive quarters in which export demand declined (Commission, 2004).

Employment

With output stagnant for much of the year, total employment in the euro area ceased growing in 2003, for the first time since 1994. In the EU as a whole, it increased by 0.1 per cent (Commission, 2004). Labour productivity grew at a slightly faster rate than in the previous year, suggesting that firms had begun shedding labour. Employment would have fallen, had it not been for a relatively resilient service sector, which was less badly affected by the downturn than the industrial and construction sectors. With a modest rate of population growth, the decline in employment translated into an increase in the average unemployment rate from 8.4 per cent to 8.8 per cent in the euro area and from 7.7 per cent to 8.0 per cent in the EU as a whole. Thus, the steady decline in the unemployment rate that took place after 1998 and that came to an end in 2002 was partially reversed, although unemployment was still below the levels recorded in 1999.

Table 2 shows the numbers unemployed in individual Member States expressed as a percentage of the civilian labour force for the period since 1964. The final column shows the European Commission's forecast for 2004.

The countries that experienced the biggest rise in unemployment were those in which output was stagnant or declining, notably, the Netherlands, Germany, Portugal and France. By way of contrast, unemployment continued falling in Greece and the UK where output was growing above the EU average. In Spain, despite relatively strong output and employment growth, unemployment remained the highest of all Member States.

A continuing concern for the EU remained Europe's relatively low employment rate, defined as the ratio of employed persons aged 15–64 in the

Table 2: % Share of the Civilian Labour Force Unemployed in EU Member States, 1964–2004

	1964 –90	1991 –5	1996 –2000	1999	2000	2001	2002	2003 Estimate	2004 Forecast
Belgium	5.7	8.3	8.7	8.6	6.9	6.7	7.3	8.1	8.3
Denmark	4.1	8.1	5.1	4.8	4.4	4.3	4.6	5.6	5.8
Germany	3.2	7.1	8.7	8.4	7.8	7.8	8.6	9.3	8.4
Greece	4.5	8.3	10.6	11.8	11.0	10.4	10.0	9.3	8.4
Spain	6.8	17.1	14.9	12.8	11.3	10.6	11.3	11.3	10.9
France	5.4	10.7	11.0	10.7	9.3	8.5	8.8	9.4	9.6
Ireland	9.7	14.5	7.8	5.6	4.3	3.9	4.3	4.6	5.0
Italy	6.7	10.0	11.3	11.3	10.4	9.4	9.0	8.7	8.6
Luxembourg	1.1	2.5	2.6	2.4	2.3	2.1	2.8	3.7	4.7
Netherlands	4.9	6.1	4.2	3.2	2.9	2.5	2.7	3.8	5.3
Austria	2.1	3.7	4.2	3.9	3.7	3.6	4.3	4.4	4.5
Portugal	5.2	5.7	5.6	4.5	4.1	4.1	5.1	6.4	6.8
Finland	3.9	13.3	11.7	10.2	9.8	9.1	9.1	9.0	8.9
Sweden	2.2	7.2	8.0	6.7	5.6	4.9	4.9	5.6	6.1
UK	5.4	9.2	6.5	5.9	5.4	5.0	5.1	5.0	5.0
EU-15	5.1	9.5	9.2	8.7	7.8	7.4	7.7	8.0	8.1
Euro area	5.1	9.6	9.9	9.4	8.5	8.0	8.4	8.8	8.8

Source: Commission (2003, 2004).

total population of the same age group. Although this has been increasing in recent years, the rate was estimated at 62.4 per cent in 2003 in the euro area, still well below that of other advanced industrialized countries (Commission, 2003). The Lisbon summit of 2000 committed the EU to achieving a target employment rate of 70 per cent by 2010, with an intermediate target of 67 per cent by 2005 added at Stockholm in 2001. The EU looks hard pushed to achieve these targets by the deadlines set.

In a similar vein, the growth in the EU's labour productivity continues to lag behind that of other advanced industrialized countries. Productivity grew by only 0.4 per cent in the euro area in 2003, compared with 2.2 per cent in the USA, 2.9 per cent in Japan and 1.3 per cent in the United Kingdom. Indeed, for the whole of the period since the mid-1990s, productivity growth in the euro area lagged behind that of the USA, Japan and UK (Commission, 2004).

Inflation

As measured by the HICP, inflation fell in 2003 to 2.1 per cent in the euro area and 2 per cent in the EU as a whole. Quarterly figures for the HICP show that the inflation rate in the euro area was declining steadily throughout the year, although a small increase occurred in the final quarter. The European Commission is forecasting a further reduction in the HICP during 2004 to a rate of 1.8 per cent for the year as whole. Given that output in the euro area was growing at a rate well below both trend and potential output, it may seem surprising that inflation remained stubbornly high. One explanation is that the HICP was artificially inflated by a sharp rise in the price of food and energy. In particular, the continuing high level of world oil prices pushed up energy costs. Despite the global economic downturn, world oil prices remained high during the year due to a combination of demand-side and supply-side factors. On the demand side, rapid economic growth in the Asian region, especially China, exerted an upward pressure on fuel prices. On the supply side, a depletion of oil stocks and OPEC-induced cuts in production quotas helped sustain relatively high prices.

However, so-called 'core inflation', which omits volatile elements such as energy costs and the prices of unprocessed food, also remained high, suggesting that the underlying rate of inflation remained strong. This is all the more surprising given that the appreciation of the euro should have lowered prices. As world oil prices are fixed in US dollars, the strong rise of the euro against the US dollar should have cancelled out some of the effect of rising oil prices. Although this was undoubtedly the case, the average rate of inflation in the euro area was kept high by the relatively fast rates of growth experienced by certain individual Member States, notably Greece and Spain. Prices also continued to rise rapidly in Ireland, despite a marked slow down in expansion. Real compensation per employee, which measures wage inflation, increased by 0.9 per cent in the euro area compared with 0.4 per cent in the previous year, and was not matched by an equivalent rise in labour productivity (Commission, 2004).

Table 3 shows the annual percentage change in the HICP for individual Member States for the period from 1961 to 2003. The European Commission's forecast for 2004 are given in the final column.

Some differences continued to exist in inflation rates within the euro area. Although inflation rates fell in most of the Member States during 2003, inflationary trends remain strong in several of the smaller EU countries, such as Ireland, Greece, Spain and Portugal. By way of contrast, inflation was well below the ECB's target of 2 per cent in Germany. This created some difficulty for the monetary authorities in the euro area in determining the appropriate level for short-term interest rates. For Germany, a declining inflation rate, which is

Table 3: % Change in the Harmonized Index of Consumer Prices in Individual Member States, 1961–2004

	1961 –90	1991 –5	1996 –2000	1999	2000	2001	2002	2003 Estimate	2004 Forecast
Belgium	5.1	2.4	1.6	1.1	2.7	2.4	1.6	1.5	1.5
Denmark	7.2	2.0	2.0	2.1	2.7	2.3	2.4	2.0	1.5
Germany	3.5	3.1	1.1	0.6	1.4	1.9	1.3	1.0	1.3
Greece	11.6	13.9	4.6	2.1	2.9	3.7	3.9	3.4	3.4
Spain	10.1	5.2	2.6	2.2	3.5	2.8	3.6	3.1	2.4
France	6.7	2.2	1.3	0.6	1.8	1.8	1.9	2.2	1.9
Ireland	8.6	2.5	2.6	2.5	5.3	4.0	4.7	4.0	2.1
Italy	9.1	5.0	2.4	1.7	2.6	2.3	2.6	2.8	2.2
Luxembourg	4.6	2.8	1.7	1.0	3.8	2.4	2.1	2.5	2.0
Netherlands	4.7	2.9	1.9	2.0	2.3	5.1	3.9	2.2	1.4
Austria	4.5	3.2	1.2	0.5	2.0	2.3	1.7	1.3	1.4
Portugal	13.2	7.1	2.4	2.2	2.8	4.4	3.7	3.3	2.0
Finland	7.6	2.3	1.6	1.3	3.0	2.7	2.0	1.3	0.4
Sweden	6.9	4.2	1.1	0.6	1.3	2.7	2.0	2.3	1.2
UK	8.0	3.4	1.6	1.3	0.8	1.2	1.3	1.4	1.6
EU-15	7.1	3.8	1.7	1.2	1.9	2.2	2.1	2.0	1.8
Euro area	6.8	3.9	1.7	1.1	2.1	2.4	2.3	2.1	1.8

Source: Commission (2003, 2004).

not accompanied by an equivalent cut in short-term interest rates means a rise in *real* short-term interest rates, further depressing demand.

In May, the ECB announced a revised inflation objective. In place of the former objective of keeping inflation at 2 per cent or less, it stated that, in future, it would aim for an inflation rate of 'close to – but below – 2 per cent'. This was widely regarded as a signal that interest rates would fall in the euro area. At the same time, it announced that, in future, less attention would be attached to an analysis of the money supply in making interest-rate decisions. The change, however, fell short of the call by some critics for a more symmetric inflation target with scope for inflation to rise above the 2 per cent figure in the short term. In May, the ECB lowered the Repo Rate from 2.5 per cent to 2 per cent, but calls for a further reduction in the second half of the year as growth in the euro area faltered went unheeded.

Public Finances

Slower output growth in the EU meant that several Member States experienced a marked deterioration in the condition of their public finances. The average general government balance for the members of the euro area stood at –2.7 per cent of GDP in 2003, compared with –2.3 per cent in the previous year. For the EU as a whole, the figure was –2.6 per cent of GDP in 2003 compared with –2 per cent in the previous year (Commission, 2004). The decline was due, mainly, to cyclical factors, as tax revenues fell and unemployment-related expenditure rose. Under normal conditions, such deterioration might be seen as evidence that automatic stabilizers were working in the way that they should in response to a cyclical downturn in the economy. However, given the large budget deficits and high levels of government indebtedness already existing in several Member States, any worsening in public finances is a cause for concern. The *cyclically adjusted* balance improved somewhat from –2.5 per cent in 2002 to –2.2 per cent in 2003 for the euro area and from –2.2 per cent to –2.1 per cent for the EU as a whole (Commission, 2004). This would suggest that budgetary policy in the euro area was playing a moderately contractionary role in 2003. The cyclically adjusted *primary* balance, which excludes interest payments, rose from +1.2 per cent to +1.3 per cent for the euro area, but fell from 1.2 per cent to 1 per cent for the EU as a whole (Commission, 2004).

Table 4 sets out the general government balance as a percentage of GDP for the individual Member States for the period from 1970 to 2003. The European Commission's forecast for 2004 is shown in the final column.

In 2003, three members of the euro area – France, Germany and the Netherlands – ran fiscal deficits in excess of the 3 per cent ceiling permitted under the terms of the SGP for the second year in succession. In addition, the UK ran a deficit of 3.2 per cent. In the case of France and Germany, this was for the second year in succession. In January 2003, Germany was instructed by the European Commission to draw up plans to bring the deficit below 3 per cent. In May, France received a similar instruction. By the middle of the year, however, it had become clear that both countries were likely to exceed the 3 per cent limit in 2004 also. Under the terms of the Pact, this should have led to sanctions being imposed in the event that the limits were exceeded. At a meeting of the Council of Finance Ministers (Ecofin) in November, however, it was decided to suspend the sanctions mechanism on this occasion, although the requirement for France and Germany to reduce the size of their budget deficits remained.

Several other Member States came close to running 'excessive deficits' under the terms of the SGP. These included Greece, Portugal (who had received a warning from the Commission in the previous year, having exceeded the 3 per cent limit in 2001) and Italy. The European Commission's forecasts for 2004

Table 4: Net Lending (+) or Net Borrowing (–) by General Government as a % of GDP, 1970–2004

	1970 –90	1991 –5	1996 –2000	1999	2000	2001	2002	2003 Estimate	2004 Forecast
Belgium	−6.8	−5.9	−1.3	−0.4	0.2	0.5	0.1	0.2	−0.5
Denmark	−0.5	−2.4	1.3	3.3	2.6	3.1	1.7	1.5	1.1
Germany	−1.9	−3.1	−1.7	−1.5	1.3	−2.8	−3.5	−3.9	−3.6
Greece	−5.7	−11.5	−3.5	−1.8	−2.0	−1.4	−1.4	−3.0	−3.2
Spain	−2.4	−5.6	−2.6	−1.2	−0.9	−0.4	0.0	0.3	0.4
France	−1.2	−4.5	−2.6	−1.8	−1.4	−1.5	−3.2	−4.1	−3.7
Ireland	−7.7	−2.1	2.0	2.4	4.4	1.1	−0.2	0.2	−0.8
Italy	−9.1	−9.1	−3.1	−1.7	−0.6	−2.6	−2.3	−2.4	−3.2
Luxembourg	–	1.7	3.7	3.7	6.3	6.3	2.7	−0.1	−2.0
Netherlands	−3.2	−3.5	−0.2	0.7	2.2	0.0	−1.9	−3.2	−3.5
Austria	−1.8	−3.8	−2.4	−2.3	−1.5	0.2	−0.2	−1.1	−1.1
Portugal	−4.6	−5.2	−3.4	−2.8	−2.8	−4.4	−2.7	−2.8	−3.4
Finland	3.9	−5.0	1.3	2.2	7.1	5.2	4.3	2.3	2.0
Sweden	0.6	−7.3	1.1	2.5	5.1	2.8	0.0	0.7	0.2
UK	−2.2	−5.7	−0.3	1.1	3.9	0.7	−1.6	−3.2	−2.8
EU–15	−2.9	−5.1	−1.6	−0.7	1.0	−1.0	−2.0	−2.6	−2.6
Euro area	−2.9	−5.0	−2.1	−1.3	0.1	−1.6	−2.3	−2.7	−2.7

Source: Commission (2003, 2004).

show six countries heading for budget deficits in excess of the 3 per cent ceiling. In addition to France and Germany, these include Greece, the Netherlands, Portugal and Italy (Commission, 2004). By way of contrast, the three Nordic Member States – Sweden, Denmark and Finland – enjoyed strong budgetary surpluses in 2003, which they are forecast to maintain in 2004.

In addition to the fact that budget deficits rose in several Member States, levels of government indebtedness increased in several EU countries during 2003. In 2003, the ratio of gross debt to GDP rose to 70.4 per cent in the euro area and to 64 per cent in the EU as a whole (Commission, 2004). The biggest increase occurred in three countries – France, Germany and the Netherlands – with government indebtedness rising above the 60 per cent ceiling under the SGP in all three. In Portugal, the debt to GDP ratio was close to 60 per cent, while in the UK it remained at just under 40 per cent. As in previous years, the highest levels of indebtedness – in excess of 100 per cent – were recorded by three countries, namely, Italy, Belgium and Greece. These high levels of outstanding debt place further constraints on the ability of countries to use fiscal policy to stimulate their economies. A further concern is the long-term strain placed on public finances by ageing populations in all EU economies. IMF estimates predict that public spending on old-age pensions will rise by about 4–5 per cent of GDP in several euro area countries over the next 50 years, and spending on health and long-term care will add a further 3–4 per cent of GDP in some cases (IMF, 2003). This necessitates the EU countries bringing about a significant improvement in their public finances in the next few years to avoid both increased indebtedness and the need for sharper adjustments in the future.

III. Economic Developments in the Member States inside the Euro Area

Germany

Taking the year as a whole, the Germany economy declined in 2003, with GDP falling by 0.1 per cent. GDP was falling for the entire first half of the year, pushing the economy technically into recession. This followed two years of slow growth, in which GDP grew by 0.8 per cent and 0.2 per cent respectively. The major factor on the demand side contributing to this dismal performance was private-sector investment, which fell by 1.7 per cent over the year as whole, although this was reversed in the third quarter. Private consumption was also weak, rising by 0.7 per cent after a fall of 1 per cent in the previous year (Commission, 2003). One explanation for the fall in investment was over-investment in previous years, part of the post-unification construction boom (Munchau, 2004). A further explanation has been the difficulties experienced by the financial sector, following the collapse of the Stock Market in 2001 (Munchau, 2004). Investment was also adversely affected by higher real long-term interest rates, as inflation fell to 1.1 per cent. With *nominal* long-term interest rates at 4.1 per cent, *real* long-term rates were 3 per cent, significantly higher than in members of the euro area.

A further concern in the first half of the year was the poor performance of Germany's exports, which have traditionally been a major source of growth in the economy. Exports grew by 1.2 per cent in 2003, compared with 3.4 per cent in the previous year. With imports rising by 2.6 per cent, the net contribution of the overseas sector to final demand was negative (Commission, 2003). Undoubtedly, the strength of the euro was a major factor contributing to this poor performance. With government borrowing in excess of the 3 per cent ceiling under the SGP for the second successive year, the authorities were also constrained in their power to combat the recession through fiscal stimulus.

In 2003, Germany experienced one of the steepest rises in unemployment in the euro area, with unemployment rising to 9.3 per cent of the labour force (Commission, 2004).

In March, the Schröder administration announced a package of reforms, known as *Agenda 2010*, to stimulate the economy. The measures were, mainly, supply-side measures aimed at cutting wage costs and increasing flexibility in the economy. They included measures to shorten the period during which unemployment benefit could be received, increased pension contributions to tackle the deficit in pensions funds, and a reform of Germany's system of healthcare benefits. Towards the end of the year, agreement was also reached with the opposition parties to bring forward planned tax reductions.

France

As with Germany, France barely grew at all during 2003. Taking the year as whole, GDP rose by 0.2 per cent. Although GDP fell in the first half of the year, the French economy narrowly avoided a recession in the technical sense. As in Germany, a fall in private-sector investment for the second year running, and weak export demand were the major factors contributing to stagnation from the demand side. Private consumption also remained sluggish, suggesting low consumer confidence. The virtual stagnation of output saw unemployment rise from 8.8 per cent to 9.4 per cent of the civilian labour force (Commission, 2004).

As in Germany, the state of public finances acted as a constraint on fiscal policy. At –4.1 per cent of GDP, the general government balance was in deficit for the second year running, with a deficit of 3 per cent forecast for 2004. Having received a formal warning from the European Commission, France was required to produce a programme for reducing the deficit by 3 October. Failure to do so would have led to sanctions being imposed under the rules of the SGP. The 2004 budget did contain a number of measures for controlling public spending, but, nevertheless, was insufficient to prevent the 3 per cent ceiling being exceeded for a third year running. At the same time, the ratio of government debt to GDP was forecast to rise to 63 per cent, breaching the 60 per cent ceiling under the SGP rules. In subsequent negotiations, the Commission accepted that France would need an extra year to bring the deficit below 3 per cent, but required more stringent action by the French government to reduce the deficit further in 2004. Some breathing space was provided by the decision by finance ministers in November to temporarily suspend the sanctions mechanism for Member States that failed to adhere to the SGP rules.

Italy

In 2003, Italy's GDP grew at a rate of only 0.3 per cent. With GDP falling in the first two quarters compared with the previous quarter, the Italian economy fell briefly into recession. The immediate cause of the downturn was a sharp drop in private-sector investment and a decline in exports due, in part, to the strength of the euro. Unlike France and Germany, however, employment remained robust, with the unemployment rate falling from 9 per cent to 8.7 per cent. As output was hardly rising, the major reason for this was that employers were hoarding rather than shedding labour in the face of weak demand. As a consequence, productivity fell by 0.2 per cent (Commission, 2003). With wages increasing strongly, unit labour costs increased, reducing the competitiveness of Italian products. One consequence was that inflation rose from 2.6 per cent to 2.8 per cent.

Despite the subdued state of the economy, the government's budget deficit actually fell from 2.6 per cent to 2.3 per cent of GDP. However, the outcome relied heavily on a series of one-off measures, including a tax amnesty. In 2004, the deficit is forecast to increase to 3.2 per cent, taking the deficit above the 3 per cent ceiling under the SGP. Even this is very dependent on the enactment of one-off measures, including sales of public assets. With a ratio of government debt to GDP of 106.2 per cent, Italy has the highest level of government indebtedness in the EU. This necessitates running a large primary budgetary surplus (the budget balance remaining after the payment of interest charges on government debt) if the level of debt is to be reduced. Yet, in 2003, this fell from 3.5 per cent to 2.9 per cent.

Spain

While the other large economies of the EU all experienced declining growth, Spain enjoyed faster growth in 2003. Real GDP grew by 2.4 per cent compared with 2 per cent in the previous year. A strong rise in private consumption, fuelled by income tax cuts, was a major factor contributing to domestic demand. Despite the appreciation of the euro, Spain enjoyed considerable growth in her exports, although this was more than offset by an increase in imports. Government consumption spending also grew at the fastest rate of any country in the euro area, helping to sustain domestic demand. With buoyant tax revenues, a balanced budget was achieved for the second year running, despite rising public spending. With a rising level of economy activity, employment grew by 1.8 per cent, sufficient to stabilize the unemployment rate. At 11.3 per cent, however, Spain still has the highest rate in the EU. Despite the relatively high level of unemployment, inflationary pressures remained strong, with the HICP rising by 3.1 per cent. Quarterly figures, however, show that the HICP was falling steadily throughout the year – from a relatively high rate of 3.8 per cent in the first quarter to 2.8 per cent in the final quarter (Commission, 2004).

Other Member States

Among the other EU economies belonging to the euro area, the only country to enjoy relatively strong growth in 2003 was *Greece*, where real GDP grew by 4.2 per cent, compared with 3.9 per cent in the previous year. The major factor contributing to this expansion was investment spending, which grew at an annual rate of 12.6 per cent (Commission, 2004). Much of this was linked to preparation for the 2004 Olympics, although structural funds from the EU made a major contribution. With real wages rising at a rate of 4 per cent, private consumption also grew strongly, further assisted by tax reductions. Rapid employment growth helped to reduce unemployment to 9.3 per cent of the civilian labour force. On the other hand, inflation remained high at 3.4 per cent as measured by the HICP, although with the rate falling over the course of the year (Commission, 2004).

Five other Member States enjoyed growth rates a fraction above the average for the Euro area. Whereas, in 2002, *Ireland* had been the fastest growing economy in the EU with GDP rising by 6.9 per cent, growth fell sharply in 2003, with GDP increasing by only 1.2 per cent. GDP fell in the first quarter of the year before rising in the second quarter. After declining again in the third quarter, growth was resumed in the final quarter. The major factors contributing to slower growth were a decline in private- sector investment and declining export demand. Slower output growth brought a welcome easing of inflationary pressures, with the HICP falling to 4.0 per cent in 2003. The rate of real wage increases also fell to 1.3 per cent, significantly below the levels recorded two years ago.

With 1.9 per cent GDP growth in 2003, *Finland* also enjoyed a rate of growth above the average for the euro area as a whole. Although this was below the rate of the previous year, it was a faster rate of increase than the two previous years, suggesting some pick up in economic activity. Rising private consumption, supported by tax cuts and wage increases, played the driving role in the revival of economic activity. Despite negative employment growth, the unemployment rate fell to 9 per cent of the civilian labour force.

The GDP of *Luxembourg* grew by 1.8 per cent in 2003 over the previous year. This compared with a rate of 1.2 per cent and 1.3 per cent in the previous two years, suggesting some modest recovery. However, this compares poorly with an average rate of GDP growth in excess of 7 per cent in the second half of the 1990s, when Luxembourg was the EU's second fastest growing economy.

Neighbouring *Belgium* managed a 1.1 per cent increase in GDP in 2003, an improvement on the rate of 0.7 per cent in the previous year. With exports declining by 1.1 per cent over the year, Belgium relied on private consumption spending to ensure any increase in aggregate demand. After a decline in the previous year, private-sector investment grew at a modest rate. With total employment declining, unemployment rose to 8.1 per cent of the labour force.

With a growth rate of only 0.7 per cent, the growth of *Austria* was only a fraction above the average rate for the euro area. This compared with 1.4 per cent in the previous year. Although unemployment was relatively low at 4.4 per cent of the labour force, this represented a small increase on the previous year.

The remaining two members of the euro area both experienced declining output. The GDP of the *Netherlands* fell by 0.8 per cent. In the first half of the year, the country experienced a recession, with GDP falling in two successive quarters. Only in the final quarter did output increase. All components of demand were weak: private consumption and private-sector investment both fell for the second successive year, and exports also fell. Employment fell by 1 per cent over the year as a whole and unemployment rose to 3.8 per cent of the labour force. A further concern for the Netherlands was the marked deterioration in public finances. The budget deficit rose from 1.9 per cent in 2002 to 3.2 per cent in 2003 exceeding the 3 per cent ceiling under the SGP and necessitating the introduction of deficit-reducing measures (Commission, 2004).

Like the Netherlands, *Portugal* also experienced a severe reduction in output, with GDP falling by 0.7 per cent over the year. GDP declined in the final two quarters of the year, pushing the economy into recession. Portugal's recession was the result of a process of economic adjustment to a series of economic imbalances incurred in the period of rapid growth of the late 1990s. These included high levels of private-sector indebtedness and excessive public-sector borrowing. Despite the efforts made in previous years to reduce government borrowing and due largely to declining tax revenues, the budget deficit increased to 2.8 per cent of GDP, only just below the 3 per cent ceiling permitted under the SGP. Current forecasts show the balance exceeding the 3 per cent limit in 2004 and 2005 (Commission, 2004).

IV. Economic Development in the Member States Outside the Euro Area

The three countries outside the euro area achieved mixed performance. With a growth rate of 2.2 per cent, compared with 1.6 per cent in the previous year, the *United Kingdom* was one of the fastest growing economies in the EU, second only to Greece and Spain. After a modest slowing down in economic activity in 2002, growth picked up through the course of 2003. As is well known, the major reason for this was the buoyancy of private consumer spending, helped by rising real incomes and the effect of continued house price inflation on consumer wealth. With inflation at 1.4 per cent, one of the lowest levels in the EU, and real wages increasing by 2.8 per cent, households were able to increase their spending (Commission, 2004). Despite predictions to the contrary, house price inflation continued at a relatively rapid rate of 17 per cent over the year as whole (Commission, 2003). A reduction in short-term interest rates by the Bank of England to 3.5 per cent in July may also have boosted consumer confidence. Whereas the ECB was required to achieve an inflation target of below or close to 2 per cent, the Monetary Policy Committee of the Bank of England operated a symmetrical inflation target of 2.5 per cent, which left greater scope for interest rate cuts.

A further factor in the somewhat stronger recovery in the UK was rising government spending. With public consumption spending rising by 1.8 per cent a year (with the biggest increases concentrated on health and education), fiscal policy gave an important stimulus to growth. During the year, the general government balance swung from a deficit of 1.6 per cent in 2002 to one of 3.2 per cent in 2003. In cyclically adjusted terms, the deficit rose from 1.4 per cent to 2.8 per cent of GDP. This pushed the UK budget deficit above the 3 per cent limit under the SGP, although the deficit was forecast to fall to 2.8 per cent in 2004 (Commission, 2004). The Chancellor's so-called 'golden rule' for public finances differs somewhat from that of the SGP in that it aims for budgetary balance of tax revenues and public consumption spending over the course of the business cycle.

Although growth in *Sweden* was above average for the EU as whole, at 1.6 per cent, it was down on the previous year. Like the UK, Sweden experienced a relatively mild downturn, with positive growth in all quarters of the year, but the economy has been slow to recover. However, Sweden did enjoy a relatively strong expansion of export demand during the year, after two disappointing years. Private consumption also remained relatively buoyant due, in part, to rising house prices and a positive wealth effect. Nevertheless, the growth in output was not sufficient to prevent a rise in the rate of unemployment from 4.9 per cent to 5.6 per cent of the labour force. With a budget surplus of 0.27 per cent of GDP and debt to GDP ratio of 51.9 per cent, however, Sweden enjoyed relatively strong public finances, leaving room for a fiscal stimulus to the economy.

Of the countries outside the euro area, the economy of *Denmark* was the most sluggish. During the year GDP was stagnant, falling in the second and third quarters and taking the country into recession. Export demand was weak due to an effective appreciation of the krona, while domestic demand was adversely affected by declining private-sector investment and weak private consumption by households. As a consequence, the unemployment rate rose from 4.6 per cent to 5.6 per cent of the workforce (Commission, 2004). Like Sweden, public finances were strong, with a budget surplus of 1.5 per cent of GDP and government debt to GDP ratio of 45 per cent.

Conclusion

The most recent forecasts of the European Commission paint a relatively optimistic picture of renewed growth in 2004. Forecasts for 2004 are that GDP in the euro area will increase at a rate of 1.7 per cent and for the EU as a whole at a rate of 2 per cent (Commission, 2004). Although this is less than the growth rates forecast for other regions of the world (4.2 per cent in the USA and 3.4 per cent in Japan), it would represent a significant recovery if achieved and sustained. Growth is predicted to pick up gradually over the course of the year, rising to annual rate of 2.4 per cent for the euro area and the EU as a whole by the final quarter. There are, however, considerable downsize risks.

A major concern continues to be the strength of the euro, which has risen by 46 per cent against the US dollar over the past two years. The decline in value of the US dollar was, in several respects, long overdue and widely foreseen. Unfortunately, however, the brunt of this adjustment has fallen on the euro, due largely to the reluctance of other countries to allow their currencies to rise. The Asian countries and China, in particular, have resisted an appreciation of their currencies, preferring to buy more dollar assets instead. It remains to be seen whether the dollar has reached a natural floor or whether a further depreciation is in store. If the latter, the prospects for a sustained recovery of the euro area economies is less assured.

On the other hand, growth is still possible, providing adequate domestic demand can be generated. This depends on households being willing to spend in sufficient amounts and businesses to invest in a way that was not true in 2003. To quite a large extent, this is a matter of confidence, although business investment may still be constrained by excessive corporate indebtedness. Monetary policy can play a part, but, with inflation only a little below the 2 per cent target, scope for further interest rate reductions is limited. With fiscal policy in several countries constrained by the rules of the SGP, there may be little that can be done at the macroeconomic level to boost demand.

That leaves structural reform as the only remaining option. Measures to tackle the pensions crisis and raise employment levels are important for lifting consumer confidence. Consumers will spend more and save less if they have greater assurance about the future. Measures to bring down prices by increasing competition can play a key part in lowering underlying inflation in the EU. Lower inflation would provide more room for the ECB to lower interest rates without jeopardizing the inflation target. Reforms in the financial sector may also help in enabling companies to bring about swifter adjustment in their balance sheets. Finally, trade liberalization may have a part to play in lowering prices and opening up markets to more competition.

References

Commission of the European Communities (2003) 'Economic Forecasts, Autumn 2003'. *European Economy*, No. 5/2003 (Brussels: Directorate-General for Economic and Financial Affairs).

Commission of the European Communities (2004) 'Economic Forecasts, Spring 2004' (Brussels: Directorate-General for Economic and Financial Affairs).

Economist (2003) 'Flying on One Engine – A Survey of the World Economy'. September.

IMF (2003) *World Economic Outlook 2003*, September (Washington DC: International Monetary Fund).

Munchau, W. (2004) 'Grounded: Why Germany's Once Soaring Economy is Failing to Take Off'. *Financial Times*, 1 April.

OECD (2003) *Economic Outlook* (Paris: Organization for Economic Co-operation and Development).

Developments in the Economies of the Applicant States

DEBRA JOHNSON
University of Hull

I. Context

Undermined by continuing uncertainty and tension from the build-up to the war in Iraq, and from the outbreak of severe acute respiratory syndrome (SARS), consumer and business confidence and world economic activity stagnated in early 2003. By early summer, although many security issues remained unresolved, geopolitical tension had significantly reduced and the SARS crisis was under control. Stock markets began to show signs of recovery and world GDP growth and trade accelerated during the second half of the year.

The US economy, helped by expansionary fiscal policy and a depreciating currency, is forecast to grow by almost 4 per cent in 2004. Twin budget and trade deficits could ultimately restrain US growth, but the emergent world recovery is also looking promising in Asia and is starting to take hold in Latin America. After two years of negligible growth, Africa too saw improvements in 2003 and Russia continues along the strong growth path that began with the oil price-driven recovery that helped pull it out of its 1998 financial crisis.

The economic performance of the European Union (EU) reflected that of the rest of the world – continuation of the weak performance of 2002 into the first half of 2003, with some signs of recovery later in the year. However, recovery had been anticipated earlier. Consequently, between spring and autumn, the Commission's 2003 growth forecasts were revised downward to 0.4 per cent from 1 per cent for the euro area and from 1.3 per cent to 0.8 per cent for the EU-15. Euro area growth is forecast to accelerate to 1.8 per cent and 2.3 per cent in 2004 and 2005 respectively, compared to 2 per cent and 2.4 per cent based on the EU-15.

In 2003, as in recent years, the economic growth of the applicant (now mostly acceding) countries surpassed that of the EU, reaching 3.1 per cent (up from 2.3 per cent in 2002).[1] However, aggregate figures mask trends in individual applicant countries. Higher aggregate growth largely occurred because of improved Polish performance and continuing buoyancy in the Baltic states. For most other acceding countries, growth decelerated in 2003. Nonetheless, apart from Malta, growth, driven by domestic demand, remained significantly above the euro area average in all acceding countries. EU recovery and accession will boost growth in the acceding countries to 3.8 per cent in 2004 and 4.2 per cent in 2005. Bulgaria and Romania, with an accession target date of 2007, have put stop–start reform behind them. Similarly, Turkey has recovered well from its recent financial crisis and has begun the long process of restructuring and reform in line with the *acquis*.

Table 1: Real Growth in Gross Domestic Product (GDP), Annual % Change

	1997–01	2002 Outturn	2003 Estimate	2004 Forecast	Real GDP in 2002[a] (1989=100)
Cyprus	4.2	2.0	2.0	3.4	n/a
Czech Republic	1.0	2.0	2.2	2.6	105
Estonia	5.2	6.0	4.4	5.6	93
Hungary	4.5	3.3	2.9	3.2	112
Latvia	6.1	6.1	6.0	5.2	77
Lithuania	3.6	6.7	6.6	5.7	77
Malta	3.4	1.2	0.8	2.7	n/a
Poland	4.2	1.4	3.3	4.2	130
Slovakia	3.3	4.4	3.8	4.1	109
Slovenia	4.2	2.9	2.1	3.1	118
AC-10	n/a	2.3	3.1	3.8	n/a
Bulgaria	2.0	4.8	4.5	5.0	80
Romania	−1.0	4.9	4.6	4.9	87
Turkey	1.2	7.8	5.1	4.5	n/a
CC-13					
EU-15	2.6	1.0	2.0	2.6	n/a

Source: Commission (2003), [a]EBRD (2003)
Note: AC-10 = countries scheduled for accession in 2004; CC-13 = candidate countries, i.e. the AC-10 plus Bulgaria, Romania and Turkey.

[1] It should be noted here that the term 'applicant states' is used in the title of the chapter to highlight the continuity of analyses begun in the 2002–03 issue of the *Annual Review*. The author does, nevertheless, recognize that the term 'acceding and candidate countries' is now often more commonplace.

II. Preparedness for EU Membership

In addition to laying the institutional and policy groundwork for enlargement, structural reforms, adoption of the *acquis* and improved governance have boosted growth and economic efficiency, giving the acceding countries more than a fighting chance of competing successfully in the single market. The current strong levels of private consumption and investment are indicators of growing consumer and business confidence.

As the accession date of May 2004 approached, it became apparent that the economies of the ten acceding economies are relatively robust, having survived a difficult international economic climate rather well, and that their level of integration in terms of trade and investment with current EU members is increasing. In the mid-1980s, less then 20 per cent of Polish, Hungarian and Czechoslovakian exports went to the European Community (EC), compared to 40 per cent in 1991. By 1995, Poland, Slovenia and Hungary sent 70 per cent, 67 per cent and 63 per cent, respectively, of their exports to the EU. In 2002, of the ten acceding countries only Lithuania sent less than 60 per cent of its exports to the EU. Given the high levels of dependence of the acceding countries on EU markets, it is a testament to their increasing competitiveness that the poor performance of their major export market did not have a more deleterious impact upon them. Indeed, export growth remained strong in most of the acceding and candidate countries. However, the even stronger growth of imports, driven largely by strong domestic consumption and investment, meant that trade had a negative net impact on growth in most of the economies in question.

The central and eastern European economies continue to attract large inflows of foreign direct investment (FDI). Moreover, much of this FDI originates from the EU: according to the European Bank for Reconstruction and Development (EBRD), the Netherlands and Germany, for example, account for over half the accumulated FDI in the Czech Republic, and for about 44 per cent of total FDI in Hungary. FDI inflows into central and eastern Europe as a whole were significantly down in 2003 compared to 2002. This was largely because the 2002 figures were distorted by large one-off investments in the Czech and Slovak Republics, which lifted FDI in those countries in 2002 to 13 per cent and 17 per cent of GDP respectively. A more representative average for the region is 4–5 per cent – an FDI level that is, nevertheless, highly significant.

Trade and investment integration and adoption of the *acquis* do not, however, in themselves guarantee economic success. Further structural reform and continuing sound macroeconomic management are also needed. For example, the EBRD has expressed concerns about the quality of public administration at all levels in several acceding countries. Unless these administrative problems

Table 2: FDI Inflows in the Transition Economies of Central and Eastern Europe
(US$ m)

	1990	1995	2000	2002 Estimate	2003 Projection	Cumulative FDI Inflows 1989–2002	Cumulative FDI Inflows Per Capita 1989–2002
Bulgaria	4	98	1 003	430	900	4 390	560
Czech Rep.	n/a	2 526	4 943	9 029	5 000	36 645	3 554
Estonia	n/a	199	324	153	200	2 503	1 846
Hungary	311	4 410	1 123	598	1 341	22 534	2 253
Latvia	n/a	245	400	388	350	3 040	1 304
Lithuania	n/a	72	375	714	550	3 540	1 024
Poland	0	1 134	8 171	3 700	4 000	38 552	1 007
Romania	−18	417	1 051	1 080	1 350	9 008	415
Slovakia	24	194	2 058	4 007	1 500	9 636	1 791
Slovenia	−2	161	71	1 748	100	3 396	1 702

Source: EBRD (2002, 2003).

are rectified, effective implementation of the *acquis* will not happen, and there
will be limited capacity to absorb EU funds. Developing the depth and breadth
of the financial markets, continuing restructuring of strategic sectors such as
energy, heavy industry and agriculture, and wholesale increases in the quantity
and quality of infrastructure provision of all types are also needed to underpin
transition and accession.

As well as continuing with structural reforms, the ten acceding countries
are also seeking nominal convergence to enable them to adopt the euro. Indeed,
the majority of acceding candidates have expressed their intention to join the
euro area as soon as possible. In order to do so, they will have to comply with
the Maastricht criteria and with the terms of the Stability and Growth Pact
(SGP).

Given that admission to the euro area requires membership of ERM2 for
two years, the earliest possible date for admission to the euro area is 2006.
In terms of the other convergence criteria, the inflation performance of many
aspirant euro area members is not too bad, although Slovakia's success in
controlling its inflation has been undermined in the short term by accession-
induced indirect tax hikes and increases in administered prices. Perhaps the
biggest threat to inflation control in the region is the depreciation of local
currencies that began in 2003, a positive factor for exports but not so good for
inflation. The inflation news for countries scheduled to accede after 2004 is

Table 3: Indicators of Real and Nominal Convergence, 2003

	Inflation (%)	Long-term Interest Rates (%)	Govt. Balance/ GDP	National Debt/ GDP	Unemploy- ment (%)	Current Account/ GDP
Cyprus	4.3	4.6	−5.2	60.3	3.9	−4.4
Czech Rep.	0.0	4.1	−8.0	30.7	7.8	−6.6
Estonia	1.6	6.4	0.0	5.4	8.6	−15.2
Hungary	4.6	6.5	−5.4	57.9	5.6	−6.2
Latvia	2.5	5.1	−2.7	16.7	12.4	−8.6
Lithuania	−0.9	5.1	−2.6	23.3	12.3	−5.7
Malta	1.3	5.8	−7.6	66.4	7.0	−6.6
Poland	0.7	5.9	−4.3	45.1	20.6	−2.9
Slovakia	8.5	4.9	−5.1	45.1	17.7	−3.8
Slovenia	5.9	5.5	−2.2	27.4	6.4	0.5

Source: Commission (2003).

good. Bulgarian inflation has fallen dramatically and to Maastricht-compliant levels. Although inflation is way above such levels in Romania and Turkey, it is heading in the right direction.

The fiscal criteria, especially the budget deficit, pose the biggest threat to the euro aspirations of the acceding countries. Although the Baltic states appear to have their deficits under control, Poland, Hungary and the Czech and Slovak Republics do not. Indeed, expansionary policy in Poland looks set to delay Polish adoption of the euro until 2008 at the earliest. The other three may achieve their deficit targets earlier, but they will need to maintain a tight grip on spending. This may be difficult given the pressure to increase expenditure to comply with other accession requirements, to co-finance EU projects and/or to improve infrastructure provision. Of course, reform of the SGP as a result of the euro's current internal problems could change the picture as would a sustained economic upturn.

Another key challenge for acceding countries is reduction of their endemic labour market inflexibility. This is reflected in persistently large and increasing differences in regional unemployment, even within the smaller countries. In Bulgaria in 1991, for example, there was a 16 percentage point differential between regions with the lowest and highest levels of unemployment: ten years later the differential had increased to 22 percentage points. Similar trends were observable in most countries: at best, there was no change. These differentials imply limited domestic labour mobility and have arisen, in part, because of the absence of a functional housing rental market and inadequate mechanisms for transmitting labour market information to job-seekers across regions. Better integration and operation of labour markets is required in all acceding and candidate countries to facilitate macroeconomic and social stability, to ease further integration into the single market and to ensure that eventual euro area membership does not create long-term adjustment problems.

III. Economic Developments in Individual States

Poland

The Polish economy accounts for approximately half the GDP of the acceding countries, and therefore has a significant impact on the aggregate growth of this group. After several years of sustained growth, Polish growth decelerated to 1 per cent in 2001 and 1.4 per cent in 2002. However, GDP growth rebounded to 3.3 per cent in 2003. Consequently, despite the fact that growth in most acceding countries was lower in 2003 than in 2002, Poland's improved performance helped push GDP growth for the region from 2.3 per cent in 2002 to 3.1 per cent in 2003.

Poland's economic resurgence was assisted by recovery in both external and domestic demand. Despite weak growth in the EU, the major destination for Polish exports, the external sector benefited from zloty depreciation and exports grew stronger, helping to reduce the current account deficit. In the longer term, stronger domestic demand could aggravate the deficit once more by sucking in imports.

On the domestic demand side, both investment and private consumption made important contributions to growth. Despite upward pressure on unemployment, real increases in social transfers and wages, plus a vibrant black economy, combined to boost consumer spending and confidence. The European Commission forecasts that annual investment growth will be 12 per cent in 2005 to become the main driver behind Polish growth. One positive factor of the subdued performance of 2001 and 2002 was the decline in inflation from 10 per cent in 2000 to less than 1 per cent in 2003. A weaker zloty, plus the renewed growth spurt, will lead to the return of inflationary pressure, but is unlikely to cause a breach of this particular Maastricht criterion.

Two big challenges continue to confront Poland's economic policy-makers – public finances and unemployment. Poor planning, an inefficient social welfare system and large agricultural and industrial subsidies ensured that the budget deficit target of 3.9 per cent of GDP was easily breached. Fiscal deficits will remain above 5 per cent for some years, delaying Poland's entry into the single currency and pushing up public debt as a percentage of GDP to levels approaching the 60 per cent Maastricht criterion, the limit also set by the

Polish constitution. In October 2003, the government announced controversial measures, including increasing the retirement age for women to that of men and curtailing automatic indexation of some benefits, to tackle the deficit. Accession pressures on expenditure, the co-financing component of financial inflows from the EU, and declining tax revenues resulting from tax reform render any immediate improvement in public finances unlikely.

Demographic trends and enterprise restructuring, especially in traditionally strong sectors like agriculture, coal and steel, have helped push unemployment over 20 per cent, the highest level in the acceding countries. Accelerated growth will help arrest this trend, but unemployment will not start declining until 2005. Any employment growth will come initially from the thriving small and medium-sized enterprise sector.

Overall, the outlook for Poland is much improved compared to two years ago, but the sustainability of its recovery will depend on the robustness of EU growth and the containment of its fiscal deficit. Failure to meet the latter challenge will delay Polish entry to the single currency and/or necessitate the implementation of a deflationary policy to bring Poland into line with Maastricht requirements.

Hungary

From the mid-1990s until 2002, Hungary's strong growth was based on a dynamic export sector composed of firms benefiting from inward FDI and integration into European production networks. In 2003, this small, open economy, despite unfavourable external trends, grew at 2.9 per cent compared to 3.3 per cent in 2002. This achievement was attributable entirely to domestic demand, especially private consumption, the result of a steady increase in real wages in both the public and private sectors and in the minimum wage.

However, these real wage increases exceeded productivity growth and translated into an increase in real unit labour costs and declining competitiveness. The impact of this has so far been limited: a few manufacturers have moved to lower cost countries, but Hungary continues to attract investment because of its skilled labour force and supportive government policy. However, if Hungary is to remain an attractive location, it must arrest its declining competitiveness. There are signs that wage increases are slowing and that adjustment is taking place via reduction in working hours and lay-offs. Although not good news for employment, this may help restrain wage demands.

One factor behind wage growth was labour shortages. Unemployment did increase marginally in 2003 to over 6 per cent but aggregate figures hide labour market tightness and skill shortages in central and western regions. Measures to improve low labour participation rates, to increase labour mobility and labour market flexibility and to improve infrastructure, are needed to correct labour market imbalances in the long term.

Public finances also remain problematic. Hungary's budget deficit soared to over 9 per cent of GDP in 2002, partly in response to one-off factors equivalent to 3 per cent of GDP. Notwithstanding these factors, the budget deficit has crept up steadily since 1999 and reached 5.4 per cent in 2003, reflecting a significant overspend in many categories of expenditure ahead of local and general elections. The 2004 budget represents a significant, much needed tightening of fiscal policy and holds out the possibility of meeting Maastricht fiscal criteria by 2006.

The deceleration of the inflation rate was reversed in 2003. This trend is expected to continue in 2004, largely as a result of a weaker currency, increases in regulated prices and indirect tax changes. The latter two factors are one-off measures and should allow for a return to lower inflation by 2005.

In the medium term, the net contribution of exports to growth is forecast to remain negative, although less so. Although private consumption growth is expected to fall from its 2003 peak, it will remain, along with investment, the mainstay behind growth in 2004 and 2005. These trends entail continuing strong imports. However, assuming the recovery in Hungarian export markets occurs, some acceleration of export growth will occur and will help reverse the widening of the current account deficit that began in 2003.

Czech Republic

Despite continuing problems in its main export markets, the Czech economy demonstrated solid growth of 2.2 per cent in 2003. Indeed, growth accelerated during the course of the year, driven largely by strong household consumption and the beginnings of an investment recovery.

The buoyancy of household consumption and investment was assisted by substantial growth in real disposable income, low real interest rates and a rapid expansion of consumer credit. The resulting feelings of consumer wellbeing were intensified by falling prices in early 2003, the result of lower than expected increases in food and regulated prices, and a strong currency. By the end of the year, the reversal of these trends was underway: the currency had begun to weaken and food prices to increase. Higher indirect taxes resulting from EU accession will push inflation to over 3 per cent in 2004. However, inflation will fall again in 2005. To date real wage increases, key factors behind the strong domestic consumption growth, have not damaged competitiveness because productivity growth has managed to stay ahead of them.

The European Commission forecasts growth of 2.6 per cent and 3.3 per cent in 2004 and 2005 respectively. Given the 2004 slowdown in domestic demand and attempts to restore fiscal balance, growth will rely, at least initially, on stock-building, continuing investment growth and on the strength of EU recovery. The Czech Republic's trade account has been in deficit for some years, but the combination of sluggish export markets and buoyant domestic demand increased its negative contribution to growth from 2001. Some improvement is possible in 2004 given slower domestic demand, but this could be reversed in 2005 if investment growth continues to accelerate and draw in imports. Nevertheless, Czech exports, despite the inhospitable external environment, were helped by a depreciating currency and continued to perform well.

The two negative factors in the Czech economic situation are public finance and unemployment. In 2002, the government deficit as a percentage of GDP reached 7.1 per cent and deteriorated further in 2003 to 8 per cent. Fiscal reform plans are in place with the intention of reducing the deficit to 4 per cent of GDP by 2006.

Persistent labour market problems continue to cast a shadow over the Czech economy. The survey-based measure placed unemployment at 7.8 per cent at the end of 2003, whereas registered unemployment levels at the end of 2003 were 10.3 per cent. Whatever the true figure, labour markets have been adversely affected by economic and enterprise restructuring: many firms have closed or face closure because of their lack of reform and inability to compete in open markets. At the end of 2003, job losses were announced across many key sectors. Fiscal reform pressures will also add to jobless totals as the public sector sheds workers. The Czech Republic is also affected by labour market inflexibilities and by big regional unemployment differences.

Smaller Acceding Countries

GDP growth of *Slovakia* decelerated to 3.8 per cent in 2003 from 4.4 per cent in 2002 as a result of a slowdown in domestic demand growth. Public and private consumption were constrained by tighter fiscal policy and increases in administered prices. Investment was also disappointing. The surprisingly strong performance of the export sector prevented further weakening. By the end of 2003, domestic demand began to accelerate again, a trend that is forecast to continue into 2004, leading to growth of over 4 per cent.

Slovakia is gradually winning its fight against its twin fiscal and current account deficits, inflation and unemployment. Substantial progress has been made towards meeting the Maastricht budget deficit criterion of 3 per cent of GDP by 2006. The 2003 deficit was close to the target of 5 per cent, a significant improvement on the 10 per cent prevailing in 2000. A key part of the government's fiscal strategy is direct and indirect tax reform, combined with expenditure cuts.

After its success in reining back inflation from 12 per cent in 2000 to 3.3 per cent in 2002, Slovakia experienced a resurgence of inflation to 8.5 per cent in

2003. Indirect tax hikes, continuing adjustment of administered prices, a process set to continue into 2004, underpinned the renewed inflationary pressure.

Unemployment has dogged post-transition Slovakia, peaking at almost 20 per cent in 2001. Revisions to the labour code to foster labour market flexibility should help reduce these persistently high joblessness totals. Indeed, by the autumn, unemployment had fallen to 14 per cent from 17.6 per cent at the beginning of the year. However, aggregate figures disguise big regional disparities.

Given its relative head-start in the transition process, GDP per head in *Slovenia* is above that of Greece and approaching that of Portugal, but its growth has been steady rather than spectacular in recent years. Indeed, growth has slowed somewhat since 2001 and fell to 2.1 per cent in 2003. The recovery in domestic demand held back growth by the boost it gave to imports, and export demand was restrained by weaknesses in EU markets. In 2004, growth will be underpinned by domestic demand and by a revival in EU markets.

The official position on the single currency supports adoption of the euro 'at the earliest opportunity', possibly the beginning of 2007. Slovenia's greatest challenge in achieving this comes from inflation. Price restraint is helped by a 2003 agreement that reduces public sector wage indexation. Further de-indexation will keep real wage growth below productivity growth. A depreciating currency, however, is adding to inflationary pressure. At present, Slovenia fulfils Maastricht's fiscal criteria but its budget deficit is subject to some upward pressure, but the indexation agreement, tax reform and tight controls on expenditure will help keep the budget deficit on course.

Although low by recent standards, the 4.4 per cent growth of *Estonia* in 2003 was still four percentage points above that of the euro area and originated from strong domestic demand, especially private consumption (boosted by low inflation and real wage increases of almost 9 per cent) and investment. Domestic demand will figure less as a source of growth in 2004. Increases in administered prices and interest rates will restrain real income growth. The EU's forecast of 5 per cent growth for Estonia in 2004 and improvements in the current account deficit require, among other things, export recovery.

Estonia's public finances are the healthiest of the acceding countries, but deficits at local government level are in danger of offsetting the surplus generated by the central government. Moreover, the IMF is concerned that the 2004 budget is based on the receipt of large EU grants, grants which typically take a long to materialize, for which increased capacity to manage the funds is required, and for which some co-financing may be necessary.

Unemployment remains a problem for Estonia with large regional unemployment differences persisting in the north east of the country. However, the overall unemployment figures have continued to improve, reaching 8.6 per cent in 2003 compared to 12.6 per cent two years earlier.

Despite continuing weakness of the euro area, the economy of *Latvia* remains extremely buoyant, growing 6 per cent in 2003. Growth has been driven by domestic demand, both from private consumption and from investment. EU recovery will bolster future growth. As a result of this growth, 2003 saw a slight fall in registered unemployment to 12.4 per cent from 13.5 per cent the previous year. Continuing rural and enterprise restructuring is preventing larger falls and significant problems remain in terms of high levels of structural and regional employment and skills mismatches.

At present, the local currency is pegged to the SDR, a basket of currencies in which the US dollar has a significant weight. As a result, Latvia has experienced changes in relative prices linked to dollar depreciation. So far the inflation figures, also affected by administered and food price rises, have shown a relatively small increase, registering 2.5 per cent for the year as a whole compared to 1.9 per cent in 2002. However, by December, prices were 3.6 per cent higher than in December 2002. At the end of 2003, the government approved a schedule that would peg the lat to the euro by 1 January 2005 when Latvia joins ERM2 with a view to adoption of the euro by 1 January 2008. Implementation of this schedule will help choke off inflationary pressures but will only go ahead with the agreement of the euro area. Meanwhile the Latvian external sector will continue to benefit from devaluation of the lat against the euro into 2004.

Growth of 6.6 per cent in *Lithuania* was the strongest of all the applicant (i.e. acceding and candidate) countries in 2003 and resulted from a domestic demand recovery in which both private consumption and investment played their part. Export growth of 7.1 per cent in 2003 was also noteworthy considering the desultory performance of Lithuania's main export market, the EU. Despite such high export growth, the net contribution of the external sector to growth was negative as a result of the even stronger growth for imports relating to domestic demand.

A major benefit of Lithuania's economic buoyancy is rapidly falling unemployment rates. Average unemployment for the year as a whole was 12.3 per cent. However, joblessness fell throughout the year, resulting in unemployment of 9.8 per cent on 1 January 2004. Higher economic activity and active labour market policies will continue to boost employment, but major structural rigidities, especially low labour mobility and skills mismatches, could reduce the scope to offset future job losses from enterprise and rural restructuring.

The outlook for Lithuania remains positive, and growth of 5.7 per cent is forecast for 2004. Domestic demand will remain strong but gradual recovery in main export markets and depreciation of the litas, after significant strengthening in 2002 and most of 2003, will aid the external account. The strong litas, plus declining prices for communication goods and services, housing and food and beverages, were largely responsible for disinflation in 2003. Renewed price pressure is expected in 2004 from accession-induced tax changes, wage inflation and price increases in regulated sectors, but continuing productivity growth should contain their impact. Public finances remain fundamentally sound, but the public deficit is edging up as a result of high public investment and accession preparations.

The economic problems of *Malta* continue. Growth resumed after falling in early 2003, but the outturn for the whole year was less than 1 per cent, the lowest among the acceding countries. As a small, highly open economy, Malta is vulnerable to external events such as the world economic slowdown that gave rise to lower tourist arrivals in 2002. Some of the lost tourism ground was regained in 2003 and construction and public spending surged. However, contraction of private consumption, poor export performance and destocking counteracted these factors. International recovery, especially in Malta's key technological and telecommunications sectors, should boost Malta's economy in 2004. However, the need for deep structural reforms to address competitiveness problems and for consolidation of public finances will hold the economy back.

Public finances remain a particular problem in Malta. After some success in reducing the budget deficit between 1998 and 2002, it began to climb again, reaching 7.6 per cent of GDP in 2003. Indirect tax increases should raise revenue, but they will also have a negative impact on real disposable income and will continue to depress private consumption. Small increases in employment are anticipated as a result of job creation in manufacturing and tourism.

Despite sharp falls in tourist arrivals and low EU growth, GDP in *Cyprus* grew by 2 per cent in both 2002 and 2003 with domestic demand the prime mover in both years. Investment growth, helped by low interest rates and one-off large purchases, was particularly strong in 2002, but declined to 10 per cent in 2003. EU accession, liberalization of financial and utility sectors and large-scale transport infrastructure projects will revive investment from 2004. Tourism also started to recover in the second half of 2003 – a trend that could be helped by spillover from the 2004 Athens Olympics.

Moderate increases in both private and public consumption plus gentle stock-building compensated for the 2003 slump in investment. Public consumption grew by 3.3 per cent in 2003, increasing the budget deficit to above 5 per cent of GDP, representing a significant easing of the fiscal stance. Renewed plans to rein back spending are in place and a reduction in the size of the deficit to about 3 per cent of GDP is forecast for 2005.

Unemployment in Cyprus was below 4 per cent in 2003. Flexible labour markets enable it to respond to seasonal demands by importing labour. This helps moderate wage demands and limits calls on the public purse when the economy is under pressure. Higher accession-induced indirect taxes helped push inflation to 4.3 per cent in 2003 from 2.8 per cent in 2002. Yet, this effect will have fallen out of the figures by 2004 when inflation of 2 per cent is forecast, a level which, along with a more favourable external environment, will help restore consumer confidence and contribute to domestic demand driven growth.

Candidates for Post-2004 Accession

Until 1997, the pace of reform in *Bulgaria* was slow and the contraction of GDP very severe. Since 1997, widespread and fundamental structural reform has created greater macroeconomic stability. Annual growth has been over 4 per cent since 1998; the budget deficit has fallen from 10 per cent of GDP to zero in 2003; unemployment is falling and inflation is in single figures – a massive improvement on the 1,000 per cent plus inflation of only six years earlier.

Real GDP growth in 2003 registered 4.5 per cent and was based primarily on domestic demand, especially private consumption and investment, both of which benefited from significant falls in unemployment, real increases in household disposable income and a loosening of restrictions on commercial and banking credit. Although exports grew by a creditable 9.5 per cent in 2003, strong domestic demand stimulated import growth even more and the net contribution of exports to growth shifted from marginally positive in 2002 to significantly negative in 2003.

The most encouraging economic news of 2003, however, was the fall in Bulgarian unemployment. In the early post-1997 years, intensive enterprise restructuring involved wholesale shedding of jobs. It was only in 2002, that growth became associated with falling unemployment. The 2002 fall was relatively small, but the trend accelerated in 2003. In January 2003, registered unemployment was 17.5 per cent; by September, the figure had fallen to 12.8 per cent. As in many of the acceding and candidate countries, however, wide regional unemployment differences persist, ranging from 4 per cent in the Sofia region to 32 per cent in Turgovishte.

After years of stop–go economic policy and fluctuating economic performance, *Romania* is at last showing signs of macroeconomic stability, sustainable growth and policy consistency. Although slightly below the previous year's 4.9 per cent, real GDP growth remained strong at 4.6 per cent in 2003. Export growth was high at 11.2 per cent, albeit significantly down on the 16.9 per cent of 2002, whereas import growth accelerated to over 13 per cent, thereby transforming the positive net contribution of exports to growth in 2002 to a negative contribution in 2003.

Acceleration of growth in all components of domestic demand supported GDP growth. Household spending surged on the back of rising real wages and booming consumer credit, in turn spurred by lower interest rates. Real wage growth was sustainable because it was significantly outpaced by continuing improvements in labour productivity. Investment registered 9.3 per cent growth in 2003 and FDI inflows also picked up – a sign of improving confidence in the Romanian economy.

Falling inflation, which decelerated to 14.3 per cent in 2003, is a major success for Romania: although high by regional and EU standards, the 2003 figure is a significant improvement on the 45 per cent plus inflation of 2000. Despite large increases in energy prices and minimum wages and cuts in employee social security contributions, inflation was effectively restrained by price stability of food and other staples and productivity increases. The local currency appreciated against the US dollar, with beneficial effects for inflation, but depreciated against the euro, which helped sustain exports but did not help with inflation. Despite the inflation improvements, concerns remain about overheating, and the Central Bank has introduced credit rules designed to rein in the spending spree to secure single digit inflation in 2004 and reduce the current account deficit.

Other positive news came from public finances and labour markets. Despite lower than expected revenues, the government deficit remained well within the 3 per cent of GDP range and average unemployment fell to almost one percentage point below 2002 levels, largely attributable to migration. Job losses elsewhere continue as a result of restructuring. As in other countries of central and eastern Europe, Romania exhibits large regional disparities in employment with particular problems in the north east.

The economy of *Turkey* rebounded strongly from the financial crisis of 2000–01, registering growth of almost 8 per cent in 2002. Driven by private consumption and investment, economic growth in 2003 was a robust 5 per cent and a similar outcome is forecast for 2004 and 2005.

As part of the recovery process and to assist an economic reform programme, the IMF approved a $19 billion standby arrangement to run from February 2002 to the end of 2004. Turkey is also in receipt of a $6.2 billion loan from the World Bank and an $8.5 billion loan from the US. The reform programme is intended to achieve macroeconomic stability, to address persistent structural problems and to help Turkey prepare for EU accession negotiations by bringing it into line with the *acquis*. By December 2003, the IMF had completed six out of the 11 reviews of the operation of the standby arrangement and had given a glowing report about progress to date, highlighting in particular the growing credibility of the Central Bank, big improvements in inflation and the general commitment to fiscal discipline. Specific reforms agreed in 2003 include the initial phases of tax reform, a bankruptcy law, reductions in bureaucracy surrounding FDI and some harmonization of laws with the EU. Major privatizations are planned for 2004.

Turkey has suffered from persistently high inflation for decades. For the first time in many years, inflation is falling rapidly, helped by tight fiscal and monetary discipline and by a currency that appreciated by 20 per cent during the first half of 2003. The outcome was inflation of around 20 per cent for 2003, a significant improvement over the 30 per cent of 2002 and making the prospect of single digit inflation by 2005 a real possibility. Falling inflation has also boosted consumer confidence and helped protect real incomes. The easing of inflationary pressure is also helped by negative labour market developments. Unemployment rose from 8.4 per cent in 2001 to over 11 per cent in 2003, primarily as a result of a big increase in the working age population.

Despite the appreciating currency, export growth was over 12 per cent in 2003, a major achievement considering the low level of economic activity in Turkey's major export markets and the high level of international uncertainty resulting from the Iraq war taking place just across Turkey's border. However, the net impact of Turkey's exports on growth was negative because import growth, driven by the high import content of exports, the demand for investment goods and the strong currency, was even higher than that of exports. Investment, assisted by greater economic stability and declining real interest rates, will continue to make a strong contribution to output in 2004 onwards. Despite an anticipated limited recovery in export markets in 2004, investment trends and buoyant private consumption will continue to boost imports and offset the positive contribution of exports to growth.

Conclusion

The economic performance of the acceding and candidate countries in 2003, although in most cases slightly less robust than in 2002, was encouraging in the face of an unpromising external environment. The most important factor in their growth was buoyant domestic demand, especially of private consumption and investment. Although export performance was generally highly creditable in the face of a depressed EU economy, the key market for all the countries in question, high import demand from the domestic sector meant that the contribution of the external sector to growth was negative in most cases.

The European Commission's forecasts for these economies are optimistic and are based on assumptions of a stronger international economic environment, especially on improvements in the performance of the EU itself. The Commission's forecasts for 2002 were also similarly optimistic, but had to be revised downwards in view of the subsequent uncertainty generated by geopolitical factors, uncertainty which continued well into 2003. However, the Commission's expectations may be better placed on this occasion given that the first signs of incipient recovery were already apparent at the end of 2003.

References

Commission of the European Communities (2003) 'Economic Forecasts: Autumn 2003'. *European Economy,* No. 5/2003.
Deutsche Bank (2004) *EU Monitor.* January 2004 (Frankfurt am Main: Deutsche Bank).
EBRD (2002) *Transition Report 2002: Agriculture and Rural Transition* (London: European Bank for Reconstruction and Development EBRD).
EBRD (2003) *Transition Report 2003: Integration and Regional Co-operation* (London: European Bank for Reconstruction and Development).

Chronology: The European Union in 2003

LEE MILES
University of Liverpool

At a Glance

Presidencies of the EU Council: Greece (1 January–30 June) and Italy (1 July–31 December).

Treaty of Nice enters into force.

Ten candidate countries complete ratification of EU accession treaty ensuring that enlargement of the European Union will take place on 1 May 2004.

Sweden holds public referendum on adopting the European single currency. Electorate rejects euro participation.

January
14   Commission adopts report on Lisbon strategy with a view to spring European Council.

21   Commission adopts decision on excessive deficit in Germany accompanied by recommendation on measures to be taken to reduce it.

27   Council adopts directives on minimum standards for the reception of asylum-seekers and access to justice in cross-border disputes.

February
1   The Treaty of Nice enters into force.

17   European Council holds extraordinary meeting in Brussels on Iraq crisis and declares support for UN Security Council in the disarmament process.

18   Council agrees so-called Dublin II Regulation (EC 343/2003) addressing flaws in prior Dublin Convention.

19   Commission issues favourable opinions on accession applications by ten lead-
         ing candidate countries.

21   Croatia applies to join the European Union.

March
10   Malta holds referendum on EU accession. Maltese people vote to join the EU
         by 53.6 per cent to 46.4 per cent on a 90.9 per cent turnout.

18   Council adopts decision on launching military operation in the Former Yugo-
         slavian Republic of Macedonia.

20–21   European Council spring session in Brussels devoted to economic, social and
         environmental issues associated with Lisbon strategy. Declarations on Iraq,
         Middle East, Balkans and North Korea.

21   Council decides to amend rules on voting in the Governing Council of the Euro-
         pean Central Bank (ECB).

23   Slovenia holds referendum on EU accession. Slovenian people vote to join the
         EU by 89.6 per cent to 10.4 per cent on a 60.4 per cent turnout.

April
1   Entry into force of the ACP–EC Cotonou Partnership Agreement.

8   Commission adopts communication on measures to be taken by Member States
         to ensure participation of all citizens in 2004 direct elections to the European
         Parliament.

12   Hungary holds referendum on EU accession. Hungarian people vote to join
         the EU by 83.8 per cent to 16 per cent on a 45.6 per cent turnout.

14   Council adopts two regulations to establish transit documents through Union
         to solve problems of Kaliningrad enclave.

16   Treaty of Accession signed in Athens by representatives of the EU-15 and
         the 10 acceding countries.

30   Commission adopts communication on 'Investing in research: an action plan
         for Europe'.

May
7   Commission adopts communication on 'Internal market strategy: priorities
         2003–2006'.

10–11 Lithuania holds referendum on EU accession. Lithuanian people vote to join the EU by 91 per cent to 9 per cent on a 63.4 per cent turnout.

16–17 Slovakia holds referendum on EU accession. Slovakian people vote to join the EU by 93.7 per cent on a 52.2 per cent turnout.

19   Parliament and Council adopt decision on adjustment of the financial perspective for enlargement.

19   Council adopts three decisions on accession partnerships with Bulgaria, Romania and Turkey.

27   Commission adopts communication on strengthening the social dimension of the Lisbon strategy.

31   European Union–Russia summit in St Petersberg.

June
3   Commission adopts three communications on the development of a common immigration and asylum policy.

7–8   Poland holds referendum on EU accession. Polish people vote to join the EU by 77.4 per cent to 22.5 per cent on a 58.9 per cent turnout.

13–14 Czech Republic holds referendum on EU accession. Czech people vote to join the EU by 77.3 per cent to 23.7 per cent on a 55.2 per cent turnout.

16   Council welcomes rapid launching by the EU of operation 'Artemis' in the Democratic Republic of the Congo.

19–20 European Council summit in Thessaloniki. Draft Constitution for Europe presented by President of the Convention on the Future of Europe.

25   European Union–US summit. Signing of agreement on extradition and mutual legal assistance with US on criminal law matters.

26   Council formally adopts broad economic policy guidelines for 2003–05.

July
9–10 Convention on the Future of the Europe holds last session.

14   Cypriot House of Representatives votes unanimously to approve Accession Treaty. Cyprus only one of 10 acceding states not to hold a referendum.

23   Commission adopts proposal for regulation establishing a European Centre for Disease Prevention and Control.

August
22   Commission proposes concluding UN Convention and its protocol against transnational organized crime.

September
14   Estonia holds referendum on EU accession. Estonian people vote to join the EU by 66.8 per cent to 33.2 per cent on a 64.1 per cent turnout.

14   Sweden holds referendum on adoption of the euro. Swedish people reject the euro by 55.9 per cent to 42 per cent on a 82.6 per cent turnout.

17   Commission adopts opinion on draft Constitutional Treaty and meeting of the Intergovernmental Conference (IGC).

20   Latvia holds referendum on EU accession. Latvian people vote to join the EU by 67.5 per cent to 32.3 per cent on a 72.5 per cent turnout.

22   Council adopts directive on the right of family reunification for third-country nationals.

23   Commission adopts communication on reform of the Common Agricultural Policy (CAP) for tobacco, olive oil, cotton and sugar sectors.

24   European Parliament delivers favourable opinion on the convening of the IGC.

26   Commission adopts communication on the role of e-government for the future of Europe.

29   Council adopts series of regulations implementing CAP reform.

October
4   The IGC charged with negotiating a Constitutional Treaty is opened in Rome.

13   Council adopts conclusions on dialogue with the new neighbours of Europe after enlargement.

14   Agreement on the participation in the EEA of the 10 acceding countries is signed.

16–17   European Council meets in Brussels. Discusses economic issues and internal affairs. Meeting of IGC devoted to institutional questions.

23–24 Madrid Conference on Reconstruction of Iraq.

29   Commission adopts legislative and work programme for 2004.

30   6th European Union–China summit.

November
5   Commission adopts comprehensive monitoring report on the state of prepar-
      edness for EU membership of acceding countries and a strategy document
      and report on progress towards accession in candidate countries.

6   European Union–Russia summit.

25   Council adopts conclusions assessing steps taken by France and Germany to
      remedy their excessive deficits.

25   Council adopts directive concerning status of third-country nationals who are
      long-term residents of the EU.

27–28 Council adopts protocol amending the Europol Convention.

December
8   Council adopts progress report on civilian aspects of CFSP non-military cri-
      sis management instruments.

12–13 The Brussels European Council meeting fails to agree on the contents of the
      Constitutional Treaty and the IGC is suspended. It adopts strategies on secu-
      rity and against proliferation of weapons of mass destruction and the first
      multiannual strategic programme (2004–06).

18   European Parliament adopts 2004 budget. Also deplores failure of European
      Council to agree Constitutional Treaty.

Index

Note: Italicized page references indicate information contained in tables.